1987

Twilight of Dawn

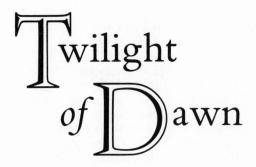

Twilight of Dawn

Studies in
English Literature
in Transition

Edited by

O M Brack, Jr.

Published for the Arizona State University Centennial by
The University of Arizona Press

TUCSON

About the Editor

O M Brack, Jr. received degrees from Baylor University and the University of Texas, Austin, and has been Professor of English at Arizona State University since 1973. He has written on biography, bibliography, printing and publishing history, and textual criticism. In addition to serving on the Editorial Committee for the Yale Edition of the Works of Samuel Johnson, he is textual editor for a ten-volume edition of the works of Tobias Smollett and an edition of Samuel Richardson's *Clarissa*. He has also edited the shorter prose writings of Samuel Johnson and Gerber's *George Moore on Parnassus*. For several years he was editor of *English Literature in Transition*.

This publication has been sponsored by the Arizona State University Centennial Commission.

THE UNIVERSITY OF ARIZONA PRESS

Copyright © 1987
The Arizona Board of Regents
All Rights Reserved

This book was set in 10/12 Bembo.
Manufactured in the U.S.A.

Library of Congress Cataloging-in-Publication Data

Twilight of dawn.

    Includes bibliographies and index.
    1. English literature—19th century—History
and criticism.   2. English literature—20th century—
History and criticism.   I. Brack, O. M.
PR464.T85   820'.9'008   86-30787
ISBN 0-8165-0964-6 (alk. paper)

The past is but the beginning of a beginning, and all that is and has been is but the twilight of the dawn.

H. G. Wells
The Discovery of the Future
1901

Contents

Acknowledgments

I wish to thank Charles Burkhart for his assistance in planning the volume, reading the contributions, and sending encouraging words when he knew I needed them. Harold Orel also read the essays and provided sound advice not only on the volume but on *English Literature in Transition,* helping to keep the journal going during the crucial first year after Hal's death. In addition to reading the essays Ian Fletcher kindly shared with me many of the problems involved in preparing a volume such as this. Special thanks are due to Lu Stitt Covert for her unfailing sense of humor and for typing, retyping, and proofreading. My greatest debt is to Robert Langenfeld. From the morning after Hal's death when we gathered in his office to see what could be done, Bob has worked selflessly to see that Hal's projects were saved and that his memory received an appropriate tribute. All of the projects except the cultural history have been saved and will eventually be published; this could not have been done without Bob's assistance.

This publication has been funded in part by the Arizona State University Centennial Commission. I am grateful to the Arizona State University Centennial Publications Committee, chaired by Bettie Ann Doebler, and to Dean Jules Heller, Director of the ASU Centennial Commission for their support.

OMB

Preface

Any period of English literature might be labeled "transition." Literature is a continuum but it also moves from one point to another, from beginnings to endings, with transitions. Pater, in *The Renaissance*, says, "The various forms of intellectual activity which together make up the culture of an age, move for the most part from different starting points and by unconnected roads. As products of the same generation they partake indeed of a common character, and unconsciously illustrate each other."[1] However valuable divisions in the history of culture may be for focusing study, it must be remembered that these divisions—a literary period in this instance—are created by scholars for scholars. Surely no writer ever thought of himself or herself as transitional, writing to prepare the way for another.

That English literature 1880–1920 has become a literary period called "transition" is due in large measure to the leadership of Helmut E. Gerber, editor of the scholarly journal *English Literature in Transition,* founded in 1957 as *English Fiction in Transition*. The difficulties in analyzing an age and finding a term to describe it were cogently presented by Gerber in a seminal essay for the English Institute in 1959, "The Nineties: Beginning, End, or Transition?" Attempting to define English literature 1880–1920 as a literary period does not mean succumbing to rigid rules and facile arguments: "We may . . . speak of the last Victorians, but in the same breath we must also speak of the first moderns. This is why we must speak of journeys out, but not out of senile Victorianism into brash but arid Modernism. The transition is from one fertile land into another, and the transition is itself through a fertile land."[2] For some, particularly the spokesmen for the Victorian establishment, the end of the nineteenth century was *fin de siècle,* a suggestion of decay, decline, decadence, death. But for most of the artists there was a sense of regeneration, a break with tradition, new beginnings. In fact most of the spokesmen for the late nineteenth century were obsessed with newness of all kinds: l'art nouveau, the New Hedonism, the New Fiction, the New Paganism, the New Voluptuousness, the New Remorse, the New Spirit, the New Humour, the New Realism, the New Drama, the New Party, and the New Woman. Emphasis may have been on vigorous experimentation but there were continuities as well. The poet who said "all is seared with trade; bleared, smeared with toil" speaks as well of the world "charged with the grandeur of God."[3]

English Literature in Transition is a fertile land, but much remains to be known about its extent and terrain. Gerber devoted his career to exploring it. In 1950 he began work on a doctoral dissertation on J. D. Beresford in characteristic style. Wishing to produce what he described in a letter to André Malraux as a "thorough and just monograph," he wrote to everyone whom he had any reason to think knew Beresford well. All of this was just to write a biographical introduction—his main concern was to analyze the psychological novels of Beresford. Another student would have been content with whatever editions of his author's works fell in his way, but Gerber set out to discover all of the printings of his author's works. His bibliography of Beresford was published in *Bulletin of Bibliography* in 1956, a portent as it turned out. Over the years numerous bibliographies appeared in the journal he edited and in 1968 he became general editor of the Annotated Secondary Bibliography Series published by Northern Illinois University Press. To this series he contributed bibliographies of Conrad and Hardy. His bibliography of George Moore, unfinished at his death, has been completed by Robert Langenfeld.

Many of Gerber's scholarly interests were directed to George Moore. In 1969 he published *George Moore in Transition: Letters to T. Fisher Unwin and Lena Milman, 1894–1910,* and his *George Moore on Parnassus,* which contains 1,200 previously unpublished letters, copious notes, and eight biographical-critical essays, was published in 1986. *In Minor Keys,* an edition of Moore's uncollected short stories with a lengthy introduction, prepared with David B. Eakin, appeared in 1985. He also contributed articles on Moore to the *Encyclopedia of World Literature in the Twentieth*

Century, to *Anglo-Irish Literature: A Guide to Research,* and to the *Dictionary of Irish Literature.* Upon examining his list of publications and professional activities, those who never met Gerber might think that he had done nothing else. In fact, he had always considered himself foremost a teacher, and his students will testify to his concern and almost unlimited patience. For those not available for conversation, there were letters—not notes dashed off in haste—but letters, often more than a single-spaced typewritten page. Numbering more than a thousand a year by late in his life these letters of style, grace, and wit were filled with warmth, news, queries, answers, encouragement. His correspondence, the seminars he chaired at the annual meeting of the Modern Language Association since 1957, and the "Editor's Fence" of *English Literature in Transition,* provided a forum for students of English literature, 1880–1920, for more than two decades.

Gerber would be pleased to know that he has again provided an occasion for an exchange of ideas on English Literature in Transition. To honor him each contributor to this volume has chosen a topic that illuminates a different aspect of this complex period. In the first essay Ian Fletcher looks at "Aestheticism," one of the *isms* often used to describe the period, and concludes that the Aesthetic Movement was only marginally connected with literature but subsisted in art in a variety of forms. Recognizing that the numerous categories devised to describe modernist art do not lend themselves readily to integration and generalization, Robert C. Schweik explores "the possibility of using the very multiplicity of analytic categories available to the historian to characterize more precisely the cultural 'place' of complex works of art," using as his example Wilde's *Salome,* and numerous European paintings of the Salome theme. The ubiquitous "nature" and "romanticism" receive treatment: Bernard J. Quint shows how the philosophy of John Duns Scotus influenced Hopkins's view of nature and Wendell Harris explores the meaning of romanticism in the 1890s, particularly as it is reflected in the work of Richard Le Gallienne. George Moore's *Confessions of a Young Man,* usually read as autobiography for the light it sheds on Moore, his contemporaries, and the cultural milieu, often puzzles readers since many of the "facts" do not agree with other sources. While not denying the autobiographical element, Robert Langenfeld shows that a new understanding of the work can be gained by examining it as farce. Arthur Symons is interesting both for his theory of autobiography and for the variety of his autobiographical writings. For about sixteen years Symons worked on his "Confessions," publishing pieces of it from 1914 to 1930. But "Confessions" was never published in its entirety and manuscript fragments in the Princeton University Library were parts of this project at one time or another. Alan Johnson discusses Symons's theory of autobiography and reconstructs this attempt at writing autobiography. According to David B. Eakin, Wilde, in his correspondence with Douglas, was little concerned with "real life" and adhered to an epistolary technique in line with his aesthetic theories. In the last of the essays on biographical subjects, Pierre Coustillas, drawing heavily on unpublished correspondence, investigates the composition and reception of Morley Roberts's controversial biography of George Gissing, published in the guise of a *roman à clé, The Private Life of Henry Maitland.*

"For Jimmy Whistler the only thing more gratifying than coining a *mot* was publishing it," Stanley Weintraub observes, and it is hard to think of another figure in the period who carried out self-advertisement with such élan. When Whistler was persuaded that it would be a good idea to collect his polemical correspondence with his contemporaries which had appeared in the newspapers for publication, a complex series of events was set in motion. Weintraub unravels the history of the publication of *The Gentle Art of Making Enemies* and the controversy surrounding it. William J. Scheik argues that Hardy's *Jude the Obscure* and Conrad's *Heart of Darkness* "comprise corresponding artistic expressions of Schopenhauerian compassion" which account for "the somewhat similar structures of the two novels" which implicate "the reader in the text in a particular complex manner." Harold Orel explores Hardy's legal knowledge and experience and considers the implications for understanding both the author and his works. For a variety of reasons Arnold Bennett felt the need to break loose at times from realism, from serious fiction. Although Bennett considered these novels a "lark," "frolic," "fantasia," "humorous," or "light," *The Card,* at least, is among his best novels. Charles Burkhart examines eight of these "entertainments" and we are invited to see them as "guides to Bennett's greater work and to Bennett himself." Finally Frederick P. W. McDowell evaluates the works of Forster either abandoned or never submitted for publication now published in *Arctic Summer and Other Fiction.*

The essays provide perceptive insights into a wide variety of literary and other artistic topics, but no collection of essays can hope to be comprehensive on such a complex period. Gerber had hoped to synthesize a lifetime of study into a cultural history. Had he lived to complete it, I'm sure that he would have felt that it was "but the beginning of a beginning." For he, perhaps more than anyone, knew the riches of the period and how much remained to be done. Hal Gerber's friends hope that this volume, even judged by his own high standards, will be a worthy tribute to his memory.

1

Some Aspects of Aestheticism

Ian Fletcher

The Aesthetic Movement is still somewhat misted despite much acute and arduous research.[1] Words such as "aesthete," "aestheticism," "soul," "Art for Art's sake," "intense," and so forth seem to derive from no center, touching groups or circles as briefly as Walter Pater's "forces" in the Conclusion to *The Renaissance* as they pass on their way to the beyond. It is not easy, moreover, within the limits of Aestheticism to isolate literary texts that are purely "aesthetic"; that are indeed all "soul" and with no more of gross meaning than the accidental play of light on some Eastern carpet. With art, or with the abstract gestures of decoration, the evidence is less tenuous: Albert Moore, for example; could those frailly robed, langorously posed girls of his ever mean anything? are they, are not we too, pleased simply by their weightlessly being? Even the most fragile offerings of the Rondeliers, though, a rondeau of Dobson, a kyrielle of Lang, can never quite formalize themselves out of meaning. And is there not a little too much of the "aesthetic teacher" about Walter Pater: what is Walter, we might say, but George Eliot in petticoats? And Swinburne seems too bent on teaching, too, teaching us to be more naughty, caught in the puritan-antinomian dialectic. As for Oscar, well, he presents so many masks and does the fat boy in so many voices that it is not altogether safe to say anything about him at all. And in any case, Oscar and Algy may be safely gathered under the orchidaceous shade of Decadence.

Considerations such as these doubtless led Ruth Z. Temple in "Truth in Labelling"[2] to suggest that "aestheticism" as a term applied to literature might disappear from our discourse. There was no movement; there was only an inventive spasm of the higher and the lower journalism. Artists of the 1880s and the 1890s care for Beauty no more and no less than other artists; nor should "aestheticism" be confused with "Art for Art's sake"; aesthetes were not all decadents; the one genus did not mechanically mutate into the other. Altogether the term was the outcome of much confusion, chauvinism, and moralism: It was not British; it was effeminate, it was . . . damme, Sir, it was French—"poisonous honey."

Elizabeth Aslin in her magistral *The Aesthetic Movement: Prelude to Art Nouveau*[3] managed to evade imaginative literature altogether. She makes one incidental reference to Pater as the inspirer of Wilde, who is accorded some space as the publicist of the movement. Attempts have been made to locate the absent center: Robin Spencer rather implausibly canvassed for Whistler; others, more plausibly, promoted E. W. Godwin; Albert Moore (who wrote poetry) may yet have his turn.[4] Wilde as sedulous ape and impresario condemns himself to the margins. And if the flavor of say "Art for Art's sake" is mid, even later nineteenth century, there may be grounds for starting elsewhere than in France and much farther back (or out of time altogether). But the line of development, if well enough known in Germany and in France, is somewhat veiled in Britain. A. G. Lehmann isolates two instances that really matter.[5]

French Etiologies

The first instance is when the slightly rickety syncretisms of the romantic group in France go out of date and fall to pieces: The "good and the true and the beautiful" come to power in 1830 for an eighteen-year reign. "Art for Art's sake," which is the thread to follow, meant nothing in the *cénacle* of Victor Hugo, Alfred de Vigny, and Sainte Beuve, but for them art is a portmanteau word covering not the plastic arts but rather implying cultivation of moral sentiments (with which we may compare Wordsworth's stricter discipline). The Good and the Truthful are accented more distinctly than the Beautiful. The cénacle in 1828 was still very much of a minority, but hoped in the person of Victor Hugo to break down resistance to its messages: his voice and his claque will tumble Jericho. But for personal and other reasons, the army disintegrates after the fall of Jericho in 1830, and "Art for Art's sake" appears as a form of *nonpossumus,* from Théophile Gautier above all, who in a new climate of ideas will have nothing to do with civilizing the people of Jericho. Now art becomes at once a *monumentum aere perennius* and a refuge, Pater's cloister of calm: at once a world of consoling hopes and dreams *and* a rehearsal for future humanity.

The first document of importance is, of course, Gautier's introduction to *Madamoiselle de Maupin* (1835), a short but emphatic affair that speaks for a generation that is still current for Wilde. The tone is off-handedly polemical, intended to frighten the bourgeoisie and spit at both respectability and revolt. If the bourgeois moralizer wants literature to improve the reader, then what happens to dramatic art if one takes "thou shalt not kill" seriously?[6] Gautier's notions about obscenity in literature prefigure the campaign for dealing with all aspects of life, culminating in *Ulysses,* when man can be altogether described—masturbation, farts, and all.

As for the so-called *Utilitarian,* critics of Gautier's friends' books, Socialists, Saint Simonians: great acrobatics about the word *utility*—of what use are music and painting; what good Utilitarian would be mad enough to prefer Michael Angelo to the man who invented white mustard? "Nothing is truly beautiful, but what is useless; everything useful is ugly."[7] Utilitarianism, in Gautier's use of the term, implies progress, but progress is a mirage; no one nowadays can eat as much as Milo of Croton who ate an ox, and there are no more deadly sins now than the seven there have always been.[8] Progress and utility and politics are inelegant as well as inoperative. The most becoming occupation for a civilized man is to do nothing or else smoke his pipe or cigar analytically.[9] Gautier has a high regard, too, for billiard players and also for good verse writers. Various forms of art are a game and a luxury, and the equivalent of this in narrative literature is disengagement.

And Baudelaire and Flaubert continue the polemic against progress (a doctrine of Belgians: Baudelaire) and Utilitarianism ("a California of lunacy": Flaubert). Among the French, "Art for Art's sake" remains an aesthetic of exclusion. Symbolism will change all that, while in England, Ritualism, the Kyrle Society, and other movements attempt some modest inclusiveness.

Some English Sources

As for England, Max Beerbohm's clever-silly dating of the Aesthetic Movement will hardly do: "Beauty existed long before 1880. It was Mr. Oscar Wilde who managed her debut. To study the period is to admit that to him was due no small part of the social vogue that Beauty began to enjoy." [10] But Beauty had been taken up by smart society before 1880. Max's essay appeared in 1894 when the Aesthetic Movement was dead, though all the aesthetes were not, and he was thinking of the birth of the "Souls" and of the mellifluous Lady Elcho and of Lady Archibald Campbell, Whistler and Godwin's patroness; but Aestheticism spread to the suburbs and the Aesthetic aristocrats took up bicycling. But, of course, Aestheticism and the Aesthetic type had existed long before 1880, and Beauty had made something of a debut long before that, though not perhaps altogether in the best circles. Graham Robertson made the disconcerting suggestion that the origins lie in the "passionate Brompton" of the 1860s with old ladies stitching those lumpy shepherds, milkmaids, and stylized flowers, that reconditely anticipate Kate Greenaway and the children's books of a mature Aestheticism. [11]

As for the connections between the Queen Anne period and Aestheticism, in 1860–61 the novelist William Makepeace Thackeray, who had a cult for that period, built himself a house in Palace Gate that could be fairly described as being in a vaguely early eighteenth-century Victorian style. But Queen Anne in purer form existed well before Thackeray's house: John Shaw's Wellington School dates back as far as 1852. But Shaw was as unversed in publicity as the dear old Ladies of Brompton. Moreover, it was in the 1860s that the manuals on the House Beautiful, furniture, dress, and the Book Beautiful begin to appear. Those constitute one of the main literary manifestations of the Movement and will be looked at later.

We might begin a discussion of the "Art for Art's sake" thread within the Aesthetic Movement with Richard Payne Knight (1750–1824), dilettante, landowner, gardener, aesthetician, poet, and most other things, who might have understudied for Mr. Rose of the New Republic with his enthusiasm for that naughty book, Les Cultes Secrets des Dames Romaines, since those mysteries, we may presume, were not to be celebrated without some aid from Monsieur Dildo. Knight's offering was concerned more with nature than with art: A Discourse on the Worship of Priapus (1786). Its author, the rumor runs, alarmed by the distress of the Philistine, tried to buy up all the copies he could find. It is, however, his views on the "picturesque" that involve him in the "Art for Art's sake" story, though the phrase was far from having become formulaic at that time in England or in France. Painting, Knight asserts, does not portray objects comprehensively; it isolates their visual qualities. Painting is a language, existing for its own sake. And great painting by no means necessarily depends on noble subject; the great painter can signify any object—flabby women (Rubens) or a flayed ox (Rembrandt) where the reality might merely disgust. [12] Indeed, the corollary might seem to be the jolie laide of Decadent theorists: the novel beauty of ugliness.

Two other significant figures in the development of visual beauty for its own sake are Sir Charles and Lady Eastlake. In the latter's famous review of Ruskin's *Modern Painters* in the *Quarterly Review* of 1856, she argues that "thought" and "ideas" are separable from, and not superior to, the language of painting itself. We seem to be listening to a Baudelaire or a Whistler when she declares "art was *not* given to man either to teach him religion or morality. . . . Art [is] not a direct moral agent to all." [13]

In a recent article, [14] Janice Nadelhaft has furnished evidence that *Punch's* polemics about those who advocated the autonomy of art touched only one of the aspects of aestheticism of which that periodical disapproved, and that its attacks on Aestheticism had begun as early as 1841. The target was a group of dramatists, influenced by German Idealist philosophers (Kant and Schiller), who called themselves the Syncretic Society, an offshoot of the London Aesthetic Institution. The Syncretics' views were antirational, and *Punch's* attacks may be seen in context of the mid-Victorian reaction against Romanticism. Westland Marston, John Abraham Heraud, and their colleagues attributed a high role to the poet. Like Gautier, the Syncretics were anti-Utilitarian; however, they remained naively devoid of Gautier's skepticism about the vulnerability of Jericho. For the Syncretics, the poet mediated between the spiritual world and *lumpen* humanity; the poet was not necessarily alienated from the public and by definition poetry should be devoted to the exploration and expression of the poet's inner life. Poetry should also expand the areas of experience commonly treated in literature. Its concern is with the cultivated individual rather than society. Marston, Heraud and their associates admired Shelley, Keats, Blake and Browning—advanced taste in the 1840s. In spite of their elitism, the Syncretics' ambition was to conquer the stage, but their programme failed at its onset. In the 1840s also, R. H. Horne in his "Essay on Tragic Influence" anticipated Pater in stressing relativism and art for art. [15] Throughout the decade, *Punch* ridiculed the Syncretics, whose self-image was Prometheus (rather than the Narcissus of the later Aesthetes).

In 1850 the Roman Catholic church re-established its hierarchy in England, and *Punch*, like your average Protestant, interpreted this action as "Papal Aggression." Celibate priesthood and floridly Italianate ritual were an affront to the English, who liked their sexes to be well differentiated. The tepidly subversive role of the Syncretics was continued by a group of young poets nicknamed the "Spasmodics," puffed by a Scots critic, George Gilfillan. Their plays were intended only for the study, allowing their work to be even more undisciplined, though spasmodic heroes were culled from the same moody stock as the Syncretics. Their brief fame, as everyone knows, was brilliantly extinguished by W. E.

Aytoun's *Firmilian* (1854), presented to the world under the pseudonym of T. Percy Jones, the humdrum name contrasting sharply with the language, incidents, and ambition of the offering. Goethe and Byron furnish models for the hero, though, as Aytoun consolingly insists in his mock review of *Firmilian,* T. Percy Jones does not carry his imitative admiration of *Faust* to the extent of personally evoking Lucifer, Mephistopheles, and Company. The review lists the principal belief of the Spasmodics: poetry is a sacred calling and anything that limits the poet's development must be disregarded or even destroyed. The group rarely, if ever, attempts anything as obvious as a plot, and they tend to the prurient. *Firmilian,* Aytoun gravely tells us, is a favorable specimen of its kind since, if not exactly burdened with a plot, it at least has "some kind of comprehensible action."[16] To accomplish his drama on the topic of *Cain,* the hero concludes that he must himself commit murder in order to feel the exquisite pangs of remorse. But after disposing of a benefactor and a number of friends, and even blowing up a cathedral crowded for a service, the hero remains unable to feel anything of the sort and his integrity forces him to abandon *Cain* altogether. The parody still reads amusingly. The hero braces himself to "Be great in guilt!" but falls into bathos when addressing his blackamoor lady (he intends a *ménage à quatre*): "the fiery song/Which that young poet framed, before he dared/Invade the vastness of his lady's lips"[17]—lines which could hardly be published in these more liberal and sensitive days. Firmilian assures us that he plans to push his best friend off a tower: "think not he dies a vulgar death/The poetry demands the sacrifice."[18] The unfortunate victim squashes in his fall, Apollodorus alias *Gilfillan* on the hunt for yet another obscure proletarian genius, announcing the fact vaporously: "I've dashed into the seas of metaphor/ With as strong paddles as the sturdiest ship/That churns Medusae into liquid light."[19]

The Ur-Aesthetic Novel

Aytoun satirized proto-Aestheticism more tellingly than the random cartoons of *Punch,* and in 1857 Charles Kingsley published a novel *Two Years Ago* (the title looks back to the close of the Crimean War) that is the first of a series with "spasmodic" or "aesthetic" antiheroes. John Briggs, a sensitive, Shelleyan youth, small of stature and feminine by nature, is brought up with, and bullied by, one of Kingsley's thuggish heros, Tom Thurnall. Tom advises Briggs, self-styled "priest of the beautiful," to change his name if he wishes to succeed: There can be no Briggs by the Helicon. When the two next encounter one another, the poet has taken the sneering advice and renamed himself "Elsley Vavasour." Elsley's uniform is described by another muscular, not too Christian lout as "nasty, effeminate, un-English foppery."[20] Poor Elsley is tall on *weltschmerz* and severely devoid of humor. Averse to action, he fails to help out in the village when cholera strikes.

Kingsley admits that Elsley has genius and that his earlier poems move the audience to a love of moral and spiritual beauty, but (unforgiveable in a poet) he allows his imagination "to run riot" in chapter 24 and his poetry becomes progressively less concerned with the state of England, with "needlewomen and ragged schools." Instead he devotes himself to the political subjection of distant Italy (Kingsley may well have had in mind Sydney Dobell's pseudonym Sydney Yendys, Dobell's closet drama *The Roman,* and his Crimean War poetry: he had met Dobell a year or two earlier). As Elsley grows older, more moody and self-absorbed, his poems lose all pretence of subject; they become mere "word-painting." The work of art's subject is—itself. Far from dissipating his melancholy by cold baths and jogging, Elsley takes to opium: a logical end for one who believes that he is sent into the world to see and not to act.

Behind such a notion of self-culture lies the philosophy of Goethe, a culture-hero for the mid-Victorians, and the great German is duly savaged: "Self-education, and the patronage of art and the theatre—for merely aesthetic purposes. . . . [He] thinks himself an archangel, because he goes on to satisfy the lust of the eyes and the pride of life. Christ was of old the model, and Sir Galahad was the hero. Now the one is exchanged for Goethe, and the other for Wilhelm Meister."[21] And one of Kingsley's several fierce women—fit mates for the straightforward Anglo-Saxon Christianized male—tells off an American aesthete: "You, the critic . . . the highly organized do-nothing—teaching others how to do nothing most gracefully; the would be Goethe who must, for the sake of his own self-development, experiment on every weak woman whom he met."[22] And the poor transatlantic aesthete is shamed into thanking the fierce one for rousing him from that "conceited dream of self-culture . . . into the hope of becoming useful, beneficent."[23] Stangrave, the New Englander, overfastidiously shrinks from action and indulges in frivolities:

> Poetry and music, pictures and statues, amusement and travel, became his idols, and cultivation his substitute for the plain duty of patriotism; and wandering luxuriously over the world, he learned to sentimentalise over cathedrals and monasteries, pictures and statues, saints and kaisers, with a lazy regret that such saints "forms of beauty and loveliness" were no longer possible in a world of scrip and railroads; but without any notion that it was his duty to reproduce in his own life, or that of his own country, as much as he could of the said beauty and nobleness.[24]

"A mediaevalising impressionist," Stangrave, and it is barely surprising that the same page leads to an attack on Pre-Raphaelitism, praised for its local honesty, but condemned for its unnatural ugliness (Millais is presumably the object). Why "copying nature," wrinkles and all, must be eschewed is because "the double vision of our two eyes gives a softness, and indistinctness, and roundness, to every outline."[25] Stangrave is, of course, converted to action. "Life," he tells us, "is meant for work and not for ease; to do a little good ere the night comes . . . instead of trying to realise for oneself a Paradise; not even Bunyan's shepherd-paradise, much less Fourier's casino-paradise; and perhaps least of all . . . my own heat-paradise—the apotheosis of loafing . . . Ah! Tennyson's Palace of Art is a true word—too true, too true!"[26] Another penitent character observes

> My Goethe fever is long-past. . . . Easy enough it seems for a man to educate himself without God, as long as he lies comfortably on a sofa, with a cup of coffee and a review; but what if that "daemonic element of the universe," which Goethe confessed, and yet in his luxuriousness tried to ignore, because he could not explain, what if that broke forth over the graceful and prosperous student, as it may any moment.[27]

It certainly breaks forth over poor Elsley, who is in a worse case as he creates rather than merely contemplates the beautiful.

Anti-intellectualism is not the only object of polemic in *Two Years Ago*. As we might expect from the sour allusions to cathedrals and monasteries, revived medievalism (even Patristic enthusiasm) in any form is suspect. Puseyites are mocked at more genially than Mr. Punch though the implication is the same: they are wolves in sheep's clothing, addicted to "bowings," "crossings," and "chanting" at St. Nepomonic's, "brotherhoods," "sisterhoods," and "all . . . gorgeous and highly organized appliances for enabling five thousand rich to take tolerable care of five hundred poor." The decade was one when several Anglican Brotherhoods and Sisterhoods were established.[28] The hysteria stems not only from patriotic and protestant affront, but from Kingsley's own psychology. He distrusted celibacy as a manichaean invention, encouraging effeminacy in men. His own view of marriage is to be gathered from those amazing drawings in which himself and his wife, nude, are presented making love, corded to a cross that floats on tumid waters, though this image fades beside one where Kingsley and his wife, at the general resurrection, wing nudely upwards in actual coition.[29] Bondage was one of Kingsley's major stimulants; one of his longer poems is on the subject of Andromeda and in the closet-play *The Saint's Tragedy* we encounter lines that might have been written by the earlier Swinburne, though it is Kingsley's men who tend to lash the women:

> Those cushioned shoulders' ice,
> And thin soft flanks with purple lashes all,
> And weeping furrows traced.[30]

Kingsley's novel presents the type of the effeminate aesthete, whether artist or critic, associated with high churchness or an aestheticized Catholicism. Such polemical presentation becomes the model for such later novels as Mrs. Margaret Hunt's *Thorneycroft's Model* (1874), Vernon Lee's *Miss Brown* (1881), and Robert Buchanan's *The Martyrdom of Madeline* (1882), to mention only a few. The figure of Lewis Seymour, painter and lounge lizard, in George Moore's *A Modern Lover* (1883), has all the characteristics of the type, but rich women and a latent philistinism, becoming a Royal Academician rather than an aesthete (self-culture and morbid inaction), are now the polemical substance.

Kingsley's Elsley had been a composite, but it was not long before a model from life was typed as "aesthete" through an existing polemical vocabulary. In the *Saturday Review* of 10 October 1863, an Oxford contemporary wrote a hostile obituary essay on the Latin Catholic convert, oratorian, and poet, Frederick William Faber, reacting ostensibly against the "gaudy" *éloge* of the Catholic newspaper *The Tablet*: "To its author, the life of . . . Frederick William Faber seems something like a superhuman marvel. To us it seems as natural and explicable as if the owner of it had been plain William Smith,"[31] or for that matter, John Briggs. Faber was flashy, not solid. As one of his fellow converts is reported to have regretfully murmured, "no bottom, no bottom." His handsomeness, we learn, was of "a feminine sort"; his manner affected, and he had initially offended his Oxford contemporaries by transforming his "scout's hole" into an oratory. Already Faber was refinedly self-indulgent (Mr. Rose of *The New Republic* was to have two main topics: self-indulgence and art), preached "lady-like sermons," and turned his gardens into "an aesthetic promenade" (whatever dubious activity that harmless phrase may mask). When converted, "he carried with him a dozen or so of his parishioners, including certain choir-boys whose parents made some unpleasant references to the fifth commandment. . . . In all the nonmasculine virtues he was admirably suited to shine, he was popular" with "a small and rather spoony set."[32] "Spoony," a synonym for sentimental devotion, though generally applied to schoolgirl "crushes," was applied increasingly to Uranian lovers: In the 1870s, Oxford aficionados of adolescent boys were described as "spooning." The anonymous *Saturday* author's piece is unified by harping on effeminacy and Uranianism: "Even his weakness for attracting (some people called it kidnapping) schoolboys was turned to its use, as a recent and unpleasant instance has shown the unadmiring world."[33] Like Gautier's tone, Faber's freedom of speech "people in general were inclined to characterise as flippancy." The conclusion is that Faber was if little else "decidedly ornamental."

Eight months earlier, the *Saturday* had been at it in a piece entitled "Aesthetical Delusions," protesting against the word "artist" indiscriminately applied to any fine art, whether the art of acrobat or rope dancer or any other romantic person who is doomed to "live his poem" instead of "writing it."[34] Those with "aesthetical sensibilities" or "artistic temperament," we are told, manifest a discontent with common life and the author finds precedents in Lydia Languish, Maria Edgeworth's tale of the "Unknown Friend," Byronism, and Wertherism, though young men in England generally evade suicide and do not become bandits. But these young men *do* believe that the artist is a "law unto himself," born to follow his own impulses; if he does not harmonize with society, then so much the worse for society. Sensibility consequently substitutes for morality: the subjectively good and beautiful become the end of life.

From its neutral origins in the eighteenth century and its prestige among Idealist philosophers, the word "aesthetic" is now rapidly becoming a pejorative term. We are told that a great scholar is able to observe of a young man that though he is "remarkable for his aesthetical tastes," he "yet evinced considerable ability." And the aesthetic young man no longer asks if this or that is right or wrong, but "how will it look if worked up into a poem and what new subtlety in human nature can I discover?" Nor does "poisonous honey stol'n from France" revolt him: No sentiment is too painful for his scrutiny. Self-analysis becomes a new and satisfying employment and like Firmilian, the ever so aesthetic young man, he performs strange acts purely from *frisson*; loses all "elementary rectitude of response," and soon "yearns morbidly for pain." Swinburne, of course, has happened since the *éloge* for Faber; "Art for Art's sake" has been asserted in the William Blake essay published earlier in the same year; Prometheus has ceded to Narcissus and the course of Aestheticism melting into Decadence has been predicted.

Visual Satire

Visual satire connects Pre-Raphaelitism and Aestheticism. The "china craze" originated with Rossetti and Whistler early in the 1860s and by the close of that decade the demand for blue Nanking was high. It was not, however, until December 1874 that *Punch* and Du Maurier first mentioned "chinamania": A little girl blubbers to her mama, "O! O!-N-Nurse has given me my c-c-cod liver oil out of a p-*plain white mug.*"[35] In the following year chinamania has become acute when a small child fails to console her mother for the loss of a favorite pot: "You child! You're not unique!! There are six of you—a complete set."[36] Aestheticism can distort normal family affections, and the types of the aesthete are already embodied in *Punch* for 2 May 1874:[37] the haggard eye, drooping mouth, and long jaw of the wife; the husband, proleptically drooping-shouldered and ineffectual. The mother mourning over her broken pot has a flowing dress and loosened hair that suits both with grief and aesthetic tendencies in the context of a tastefully simple room with bare polished floor boards and high wainscot.

Charles Lock Eastlake, nephew of Sir Charles, in the first of the manuals devoted to the "house beautiful," *Hints on Household Taste in Furniture, Upholstery and Other Details* (1868), observed that the collecting vogue of the 1860s was not confined to china, but that the smallest example of rare old porcelain, ivory carvings, metals, venetian glass, and enamels "which illustrates good design and skilful workmanship, should be acquired whenever possible and treasured with the greatest care . . . a little museum may thus be formed."[38] As far back as 1860, *Punch* had a young man offer a perplexed uncle a decanter of fantastic design, and in 1873, a girl presents her cousin with a "bit of Japanese enamel"[39] which he desecrates by dropping ash into it.

The taste for Japonaiserie was also associated with the aesthete, particularly with E. W. Godwin and Whistler. Japanese fans as wall decoration are present in 1872, and the appearance of oriental motifs— blossoms, storks, and tall female figures on firescreens and room dividers—rapidly follows. In February 1876 in "Intellectual Epicures"[40] surrounded by artistic wallpapers, Blue China, Japanese Fans, medieval snuff boxes, and his favourite periodicals of the eighteenth century, the dilettante De Tomkyns complacently boasts that he never reads a newspaper and that the events of the outer world possess no interest for him whatever.[41] De Tomkyns's pose is spineless enough, though he has not yet developed the fully attenuated aesthetic physique. His absorption in "culture" has led him into total withdrawal from everyday life, and the eighteenth-century enthusiasm is notable.

Mr. Rose of the *New Republic* and Walter Hamlin in Vernon Lee's aesthetic novel, *Miss Brown,* similarly approve of withdrawal from the ugliness of the present. De Tomkyns is juxtaposed with an old charwoman in the right panel of the drawing, who expresses a similar failure of interest in wars and "sea-sarpints."[42] And as Elizabeth James points out, *Punch's* inhumanitarian style makes the charwoman as laughable as Tomkyns so that the moral comment tends to evaporate. A similar ambiguousness—

Du Maurier shared aesthetic tastes with his victims—can be detected in later *Punch* cartoons. What is interesting in the 1878 narrative and illustration "The Rise and Fall of the Jack Spratts,"[43] an indigent painter and his "girl-wife" with Pre-Raphaelite tastes, is that aestheticism has spread to shabby bohemia: the Spratts live in a rundown red brick house, built at the time of Queen Anne; it is only the dust on their muddle of objects that harmonizes them.

Correspondences between the arts is a familiar symptom of the Aesthetic movement. *Punch*'s "Jack Easel" had commented as early as 1860 on Whistler's first work exhibited in England at the Royal Academy, "At the Piano": "The tone which he has produced from his piano is admirable, and he has struck on it a chord of colour which I hope will find an echo in his future works."[44] It was three years before the painter's first "Symphony in White" was painted. Satire of such features was not limited to the cartoon or the novel. *The Grasshopper* which ran at the Gaiety Theatre in 1877 has a character, Pygmalion Flippit, featured as a "harmonist in colours. . . . Like my great master Turner, I see things in a peculiar way, and I paint them as I see them."[45] The audience was invited to behold

> a dual harmony in Red and Blue. You observe before you . . . the boundless ocean lighted up by one of those Gorgeous Sunsets. . . . Reverse the harmony thus, and you have the equally boundless Desert . . . slumbering peacefully beneath an Azure sky.[46]

In *Fun*, an even brasher organ than *Punch*, the confidence trick element in Aestheticism (with corroboration from the Whistler-Ruskin trial) seems to confuse the production of Nocturnes with Tachism. The medium is "a pair of shoe brushes on my feet, and a bucket of any colour."[47]

Where the earlier aesthetes appear as harmless, effeminate, dangerous mainly to themselves, by the end of the 1870s, both in drama and novel, they tend to be portrayed as more self-conscious and sinister. Lambert Stryke, as the editor of *Punch*, in F. C. Burnand's *The Colonel* (1881),[48] is a confidence trickster pure and simple with his flotation of the Aesthetic High Art Company Limited that aims to cultivate "the Ideal as the consummate embodiment of the Real and to proclaim aloud to a dull material world the worship of the Lily and the Peacock Feather."[49] Stryke's enjoyment of good food has to be concealed to maintain the pretence that he feeds on beauty alone. Most of Stryke's disciples are aristocratic *dévotes*.

The Aesthetic Manuals

Punch's Mr. Fernando F. Eminate in 1877, if epicene, is nimbly topical in recommending for drawing-room decoration "lattice windows glazed with opaque glass," "sage-green or dull yellow for walls, and black furniture; not carpets" but "straw matting" on the floor and dado.[50] Pictures, of course, by "E. B. Jones and Whistler" and "delf and blue china." In one of the "aesthetic" novels, Walter Besant's and James Rice's *The Monks of Thelema* of the same year,[51] the plan for a cottage might have been designed by Fernando or appropriated by him:

> The windows were to have diamond panes, *en grisaille,* to open on hinges: the rooms, each with a dado, were to be prepared and painted in grey and green: Dutch tiles were to adorn the stoves and the fenders were of brass: no carpets, of course, but matting in wonderful designs; cabinets for the inexpensive blue and white china: chairs in black wood and rush, with tables to correspond.[52]

Eastlake's *Hints on Household Taste* (1868) had no successor—apart from its later reprintings and revisions. In 1875 though, *Punch* ran a series, "The House and the Home" by Leonardo della Robbia de Tudor Westpond Tomkyns . . . Hon. Member of the Dulidillitanty Society of the "low-toned papers" and tiled dado—the first dado in *Punch,*[53] it seems: for the dado was in *Punch*'s view both ridiculous and indispensable to the aesthetic "House Beautiful"; perhaps the noise of the word itself was pruny and prismy enough to encourage giggles.

"Soft indescribably" colors were promoted in reaction to the harsher primaries of the early nineteenth century. The Misses Garrett in *Suggestions for House Decoration* (1877) urge the suitability for the bedroom of "shades of soft olive and sage green." Not only are they "particularly pleasant and restful to the eye but altogether safe because freer from the arsenic used in the brighter greens."[54] Eastlake had advised a "delicate green or a warm grey tint" and "silver grey" as suitable backgrounds for pictures in living rooms, embossed white or cream colors for walls where water-colors were hung.[55] However, all the manuals associated with the movement did not agree: W. J. Loftie, for example, in *A Plea for Art at Home,* orthodoxly plumps for a dark-red ground as best for oils,[56] while Jakob von Falke sounds a note of caution his his rigorously and Teutonically detailed *Art in the House* (1879). The wall, he tells us, should be "absolutely quiet in tone"; it must "harmonize in colour with all, or with as many of the pictures as possible, it should be of a neutral tint. . . ." Red, that is to say, "a dark broken red, neither too fiery nor too rusty . . . of a flat tint" should be used with a border, flat in tint, or with a simple conventional hue of the same group. Alternatively Falke would allow "a decidedly broken and subdued green, something like the colour of green tea, or a dull drab."[57] No trace of Whistlerian or Godwinian chaste color here, though any mention of straw matting will suggest these sources. The engravings of the Garretts' book are specially tasteful: Godwinian coffee-tables, Morris wallpapers, etc.

All of this indicates the distance we have travelled from Eastlake's *Hints on Household Taste*. As Aslin has remarked, the illustrations in that work (although Eastlake replaced some of those in the first edition) have a mid-Victorian look that does not altogether reflect the book's modern elements. Eastlake's accenting of industrial art looks back to Sir Henry Cole's preoccupations and the establishment of the Schools of Design, but also accents his sober and pragmatic tone. Unlike the authors of later manuals, he is aware that establishing what is bad and what should not be done is easier than indicating standards of excellence. His prejudices are strong. His preference is for the English and the Gothic: French taste, so vulnerable to the rococo—"curves with everything"—and the curvilinear in furniture, rarely functional, he considers vicious. What is modern is Eastlake's approval of "fidelity to material": function must not be hidden; substance conditions form; ornament depends on the nature of the material; and art is degenerate when it directly imitates natural form, though nature remains a norm. Students should study natural form, and colors should, as in nature, be "graduated." Drawing room chairs may be light, though not rickety. The dado (presumably toned distinctively) is required to prevent monotony in the expanses of wall, floor, and ceiling. And confirming his nearness to Morris and Art and Craft, Eastlake is insistent on the superiority of wrought to cast iron, of handicraft to manufacture; he deplores stucco. His own sympathies are clearly with the Gothic, but he recognizes that it is a condition of civilization that taste should move in cycles and he himself seems to have moved in later editions to a guarded approval of the Queen Anne style for domestic eyes, though he remains uneasy over nineteenth-century eclecticism. On the other hand, total art is condemned and unlike Morris, he does not approve of the four poster. Most of his rhetoric involves "we," as appeal to consensus, now that he detects continuous improvement in public taste. Occasionally, he uses the first person and the lively contemptuous note that is frequent in the later manuals: English carpet design with its naturalistic flora is only fit to cover the floor of the Chamber of Horrors at Madame Tussauds; as for Irish porcelain, it "glistens like wet barley sugar."[58] A circular rosette is an obviously appropriate feature for the joint where the rods intersect in an iron bedstead instead of the small boss generally introduced. The designer

insists on inventing a lumpy bit of ornament, which, possibly intended to represent a cluster of leaves, more closely resembles a
friendly group of garden slugs, and this excrescence is repeated not
only a dozen times in one bedstead, but in some thousands of the same
pattern. [59]

Eastlake shows a concern with the manufacturing industry that is not
always typical of the more florid and devoted manuals of the high
Aesthetic period. Many such works were written by women. Eastlake
appears to be writing more for men than women. He has, for example,
more to say on the topic of men's than women's clothing, but apart from
deploring male dress and observing that the old hoop is better than its
modern version, he is not at all prescriptive. [60] Falke, on the other hand,
devotes a chapter to "Woman's Aesthetic Mission." It is man who is
responsible for all beautiful works of art: female artists are few and minor
and succeed best in the minuter arts. Woman's domain is the home where
she can create "the House Beautiful" for her menfolk who are too busy
with business to visit museums. "Shall the gates of the kingdom of beauty
be therefore closed" he asks "to the countless myriads of men who cannot
visit museums and collections, and to whom all possibility of coming
under the influence of art is denied?" [61] No, for the Useful and the
Beautiful shall lie down together in the House of Art, a temple whose
artificer and priestess is the wife. "Her husband's occupations necessitate
his absence and call him far away from it. During the day his mind is
occupied in many good and useful ways, in making and acquiring money
. . . and even after the hours of business have passed, they occupy his
thoughts. When he returns home tired with work he takes pleasure in the
home which his wife has made comfortable . . . and has beautified with
works of art." [62] The home should be a temple for the tired businessman,
where he can brood more agreeably on the goodness and usefulness of
acquiring money, and a means also of keeping lonely wives out of
mischief. Falke accents the influence of beautiful objects on children and in
England, certainly, children's clothes and books became expressions of the
Aesthetic Movement. [63] Books, for example, were visually agreeable,
entertaining, and did not peddle morals. Finally, Falke insists that the
woman of the house should dress up to her "artistic surroundings," should
herself be "the noblest ornament in the ornamented dwelling." [64]

Neither of the two manuals already glanced at can be termed imaginative literature, but Mrs. M. E. Haweis's "Beautiful Houses," a set of
articles contributed to *The Queen* in 1880–81 and in the latter year
published in book form, is firmly a product of the Aesthetic Movement
and amounts arguably to a set of prose poems about the interiors of houses
belonging to and largely designed by artists such as Lord Leighton and

architects such as William Burges and the Queen Anne style architect J. J. Stevenson. She looks also at several wealthy virtuosi and the interior of the British Embassy at Rome. The volume is itself a total work of art, designed for "time-travelling" through museums not altogether imaginary, "a modern vision of the past" and involving the "beauty of inclusion," a controlled eclecticism that can contain wide margins, rich italics, catchwords, the long "s," sidenotes (anterior to Whistler's *Gentle Art*), the occasional black letter words looking back to the sixteenth century, wood cut initials, and running heads that rather remarkably extend beyond the sidenotes, unifying the page. She describes Leighton's house in the following passages:

> In Lord Leighton's house the main feature is the gradual progress and ascent to the studio, and the arrangement of the ground floor, where hall opens out of hall, reviving now antique, now mediaeval, now *Renascence Italy,* from *Florence* to *Rome,* down through regal *Naples,* on to *Cairo* itself; and yet it is not *Rome,* nor *Sicily,* nor *Egypt,* but a memory, a vision seen through modern eyes.

> Turning aside from the foot of the stairs, we pass through peacock-greeny arches, with deep gold incisions, into the third Hall, called of *Narcissus,* which strikes a full deep chord of colour, and deepens the impression of antique magnificence. A bronze statuette of the fair son of *Cephisus,* from that in the Naples Museum, stands in the midst of it. Here the walls are deepest sea-blue tiles, that shades make dark; the floor is pallid (the well-known mosaic of the *Caesars'* palaces), and casts up shimmering reflected lights upon the greeny-silver ceiling, like water itself. There is something poetic and original in thus echoing here and there the points in the story of *Narcissus*—not repeating point-blank the hackneyed tale, or showing the fair boy adoring his mirror'd self in the "lily-paven lake," but just recalling it piecemeal—the lilies in the pavement, the shining lake above, and all the joy and sorrow, the luxury and pain of his loneliness and aberration, told by the colours, the purple and the gloom, and by the boy's own attitude. There is undoubtedly here an imperial stateliness and strength of flavour; and the silence is like a throne. The deep shades of the corners are filled with tarsia work and porcelain; but, as in a well-coloured picture, these are absolutely subservient; and the impression given is purple; like a Greek midnight, circling round a point of softest green (the bronze boy), and falling into a warm grey on the floor.

> But further on—beyond this vestibule—dwells the sun! and here springs up the lovely dome as of the *Alhambra,* made of the dust of the earth, but quickened by the rainbow, even as man's body sprang from dust and received a soul. People who have not a real sense of colour cannot understand the joy in it of those who have. Fine colour comes like food, like joyful news, like fresh air to fainting lungs. [65]

Disclaiming any intention of dissecting the Moorish Court, Mrs. Haweis still lingers intensely on disparate detail and evanescence of color:

> The delicate tracery of the lattices brought bodily from the *East,* and which rise to right and left, having the complexity and colour of the skeleton of a leaf, and guarded by glass outside; the fine *alhacen* of carved wood which lines the central alcove facing us, with its four rare *Persian* enamels of women's figures, and its shelves of Persian plates; the brilliant little windows that break the sunshine into scarlet and gold and azure flame; the snow-white columns of marble that stand against red at every angle; the fountain that patters and sings in its pool of chrysolite water—most perfect *colophon* to all the colours and the outer heat. Again and again we wander round and enjoy the toss of its one white jet from a bed of water wherein descending ridges step-wise have the semblance of the emerald facets of a great green stone. [66]

In describing J. J. Stevenson's house, designed like Leighton's and Burges's by the owner, Mrs. Haweis is severe on Bedford Park.

> Its handsome russet *facade* and niche holding a *Nankeen* vase, has been continually parodied by cheap builders possessed by the idea that red brick, a blue pot, and a fat sunflower in the window are all that is necessary to be fashionably aesthetic and *Queen Anne* . . . [67]

and on a sour, concluding note:

> To explain the apparent confusion of terms, I may remind readers how I have elsewhere shown that the slang term *"Queen Anne"* means almost anything just now, but it is oftenest applied to the pseudo-classic fashions of the *First Empire.* [68]

Mrs. Haweis's book on aesthetic topics appeared during the year that the movement began to decline.

Four years later, the patron and disciple of E. W. Godwin, who produced his open-air pastoral plays with their costumes delicately toned to the woodland ambience in the grounds of her house at Coombe Warren in Surrey, Lady Archibald Campbell, published a strange slim essay, *Rainbow-Music or The Philosophy of Harmony in Colour Grouping.* This amounted to a faithful reflection of the doctrines of Godwin, Whistler, and more remotely, Wagner. Her notion that certain laws "as true, though not as self-evident, as those of mathematics" operate in any work of art was illustrated by what she predictably considered to be successful applications: the color schemes of Godwin's pastoral performances and Whistler's "Peacock Room," which achieved harmony through counterpoint of blue on gold, gold on blue. And the essay concludes with a lecture on the color chromatics, "by which the seven primary colours are said to harmonise with the seven gaps in the octave."

Lady Archibald, though accurately described as the "Queen Bee" of the Aesthetes, is sharply opposed to the "House Beautiful" manuals. As for the artworks described by Mrs. Haweis, Burges's *salle de reception* in the Castle of Pierrepont is "like sitting in a Kaleidoscope." Without theme, room decoration is approached through inductive reasoning and didactic method, hardly impairing the flight of imagination. Decorative unity "is alone worthy to be designed the Grand Style." So the Imaginary Museum and the "beauty of indusiveness" approach is rejected. Lady Archibald gives us a close analysis of the Peacock Room, which concludes:

> In the mustering and opposing of these birds in feathered strife, in counterchange of golden plumes on field of azure, azure plumes on field of gold—from the glancing movement of multitudinous eyes and erected feathers and interchange of fiery tone is evolved Peace—Unity—as of ONE Plume. [69]

Lady Archibald's prose can be as lush as that of Mrs. Haweis. "The Iris Parlour" presumably refers to a real room (though this is not certain) at Inverary Castle, or her own house in Argyll, Ard Cheannglas, or even perhaps her other house at Coombe. The room is not the result of handcraft but of light and natural objects:

> Far from the sea, yet so much of the sea that within its glimmering walls the in-dweller may almost feel its air, listen for the lapping of a languid tide, and dream that from jewelled sands have been gathered all the wealth of strange conceits which bedeck the room.

> It is so far true, in that nothing but sea-wonders here find a place. Shells, large and small, shimmering with iridescent light, Venus's ears, the horned murex, rose-lipped conches, tender-coloured pectens, Triton's horns in amber and white, the graceful nautilus, the spikey spondelli, the pearl house of the sea-snail, the oyster, and the mussel, all are here. Corals peep pendant from nook and corner. A giant craw-fish from the Malay Straits combines in the tracery of its strange characteristics all the dominant hues of the room. These dominant hues are golden pink (or aurora), amethyst fading to pearl-grey, sea-green (aqua-marine), all melting in tone like the blushing dawn reflected in a calm sea. There are three lattice-windows of quaint but simple construction, all slightly differing; but as it is now evening, we see them closely curtained with aurora-colour satin of the same tint as that on the walls. On these walls are painted and on these curtains are embroidered many an Iris in delicate tint and fantastic form. Their fluttering heads and waving reeds bend hither, as if swayed by contending breezes; while others lie stricken to the ground, as if by a passing storm; their flowers vary in every tint of amethyst, pearl-grey, blue, pink, and white, and the reeds in aqua-marine and every tint of sea-green. Of nervy and resolute outline, it is the Iris of

pure convention in form and treatment; for, painted in flat colour with little shading, it suggests the spirit rather than the substance. Here and there a crystal dew-drop glistens on a petal; here and there one stands out in bold relief, shining in *Iris* tints and bathed in light; and again the water-splashes from which they rise glance with the hues of a fading rainbow; the faint water-bow itself shimmers on the wall, through which flags and flowers are seen tipped with changeful colour; gold and silver mists hover among the reeds, and add their witchery to the whole arrangement. The eye travelling the rainbow-path, or following the caprice of these wayward flowers and flags, is carried up first to a row of lustrous shells which, fixed rectangularly and about two feet apart on a pearl-grey velvet belt, support a slight shelf of gilded oak. The gilding is very pale, and seems to repeat the self-same lustre as that of the shells. This shelf divides the aurora wall from an aqua-marine frieze above, and higher still, as the eye wanders upwards, the aurora appears again on cornice and ceiling cut into by an aqua-marine oval, thus leaving the surrounding corners of aurora free, whereon ghost-like Irises have room to wave their pennons, and beck and nod their shadowy heads; a golden fishing-net at a certain angle is looped across the ceiling, and within its folds glisten the changeful light of many shells. On the pearly-grey velvet curtain, drooped low across the wide bay-window we see embroidered a tangle of ocean plants in all the colours of the room. On the door are emblazoned Landor's famous lines on the sea-shell.[70]

A description follows of M. Chevreul's color-organ of 1851, though later she alludes to that of the eighteenth-century Abbé Castel. One is led to wonder if Lady Archibald had read *A Rebours*. That her "Iris Parlour" is decadent and *symboliste,* we may gather from her rationale of the decoration:

I have been asked why I selected the Iris to accompany the sea-shell as a joint element in this decoration. On the surface of things there is, indeed, a wide divergence between the pearly tombs of the deep and the sedgy margin of some shallow pool. Yet their point of concord and bond of union is a close one. By inter-marriage of Shell and Iris is simplicity, a certain singleness of purpose accentuated—pattern given through contrast of form and line, unity throughout the colour-scheme; the shell contributing the ever-changing curvature of the volute, the spikey reed and flower-barbed shaft of the water-plant the required opposition in design. This sinuous Shell and Iris are, indeed, not only depositories of, but the symbols of, one and the same treasure—the message of peace. The shell recording in its hollows the gift of Iris; the flower, true to its name, keeping the sign of its baptism when, long ago, the goddess stepped from her rainbow-path on the white lily, which men henceforth were to call *Iris*.[71]

The Aesthetic manuals belong to the high years of the movement, 1878 to 1882, though the articles on which Mrs. Haweis's *The Art of Beauty* was based had appeared several years earlier in *St. Paul's*. There is then a hiatus, the years of the Guilds—Century and Art-Workers among others—until *The Art of the House* (1897) by the poet Rosamund Marriott-Watson, who protests against the latest fashions:

> Unhappily the same movement that dethroned the bloated common places of the day before yesterday has given birth to . . . monstrosities, human and inanimate. The decadent, the art 'square', the symbolist, the hand-painted looking glass, bedizened to distorted simulacra of Iris and Mary-lily; the "art" wall-paper with its misbegotten sunflowers and poppies, its inane mediaeval dicky-birds intermixed with geometrical patternings, its living complexion, now sour, now sallow, but ever revolting.[72]

She consoles herself, however, that the monstrosities "have mainly ebbed on to the suburbs." Her book presumably appeared because of an ambitious Art Library scheme promulgated by the publisher, George Bell.

The Aesthetic Novel

That *Two Years Ago* furnished the model for the aesthete antihero is evident enough. We are told by *Fun* on 23 February 1881 that like his Pilcox, Du Maurier's Basil Georgione was a chemist before he took to art. John Briggs himself had run away from a chemist shop to be a poet. Briggs anticipates Henry James's Roderick Hudson of 1875, a morally weak artist, and the type continues with the Hamlin of *Miss Brown*, Moore's Lewis Seymour, and the hero of Kipling's *The Light That Failed*. Elsley Vavasour had a principled dislike of the horrible. *Punch* on 24 February 1877 devotes some attention to a nasty criminal case: A couple had brutally mistreated a servant they had been sent from an orphanage. As soon as the girl arrived, the mistress of the house had complained about her servant's appearance. She was too plain and "she wished her child from the first to look only on what was beautiful."[73] Mrs. Perry applies the same criterion in *Miss Brown,* and *Punch,* solemn for once, drew a moral about "the absolute independence of Ethics and Aesthetics and the entire absence of correlation between Art and Morals."[74] The cold aesthete is memorably imaged in the Osmond of *Portrait of a Lady* (1881). James's Gabriel Nash, who "announces" Nick Dormer's talent as a painter in *The Tragic Muse,* is an aesthete of another type, but Nash too objects to ugly words that denote an ugly world: "Mr. Pinks, the member of Harsh? What names to be sure."[75] And Mr. Rose in the *New Republic,* when he enters ugly houses, often takes "a scrap of some artistic cretonne with me in my pocket as a kind of aesthetic smelling salts." [76]

In *The Monks of Thelema* (1877) those who confront and those who evade the ugliness of common life are sharply contrasted. Alan Dunlop, a solemn young aristocrat, is under Ruskin's influence and has done his bit for the road-building project, unlike his friend Paul Rondolet, Fellow of "Lothian College" (his name may owe something to the French and English Parnassian poets—or to the Rondeliers, who in their rondeaux, rondels kyrielles, and other old French forms pursued the ideal of formal purity). While Dunlop applies himself to improving his estate, Rondolet lurks effetely, like the type about to appear in *Punch* with his "long white fingers, which played plaintively about his face. . . . He spoke in a low voice as if exhausted by the effort of living among humans, and he spoke with melancholy, as if his superiority were a burden to him; he affected omniscience."

Besant and Rice offer an etiology of aestheticism as a "school of prigs . . . some of them are still at Oxford; but some may now be found in London. They lounge about sales of china . . . and they worship at the Grosvenor Gallery. Rondolet called himself, sadly, an agnostic, but he was in reality, a New Pagan." [77] Whether this anticipates Wilde's New Hedonism is not clear. Rondolet is indifferent to the ritualism of the Aesthetes, refuses to take orders, affects to be unable to pronounce his r's, and his poem "Aspasia's Apology" is a companion piece to Rossetti's "Jenny," only "even more realistic." "Above all," Rondolet tells us, "the man of Higher Culture is a critic," anticipating Pater and Gabriel Nash once more: "Literature, you see, is for the convenience of others. It requires the most abject concessions. It plays such mischief with one's style that really I have to give it up." Rondolet is an elitist, who finds it "useless and even mischievous to promote culture. Especially when such efforts lead to personally interesting oneself with the lower classes." [78] This attitude is the "Paterian" as opposed to the "missionary" attitude toward culture.

Thelema itself is a genteel, hardly Rabelaisian commune devoted to aesthetic dilettantism, with lectures and a gazette promulgating the Higher Culture. The agreeable life of the inhabitants of the abbey (actually Alan's country house) is presented idyllically rather than ironically, though the tone sometimes drifts into irony. At Thelema, "dining was no longer the satisfaction of an appetite; it became the practice of one of the Fine Arts." [79] The Canon's daughter "was aesthetic, dressed in neutral tints, parted her hair on the side, and corrected her neighbours in a low voice when they committed barbarities in art. She was not pretty, but she was full of soul, and she longed to be invited to join the order. . . ." [80] But invited, she is not. Her "soul" is not smart enough. Alan, the landowner, has a total lack of success with aestheticizing the local proletariat. Briefly he finances Rondolet's magazine, more *raffiné* than any other review. It fails, and Rondolet resorts to the lower journalism, not "writing for the common herd" but now "swaying the masses."

Robert Buchanan in the preface to his *Martyrdom of Madeline* (1882) hedges his bets by attempting to distinguish between "aestheticism proper"—he is still trying to exculpate himself from the Fleshly School Controversy of 1872—and "the cant of Aestheticism." Vernon Lee's Hamlin in *Miss Brown* of 1884 as both poet and painter is certainly based on Rossetti, the main target of Buchanan's attack, though he comes from the landed class. His refusal to ameliorate the condition of the villagers on his estate is compounded by incorporating their incestuous vice into his own poem. The analogue with Elsley Vavasour's impassive surveillance of a shipwreck as raw material for a poem is plain enough. The Pre-Raphaelite set in this novel is a simplified, coarsened version of William Michael Rossetti's circle at Fitzroy Square in the 1870s and 1880s.[81] In Buchanan's novel, Gavrolles represents the "new Aesthetic set," influenced for the worst by "poisonous honey" not exactly "stolen from France" since Gavrolles is himself a Frenchman. This set supersedes the old Bohemia, though Gavrolles seems to add a missionary keenness to his "Art-for-Art's sake" heresy. He is described as "having Communist views."[82] Buchanan's views of communist views probably owed more to contemporary reporting of the commune than to Marx. Hamlin's exotic cousin Sacha is another evil graft on the native Bohemia. Elitism in aesthetic circles is confirmed by the species of mutual admiration Buchanan disliked in Pre-Raphaelitism: He saw it as inevitably connected with the practice of several arts and the close connections between the arts: the poet writes a sonnet on the painter's "poetic" image, while the painter illustrates the painterly qualities of the poet by illustrating his work, and both are praised by the "aesthetic" critic. And Buchanan and "Vernon Lee" share an attitude of pained sensitivity to the aesthetic mode's accommodation to the erotic, though this becomes involved with Buchanan's genuine sympathy with the wrongs of women under the Victorian double standard. Even so, Buchanan still exalts woman for her traditional virtues of self-sacrifice, suffering, and patience. He does not recognize any virtue in the Pre-Raphaelite and Aesthetic Movement's concern with women of the lower classes and with the "unchaste" woman. What he observes is the reduction of woman to the role of sex goddess: the Lucrezia Borgia of Swinburne's verse or her worship by Vernon Lee's Cosmo Clough (a version of Arthur O'Shaugnessy), in the physical distortion of Rossetti's later mannerism, the convulsed necks in the "Astarte Syriaca" corresponding to the painter's psychic distortion of woman, and that Zolaesque lingering over the degradation of women in the person of the prostitute. The stately Lecky, speaking for enlightened Victorian males, eloquently salutes the fallen woman as antinomy incarnate:

> herself the supreme type of vice [she] is ultimately the most efficient guardian of virtue. But for her, the unchallenged purity of countless happy homes would be polluted, and not a few who in the pride of their untempted chastity, think of her with an indignant shudder, would have known the agony of remorse and despair. On that one degraded and ignoble form are concentrated the passions that might have filled the world with shame. She remains, while creeds and civilisations fall, the eternal priestess of humanity, blasted for the sins of the people.[83]

To descend from that paean—we need only chaperone, not lock up our daughters—let us glance at the heroine of Mrs. John Lillie's novella *Prudence,* who in the first chapter appears at an "aesthetic gathering" in "passionate Brompton" alarmingly without a chaperone. A male friend has brought her to the door and will call for her at one o'clock in the morning. *Prudence* was to be published in Britain, but appeared first in *Harper's New Monthly Magazine* between December 1 88 1 and May 1 88 2, altogether appropriately, for the action conforms to the by now familiar contrast between Europe (ruined Paradise) and America (wilderness becoming Eden), a *topos* doubtless deeply reassuring to its transatlantic audience. Aestheticism is part of that ruined Paradise, but is mildly treated. The principal characters, with the exception of an absurd and absurdly named English aristocrat, Barley Simmonson (desperate evasion of libel?), are all transatlantic. Aestheticism has been taken up by society and has claimed two charming, cultivated sisters, the younger, unmarried, Helena, a sympathetic critic of the movement. Prudence, a simple sweet thing from Ponkamak, precipitates the action when the Aesthetes take her up as an animated Boticelli or, as one genial hostess observes: "The child is like the Pompeian Psyche." In fact, she is like her pretty silly self, but plays her role capitally by acting as passive vehicle for specially designed aesthetic dresses; like the girls of Albert Moore (whose work is alluded to when the Bromptonians visit the Grosvenor Gallery), Prudence *means* nothing at all. Her hopeful suitor, an American clergyman, discovers this. Helena falls in love with this young Hickory figure, who seems to her a forcible emblem not of London, Washington, or Boston, but "the fervider, more intrinsically American life which has for its background, as it were, the cañons of Colorado, the ranches of California" [84] very much "as it were." Helena nobly precipitates the two toward one another, but

Prudence is already absorbed in being the idol of the Aesthetes and the watercoloring, arpeggio doodling Barley Simmonson is on the verge of proposing. Fortunately, another wealthier, moderately Hickory young American turns up and marries Prudence instead. Barley rapidly transposes his loss into sentiment and the reader is left wondering idly if Helena will ever again see her "fervider intrinsically" Yankee preacher. But even the fervider sees some good in Aestheticism, and Helena gravely observes that "the false ground of aestheticism is only in the establishing a standard of feeling." This rather baffling remark is given point by Barley who clearly is quite unable to establish any standard of feeling. It hardly requires the narrator to mock aestheticism when he is on stage. Even the peerage it seems can be aestheticized: "Then we may wear laurel in Westminster; then we may assemble as one palpitating, perfect soul." [85]

The preoccupations of the novels of Kingsley, Mrs. Hunt, Vernon Lee, Mrs. Lillie, and others are more magisterially addressed by Henry James through *The Tragic Muse* of 1889, and in Gabriel Nash we at last encounter a sufficiently subtle species of "aesthete," though one with a decadent fear of his own image: He seems to lose identity as Nick Dormer's portrait of him advances, and finally, like the Cheshire Cat, even his epigrams disappear.

The Kyrle Society

"Missionary" aestheticism is best exemplified by the history of the Kyrle Society. It would require a far abler and more sociological pen than mine to write that history; all I can do is mention and let fall salient moments. The Kyrle's origins have been traced to the appearance of a brief pamphlet in December 1875, "A Suggestion to those who love Beautiful Things" by Miranda, sister of the famous housing reformer, Octavia Hill. Miranda suggested that a "Society for the Diffusion of Beauty" along the lines of the "Society for the Diffusion of Christian Knowledge" might be formed for "helping the great work of making beautiful places for the poor . . . our towns are growing so enormously . . . there is less and less possibility of beautiful country objects being within the reach of the poor in their daily lives" for they were beyond walking distance. [86]

A small committee had actually begun work in October 1875 and its first, paradigmatic efforts included the planting of flowers on barren land, the draping of ugly buildings with creepers, the provision of window boxes and flowers, the painting of walls in St. Jude's church in the slums of Whitechapel with panels of wildflowers, and those of an institute building with sketches of the countryside, along with the carving of brackets.

Miranda wrote plays for slum children and organized drama for the adults; oratorios were sung at churches in poor areas of London before working-class audiences and in public gardens on evenings of summer. More than a tinge of Ruskinism seems to color such activities. The Kyrle Society published its first annual report in December 1876, and became a national organization in June 1877 when it acquired Prince Leopold and Princess Louise as president and vice-president respectively. The real work, though, was done by devoted bands of middle-class persons up and down the country. Often the same family would provide officers for the various activities through several generations. The national committee members included William Morris, G. F. Watts, Mrs. Alfred Hunt, whom we have encountered already as author of *Thorneycroft's Model*, and the faintly incongruous figure of G. A. Sala, journalist and very *bon viveur*.

The society's name derived from the philanthropist John Kyrle of Ross in Herefordshire, celebrated in lines 249 to 280 of Pope's *Epistle to Bathurst* as one who on limited means provided considerable service to the local poor. The society was never to control much money, and appeals in the newspapers for funds and volunteers were not infrequent. Octavia, the more forcible of the Hill sisters,[87] was active in the more public activities of the society, the Open Spaces Committee, which began by transforming old churchyards of the inner city into gardens, preserving open spaces in the suburbs, so becoming the ancestor of the present National Trust. *Punch,* which seems not to have become aware of the Kyrle Society until 1881, directed its satire mainly against the notion of offering beauty to the poor in place of bread, and feared the unsettling of those whose labor sustained the social order. A few verses from "A Kyrley Tale" to the tune of "A Norrible Tale" will make the point:

Oh a curious tale I am going to tell
Of the singular fortunes that befel
A family which late resided
In a slum by High Art much derided.

They never dreamed of the Weird Intense,
Though a family of undoubted sense,
Till a Kyrle Man came with his lyre and lily,
And drove that unfortunate household silly.

He came, soft carolling, "Lo! I come!
My mission's the bringing of Beauty home!"
And he opened the door, and he led her in,
A weariful damsel pale and thin.

With eyes as dusk as the veil of Isis,
Like an incarnation, she seemed, of Phthisis.
When in he ushered this spectral Psyche,
The family's comment all round was "Crikey!"

But the spell was on them, they stood and gazed
Till their souls grew dim and their sight grew dazed;
From the youngest child to the father burly
Their views of life straight before, grew Kyrly.

The father—he was a hearthstone vendor—
Strove to make his street-cry as subtly tender
As Chopin Nocturne, and pined to a shade,
And ruined his voice, and lost his trade.

The mother—she used to go out to 'char'—
Fell madly in love with a Japanese jar,
The pot, with cold scraps, in her basket left,
And was quodded for taste, which the law called theft,

The eldest son—and he carried a hod—
Yearned his ladder to mount with the grace of a god
In Attic story, but failed and fell
From the Attic story, and ne'er got well.

The eldest daughter—a work-girl plain—
Would touzle her hair and wear gauze in the rain;
Caught cold, sought cure in a peacock's feather,
And died of High Art and the state of the weather. . . .

Clearly the satirist was ignorant of the society and its aims.[88] But not all those involved shared the same aims. William Morris, speaking as a convinced socialist to the Kyrle Society on 27 January 1881, asserted the society's aim was to fight "Carelessness, Ugliness and Squalor," and in another address at Nottingham on 16 March of that same year he used the occasion to attack laissez-faire capitalism and dilettantism: If those who work with their hands will not have art, then "we the cultivated and rich people cannot have it; if they cannot have it, if our social system forbids it to them, be sure that the day is not far distant when the cultivated part of our society will refuse art also, will have grown utterly blind to it."[89] The aim of the Kyrle Society must be to "resist such a return to barbarism, nay to a state of degradation far worse than barbarism, for that was hopeful." The Society has begun at the right end, with art. Any discussion about art as its own end, rather than for a purpose, is fruitless: A "real artist does his work because he likes it . . . when done 'tis a blessing to his fellows."[90] And Morris anticipates the natural rage of the deprived against art: the slashing of pictures, vandalism, graffiti. The Kyrle Society's work is not mere palliation of a steady social state. A note of warning is added: any decoration for the poor should be up to the standard of marketable work.

Octavia Hill in an article of 1884, "Colour, Space and Music for the People," adapted from a paper given to the Society at Grosvenor House on 24 March 1884, stresses that the Kyrle Society, in bringing joy to the poor, does not claim to bring them "the principal sources of joy." These are religious: Music, color, art, space, and quiet are "secondary gifts," but distributed with a sad inequality. For Miss Hill, the stencils on the walls of parish halls and the colored prints in squalid houses amount to a species of *biblia pauperum;* they speak of "higher things" to those who are too weary or ill-educated to read. Miss Hill emphasizes the importance of helping the deserving poor and she attacks those who have "a depraved hunger for rags, sharp need, and slums. . . . 'I should like to go where there is condensed misery,' a lady said lately in the cheeriest tone . . . there is a certain excited temper abroad which almost amounts to a longing to see extreme want."[91] Rather in the spirit of those who earlier in the century had enjoyed public executions. Unlike Morris, Miss Hill does not take large philosophical views of society: there is work to be done, economically, and in a devotional spirit.

By 1884 associations had been founded at Liverpool (1877), Birmingham (1880), Glasgow (1882), Leicester, Bristol, and Nottingham. The Birmingham Society is particularly well documented, and its activities included plays and concerts. What this illustrates is that the Kyrle was responsive to movements of taste in the arts. Its history of *Work Done and Proposals for New Developments* has a rousing cover design by Walter Crane—an angel festooned by a streamer with the bracing device "Art for All: The New Social Order Work for All." This is reinforced by the familiar "all for one and one for all": Socialism, Art and Craft and Trade Unionism. The program illustrating Pinero's "The Schoolmistress" given at Edgbaston on 13 and 14 December has *art nouveau* poppies (recalling Mackmurdo's famous design for *Wren's City Churches*). Pinero, indeed, was the favored Kyrle dramatist, but the dramatic entertainments were probably directed to the volunteers rather than to the poor. The songs, however, given at musical evenings were popular, sentimental, and insipid and illustrate Morris's warning about aesthetic condescension to the working class. Morris's influence can be detected in the record of the society's aims in 1894 as being "to revive the handicrafts amongst men to whom work has become drudgery rather than delight."[92] The most ambitious activity of these years was the new building designed by W. H.

Bidlake in 1892 for the Kyrle Hall Workshops. This embraced the activities of the society and the Birmingham Guild of Handicraft, founded in 1890, seven years after the Century Guild. Bookbinding, woodcarving, and the fashioning of doorplates were among its activities. The "simple type" of Flemish building, "quaint and unobtrusive," contained a hall, a stage, a boy's club, men's workshops, and a library.

In 1896 a May Festival was given. The program printed by the Guild of Handicraft has a Celtic-type initial letter with an elaborate tail, showing that the Kyrle was once more at the frontier of fashion. MacFarren's cantata, "May Day," was given by the Kyrle choir, and we are reminded of the May entertainments at girls' schools under the auspices of Ruskin. The program included also a song by the notorious Lord Henry Somerset, in exile for his unorthodox sexual tastes, "Come to me in the silence of the night." This, along with sentimental, morally wholesome *lieder*, set the tone. Annual reports of the Birmingham Society continue until 1908, but the Kyrle survived until much later. *The Kyrle Hall Flash* (incorporating *The Wag and Perch*), the magazine of the boys' and girls' union respectively, was still being pubished between 1942 and 1953, though by that time its original connection with the society may well have faded. The Liverpool Society "quietly ceased to exist" in 1919. Its activities had been increasingly taken over by the Corporation, and more intense Local Government spending on tree planting, seats, music for the ratepayers, etc. rendered its program nugatory.[93]

One of the more ambitious enterprises undertaken by the Society was the production and publication of the Kyrle Pamphlets. The second of those was *The Guide to the Italian Pictures at Hampton Court* by Mary Logan, Bernard Berenson's disciple, mistress, and, finally, wife. Mary's description of the pictures combines historical survey, brief appreciation, and a species of reattribution associated with the connoisseurship of Morelli, Frizzoni, Richter, and Berenson himself. The arguments in favour of such reattributions are not given, we are blandly assured, in order "to bring the work within the limits of similar publications of the Kyrle Society."[94] Still, there can be no doubt that these pages are for the educated, not the poor. The disciple of Pater stands revealed in Mary's description of Giorgione's temperament as Greek, though with a subtlety, a refinement, and feel for landscape in, for example, the Dresden Venus that goes beyond the reach of Greek art. We then pass to the "blonde manner" of Palma, and the story of the Venetian school ends with Tintoretto and Bassano's "jewel-like colouring and mysterious effects of twilight and night": hardly unorthodox descriptions. Mary will have no truck with Mannerism; we are hastily shuffled on to the *ottocento* and the piece concludes with a long examination of the Mantegna *Triumph of Caesar*.

Like Octavia Hill's housing schemes, the Kyrle was a symptom of the old paternalism; it was to be succeeded not only by the National Trust but by a new impersonal paternalism of state benefits that has now, it seems, run its course. The need for a revival of the best type of private effort as represented by the Kyrle is pointed.

The Dress Reform Movement

A further activist area was dress reform, a movement that began somewhat late and cohered only sporadically. It was to reach its consummation in the United States rather than in Britain with the apotheosis of the "bloomer." The movement's comparative failure on the cisatlantic shore stems from its proponents being highly various: men, women, aristocrats, the middle classes, with often divergent aims. Though it involved art and craft figures no less than aesthetes, and coincided with the moment when the Aesthetic Movement was already faltering, the dress movement (which could sometimes be construed as an "undress" movement) was certainly patient of a "decadent" accent, particularly in its more Hellenic form.

The first generation of Pre-Raphaelites had reacted against Victorian constrictions. Rossetti, as Leonee Ormond has pointed out,[95] disliked the "unnatural" taste of modern costume, and since reformed dress existed in painting from the 1850s it is the more remarkable that systematic reform should have taken so long to come about. But for the exalted, the beautiful, and the eccentric, all of whom might ignore fashion, dress was essentially a matter of individual style. Some generalizations emerge. That the aesthetic ladies of the late 1870s and the earlier 1880s did affect shapeless garments that ignored the waist and failed to accent the *derrière* was not evaded by *Punch* and other unkind observers. And documentation of a distinguished minority's wear can be found in Frith's well-known picture of the Private View of the Academy. There, highly fashionable dresses suavely brush the more fluent spaces of the female Aesthetes. Disciples of Art and Craft tended to stress the healthy and the useful, though the Aesthetic element saw the end as beauty of form and color: nature demanded the use of natural colors rather than synthetic (the aniline dye had been recently perfected). The artist Henry Holiday, prominent in dress reform circles, suggested indeed that Beauty should rank higher than either Health or Utility. In nearly every publication of the movement, the three values were interrelated with free motion. This interrelationship involved an attack on the tyrannous supremacy of the corset, stiffly whaleboned to create the waist. As early as 1860, Wilkie Collins in *The Woman in White* had praised the natural form of the female waist, "occupying its natural circle . . . visibly and delightfully undeformed by stays."[96]

The earlier reformers, we are told, damaged the cause by insufficiently accenting beauty and instead stressing the fact that nineteenth-century woman's costume rendered her unfit even for light home duties, frequently indeed causing those faints, so much an index of the sensibility of the heroine in contemporary novels. These arguments were barely germane to, say, Lady Elcho, who had evolved her own style of loose dress and whose home duties were seldom more arduous than entertaining Arthur Balfour in the East Room at Stanway, their "right paradise," occasionally proffering a little light flagellation. Holiday, in the first issue of the dress reform periodical *Aglaia,* suggested a modified form of rational dress for working, whether about the house or in the fields (another instance of the aesthetic mission to all classes), a loose over-dress which could be looped into sashes for walking and practical work or let down to ankle-length for a housedress, modeled on European peasant costumes and those of classical Greece, with cross-sash fastenings. Dress played a large role in dividing the sexes, and at a period when "liberation" was beginning, women became aware that dress was actually constraining their physical potential, muting health and general activity.

The Pre-Raphaelite taste was for the vaguely medieval; the taste for the Greek style was furthered by the elaborate machine paintings of Leighton and Alma Tadema and the glowing, timeless idylls of Albert Moore. E. W. Godwin, another hierarch of the movement, wrote extensively on dress reform, advocating "freedom of the body" and designing Greek costumes for his meticulously archaeological reconstruction of a Greek theater at Hengler's Circus, Regent Street, where John Todhunter's play, some way after Euripides's *Helena in Troas* (1886) was performed, with Mrs. Oscar Wilde swirling whitely among the chorus. However, the taste for Greek costumes dates as far back as the neo-Greco movement of the early nineteenth century, to Lord Guilford's vision of the boys of the Ionian Academy at Corfu at work and at play in the chlamys. Whatever the nature of Lord Guilford's antiquarianism, boys in chiton and chlamys became part of the vision and vocabulary of the "New Hellenism" of Wilde and others, and the photographs of Sicilian youth so prized by homoerotic collectors show them, when not nude, in Greek apparel, appropriate to that island's antique past. The late nineteenth-century versions of Greek dress are hardly precise archaeologically since the loose long robes were fastened with stylish unconcern at the shoulders so that they could take the wind and be curved into fetching arabesques. Oscar Wilde, it need hardly be said, approved, suggesting that such designs would form the costume of the future. Such recourse to Greek practice, so April Dunnett points out, lent authority and respectability to dress reform. This was indeed part of the time-travelling inherent in the Aesthetic Movement (compare the costume conversazione popular at Bedford Park round about 1880). Leonee Ormond reminds us of how the aesthetic ladies had loose, long, flowing waistless dresses with "leg of mutton sleeves and no bustles—a mixture of motifs, from any period that was sufficiently distant and romantic. They favoured large floral patterns and restrained colour schemes." [97] The dresses were worn without petticoats, and they produced that drooping effect familiar from *Punch* cartoons.

In the late 1880s, a few issues of a Gazette had been published by the Rational Dress Society, but the full spectrum of the movement is better gathered from the periodical *Aglaia,* which ran to three numbers between July 1893 and October 1894. *Aglaia* was the official organ of the Healthy and Athletic Dress Union, which included men and women of several social classes. The general principles involved no corsets, free play for the limbs, low heels for shoes, and lightweight clothes for work and recreation: economy through simple dress free of changes in fashion.

Throughout the English movement toward dress reform, Beauty may have nominally been the highest factor, but Health seems to predominate—certainly as a means to Beauty. *Aglaia* alludes to one of the Graces, Adornment. Her sisters, Thalia and Euphrosyne, who share the cover design, represent pastoral health and joy, along with the practice of homely skills such as weaving (we are reminded of Morris at the loom). Only under *Aglaia*'s aegis may Health and Utility flourish. As April Dunnett remarks: "the stated principles of the Union fail to mention Beauty or artistic taste at all; only health and economy." [98] But both are probably taken as read. *Aglaia*'s tone is persuasive; even the corset is mildly censured. The dresses illustrated combine classicism with the folk and the medieval, signs of Art and Craft once more merging with older Aesthetic influences. Several years later such dresses were advertised in Liberty Catalogues. But by the end of the century, rational, utilitarian, brashly medical (think of Jaeger suiting!), the English movement faded.

Yet Aestheticism survived the century and precisely in those aristocratic circles where it first became prominent. In Oxford, as in London, 1895 and all that had finally blanched the movement of its frivolity, its elegance, and its public. But in their country houses the "Souls"—their nickname which, like the Decadents they sometimes shruggingly accepted—continued to be hospitable to literature and art and in turn inspired the authors of *Dodo* and *The New Machiavelli* and the somewhat more tepid fictions of the Honourable Maurice Baring.

"Soul" and "The Souls"

A lustre of ladies, like elusively tinted moths fluttering round the thin flame of Arthur James Balfour, statesman and philosopher (of whom it has recently been remarked that though the flesh was willing, the spirit was bleak), were themselves not only inspirers of literature and art, their images descending to us from the hands of Poynter, Watts, Burne-Jones and J. S. Sargent, but talented artists also. Violet, Duchess of Rutland, was a painter; Nina Cust (never quite accepted into the group, the too grave wife of one of the more dashing members) a sculptress; and Lady Elcho created her own luminous ambience, tasteful yet inexpensive. Poynter's watercolor illustrates her, aesthetically habited, among the vases accented with flowers, oriental screens, and flame-colored fishes mildly drifting through their vast bowls in that paradisal, if piercingly cold "East Room" behind Stanway's warmly golden stonework (light flagellation of Balfour by Lady Elcho may well have been a physical as much as a psychological solatium). Lady Elcho's exquisite and ingeniously designed playing cards are as evocative in their manner as Conder's fans. Lady Desborough, an alarming beauty, was captured by Sargent as Selene in black chalk, the upcurved moon tangling faintly in her hair. The Duchess of Rutland, it was said, found Morris's colors too vulgarly bright and would put out his curtains and rugs on the lawns to fade them in the sun, Morris reportedly acquiescing. In their intellectual gaiety, their intense interrelationships, their treatment of politics as game and the drawing room games of their own devising with a high seriousness, they carried life as art far beyond the interiority of Pater and the iridescent talk of Wilde.

As Mark Girouard has splendidly shown, "The Souls" consummated the chivalric ideals of the century: the women of the circle tended to be the more formidable and claimed the right to pursue a cult of passion between the sexes: "Unlimited licence in love, save for the one connubial act" and some, Lady Desborough certainly, exceeded when it so pleased them that limit, though her finer pleasures seem to have consisted in the subjugation of numbers: "the chase was more important than the kill." In conflating siren with *grande dame,* the women of the sect practiced a species of *amour courtois* and indeed not merely their decor, but their friendships and ideals also, were more than tinged by the revived medieval and the Pre-Raphaelite: The *Morte D'Arthur* furnished exempla, all banners and adultery. And as Mark Girouard points out they were wealthy enough to build or better refurbish actual castles: those ladies needed richly suggestive backgrounds, though Stanway, most beautiful of backgrounds, was modest enough. Pre-Raphaelitism, Aestheticism—they inherited many of the cultural ideals of the nineteenth century and their enthusiasms extended to Wagner, Rodin, and bicycling, while Balfour, in moments not given to Lady Elcho and the House of Commons, threw off his somber theorems as to Philosophic Doubt. The painters they admired were admitted to the circle, and even to its rites, as the tensely passionate friendship between Burne-Jones and Lady Windsor witnesses.

"The Souls" had inherited their attitudes from an older generation of hostesses, "the Aunts" as they called them, but their children were not to inherit. For twenty years the women moved, part of society, yet superior to it; the men were continuously and conspicuously in government, but their male children in particular were shadowed by their splendid mothers. The world shifted in 1914 and the trenches claimed, almost without exception, those sons, some gifted but all restless. Still, Barrie, George Moore, and others were to be found at Stanway in the early 1930s. "Anima dilectissima," Lady Elcho died in 1937. Perhaps the "Souls" were not as elect, not so clever as they themselves thought, but not since the Heian world of Japan in the tenth century, and not for a long time to come, is such a circle likely once more to cohere.[99]

But where does all this leave us? The aesthetic movement, we may conclude, is only marginally connected with literature: it subsisted in satire, in parody, and in the furtive cadences of Pater; and it subsisted in art, the remote glow of Albert Moore's flower maidens lost in timeless reverie, their world, in Ruskin's phrase, "without facts," as though they only lived as part of the design of an oriental carpet. Essentially centrifugal then, Aestheticism, before it finally dissolved, became fully embodied in a total art of love and friendship, vivacity and style, more passionate than Brompton could ever have kindled.

2

Collecting the Quarrels

Whistler and *The Gentle Art of Making Enemies*

Stanley Weintraub

For Jimmy Whistler the only thing more gratifying than coining a *mot* was publishing it. When Walter Sickert fathered one, and wanted to insure its publication, he attributed it to Whistler, which gained it the front page of the *Westminster Gazette,* directly under the leading article. "Very nice of you, very proper, to invent *mots* for me," the Master said. "'The Whistler *Mots* Propagation Bureau!' I know! Charming! Only when they are in languages I don't know, you had better advise me in good time, and send me a translation. Otherwise I am congratulated on them at dinner parties, and it is awkward."[1]

People even noted Whistler's *mots* in their diaries, one such entry by Thomas Sergeant Perry in 1888 reporting, "Whistler is mistaken for a hatter's clerk and addressed, 'This hat doesn't fit.' 'True, and your coat is damnably ill cut, and I don't like the set of your trousers.' Going to Collinses he finds an obviously unfinished picture in Whistler's style, a frame like his own. C. asks for advice. 'Leave it as it is.' C. apologizes for the frame, a copy of one of Whistler's, saying, 'You see, I took a leaf out of your book.' At the foot of the steps W. says, 'It must have been a flyleaf.'"[2] The squibs and polemics by which Whistler advertised himself were indispensable to his existence. As much as the Victorian artistic establishment would have had it otherwise, he would not be ignored. "I have seen Whistler," Sickert once wrote, "spend mornings of precious daylight showing Nocturne after Nocturne to the football correspondent of a Fulham local paper."[3]

Whistler's quarrelsome tone, often astute and clever, could degenerate easily into sheer silliness, for he was poorly educated and haphazardly self-educated. In Max Beerbohm's unfinished *The Mirror of the Past,* unpublished in his lifetime, Max parodied a taunting Whistler letter of the type reproduced in *The Gentle Art.* "Furious but amusing," it is sent to the mythical Sylvester Herringham, a one-time friend of Dante Gabriel Rossetti, who had commented on Whistler's notorious inability to complete a commission on time. "Is perfection," Whistler retorts, amid ejaculations in French and German, "to be timed by the stop-watch, and must the painter in his wisdom compete with the perspiring fleet ones [hurrying bicyclists] of Lil[le]y Bridge? Was it between the fish and the soup that your Darwin knew Man a Monkey?"

Herringham's curt reply gets to the heart of Whistler's style and methods as seen by his detractors. "Your note has reached me. In so far as I can extract any meaning from its polyglot and illiterate verbiage, I deduce (1) that you are angry, and (2) that you are, at the same time, attempting to be funny. As to the reason for your anger I am as profoundly indifferent as I am depressed by your efforts to be funny."[4] Whistler, in Max's fantasy, replies with further polyglot invective, as he might have in life, always eager to supply the last word, and, if he could, to get it into print. His letters on professional issues were always intended to educate a larger public more than to explain or exculpate Whistler himself. Had the Herringham correspondence existed, he would have included it in *The Gentle Art,* risking the likelihood that despite his giving himself, always, the last word, his antagonist might have already furnished the reader with the more persuasive one.

Among the Americans in London whom Whistler knew in the late 1880s was Sheridan Ford, who wrote for the *New York Herald* and the Irving Bacheller Syndicate, and who had published *Art: a Commodity* (1888). Having written several columns on Whistler, Ford had occasion to root through the newspaper files in which the record of the artist's jousts with his contemporaries had appeared, and came up with the idea that the exchange of correspondence was worth preserving as a book. It meant a second wind for the old antagonisms, and possible income, which Whistler was only too willing to share if Ford did most of the work. As his collaborator searched newspaper files in the British Museum, Whistler went through boxes of correspondence and clippings he stored at home, often taking an already printed letter and repolishing the text in order to sharpen a barb or improve his own position in an old controversy.

Originally the collection bore the commonplace and not altogether accurate title of *The Correspondence of James McNeill Whistler;* and the type was already being set by Messrs. Field and Tuer of the Leadenhall Press when the author, urged on by his wife, Trixie, decided to cancel the agreement, pay off the editor with a pittance, and order him to proceed no farther with the publication. The printers, receiving a similar notice from Whistler's solicitor, George Lewis, obeyed; and it may have been preliminary to that action that Lewis, at his office in Ely Place, asked, "But, my dear Jimmy, would it be quite just—?"

"My dear George," Whistler interrupted, "when I pay you six-and-eightpence, I pay you six-and-eightpence for *law,* not justice."[5]

The law was on Whistler's side. He owned the rights to his own writing, although he had instructed Ford earlier to secure permissions in his own name from the newspapers involved, which Ford had accomplished. As Ford recalled the episode, when he was "measurably within sight of the promised land of printer's proofs, Mr. Whistler, one fine morning, sweetly asked to have sent [to] him everything collected in the way of copy. The strangeness of the request sowed the seed of distrust. . . ." On asking why, Ford was "blandly informed that Mr. Whistler wished to convey the matter entirely out of Mr. Ford's hands and entrust it to Mr. Whistler's *cher ami,* one Theodore Duret, of Paris, who would kindly take charge [and] . . . substitute his own name on the title-page. . . ." Duret, a friendly and Anglophile Parisian critic whose portrait Whistler had painted as *Arrangement in Flesh Colour and Black* (1884), would not be involved and may not even have known that his name would be mentioned. Still, Ford had no intentions of presenting Duret with Whistler's gift, and angrily stamped out.

Quickly, Whistler rushed off a note to Ford (19 August 1889) of more than usual ambiguity. "Let us have no wrong impressions. I thoroughly know that you are just the man to bring to its completion the work in question, and how lucky I am in having interested you in it." Dropping any suggestion of Duret, Whistler declared that his involvement in painting had to be "made anterior to more literature," and that the "proposed publication" would have to be postponed "for awhile." But he was prepared to be generous. "Do let me recognise slightly the time and care you have taken to give the collection the shape it already has. I enclose, therefore, [a] cheque for ten guineas. I do not in this way pretend to value the pains you have been at, but in all fairness to each of us you must allow me to see that you are not so far absolutely the loser."[6]

In frustration and fury, Sheridan Ford decided that the letter required a Whistlerian reply. "No! no!" he wrote the next day, "believe me, you state the case clumsily. What you meant to say was, how lucky you were in my having interested you in yourself." Returning the check he added, "Shall I have a brutal philanthropy thrust upon me and be buried by the vulgar cheque of commerce? Credit it not, though chaos reign in Chelsea! Know also that I am endowed in perpetuity by an all-wise Providence, that Truth may triumph and the foolish in high places be put to shame." He directed Whistler to bestow the ten guineas "on the unworthy poor of your parish, lest ridicule come down upon you and it be gleefully set down, by some historian of an idle day, how the Brush sought vainly to besmirch the Pen." And in attention-seeking Whistlerian style, Ford offered the letter for publication. A day later it appeared in the *St. Stephen's Review*.

As far as Ford was concerned, the exchange merely furnished more copy for *his* book, to which he added these as well as other unanswered letters to Whistler he would write, culminating in bitter verses, "Hic Jacet the McNeill," which he dated 20 January 1890 and identified as "Refused publication by the *St. Stephen's Review*." No one would mourn Whistler, he began, because Nature, who endowed Whistler with "a subtle sense of form and colour," had nevertheless "denied him heart," engendering in him a taste for "unmeritable private feuds" and "a feminine love of notoriety" despite his "brave true words in the cause of Art." The closing lines confirmed that Ford had burnt his bridges to Whistler:

May he make his peace with God;
he never did with man.

Despairing of publication in England, and unwilling to discard the work he had done, Ford then took his copy, old and new, to Belgium and had the small book printed in Antwerp. There the printer, aware of the interest of the work he had set in type, objected to the unimaginative title, and Ford challenged him to pick a better one. He did, pointing to a paragraph in the introduction, where the compiler had written, "This collection of letters and miscellany covers something over a quarter of a century, from 1862 to the present year. It illustrates the gentle art of making enemies. . . ." "There's your title," said the printer. "Don't use this other thing."

Put into type once more as *The Gentle Art of Making Enemies,* two thousand copies were printed and ready for delivery when George Lewis appeared in Brussels and had the *Procureur du Roi* confiscate the copies and the type. Still determined not to be thwarted, Ford then pawned his watch and his wife's jewelry and found another English printer, in Ghent, who printed the title page as "Paris: Delabrosse & Cie, 1890." Ford had acquired (for Whistler) permission to reprint the Master's stings and barbs first published by "Atlas" in *The World,* and prudently prefaced his collection with editor Edmund Yate's 19 September 1889 grant of "liberty to reprint Mr. Whistler's letters and other matters concerning him, which have appeared in these columns." Nothing could have appeared more legal or authentic. Then he added an amiable dedication: "To all good comrades who like a fair field and no quarter these pages are peacefully inscribed." Even the introductory note had the appearance of being free from rancor, Ford denying the existence of any "soulful intimacy between Mr. Whistler and myself," and commending the book "to Mr. Whistler's enemies, with the soothing assurance that should each of them purchase a copy the edition will be exhausted in a week."

Four thousand copies were printed, those with a grey-green paper cover for European distribution, and those with a similar cover imprinted in red, bound from sheets by the firm of Frederick Stokes and Brother in New York, which later disclaimed involvement with the book. Most of the Stokes edition was destroyed by a warehouse fire, and few of the "Delabrosse" edition were sold over the counter, for Whistler persisted in his suit to ban any distribution of his book, and had gone ahead with preparations of his own edition, even to adopting Ford's title—which appeared nowhere else in the book—and adapting Ford's device of butterfly silhouettes—the Master's hallmark—to grace each Whistler note.

Prudently Ford remained in Paris when George Lewis, aided by Belgian lawyers Edmond Picard and Albert Maeterlinck, took the matter, after months of legal delays, to the Belgian courts in October 1891. Whistler and M. Kohler, the Antwerp printer, were the only witnesses. "What religion do you profess?" asked the presiding judge before the administration of the customary oath. There was silence, while the artist pondered the unexpected question. "You are, perhaps, a Protestant?" pursued the judge, hoping to relieve the awkward situation. Whistler— whose first appearance in church since his mother died had been at his belated wedding in 1888—shrugged his shoulders, as if to leave it up to the judge, and when he was asked his age (he was now dyeing his carefully barbered locks) he objected and was upheld. But he did deliver his testimony, and Judge Moureau condemned Ford—in absentia—to a fine of 500 francs (then £20) and an indemnity of 3000 francs (£120), to be paid, with costs, or three years' imprisonment in default of payment. Since Ford never appeared in Belgium afterwards, only his confiscated books remained imprisoned, mildewing in the damp cellars of the Palais de Justice.[7]

In Paris, too, Ford was checkmated, the American ambassador, Whitelaw Reid, introducing Whistler to the *Procureur de la Republique,* who saw to it that the book was suppressed. When what Whistler called "the true book" appeared he sent an inscribed copy to the ambassador, "a souvenir of flattering courtesies, and most effective aid in pursuit of The

Pirate." As American journalist George Smalley put it in one of his dispatches from London to the New York *Tribune,* "Nowhere was there rest for the sole of Mr. Ford's publishing foot."[8] Unrepentant, Whistler wrote of Ford to a friend, "The horse pond is for him a mild sentence."

While Ford was being treated badly and reacting accordingly, Whistler, having appropriated Ford's title and ideas, set about creating his own edition, and improving his own legend. He had become close to the young publisher, William Heinemann, and he called his "publisher, philosopher and friend," and together they planned the book. Whistler drove to Heinemann's office almost daily at eleven, to extricate him from his morning's work and to breakfast at the Savoy, where on the balcony overlooking the Embankment, deserted between the customary dining hours, they would go over such tiny details as the arranging of a single butterfly on a page. That Heinemann might have other business or might already have had breakfast was preposterous to Whistler, and if the publisher did, he concealed it with real enthusiasm for the project.

The Ballantyne Press was entrusted with the printing, but Whistler chose the type, spaced the text, designed an asymmetrical title page and drew expressive butterflies for each entry which laughed, mocked, stung, drooped over the famous farthing damages of the Ruskin libel trial, or triumphed in gay flight, adding an appropriate flower of ego and eccentricity. A "publisher's note" prefaced the book, explaining it as the reaction to "a continued attempt to issue a spurious and garbled version of Mr Whistler's writings," with only the Heinemann version as under Whistler's "own immediate care and supervision." Following were six pages of extracts from the London and Paris press—originally planted by Whistler—about the "extraordinary piratical plot" of a carefully unnamed villain. Then came Whistler's title page (p. 40).

The dedication was in the same spirit: "To the rare Few, who, early in Life, have rid Themselves of the Friendship of the Many, these pathetic Papers are inscribed." It became Whistler's artistic autobiography and testament. It included—as Ford could not—Whistler's carefully edited condensation of the disastrous Ruskin libel trial, in which Whistler had won only a symbolic farthing's damages; his *Piker Papers,* about a case of mistaken artistic identity; his *Ten O'Clock Lecture* with its magical evocation of the way in which art trains the eye to perceive a romantic reality; his favorite exhibition catalogue texts; and interviews and newspaper encounters with the critics, from 'Arry Quilter to Oscar Wilde. It necessarily omitted Ford's thirty small-format pages of introductory essay, "Mr. Whistler as the 'Unattached Writer'," by which Ford meant the critic characterized by "complete intolerance," belonging to no school or party. Mostly stitched together from Whistler's own comments, reprinted in full

THE GENTLE ART

OF

MAKING ENEMIES

AS PLEASINGLY EXEMPLIFIED
IN MANY INSTANCES, WHEREIN THE SERIOUS ONES
OF THIS EARTH, CAREFULLY EXASPERATED, HAVE
BEEN PRETTILY SPURRED ON TO UNSEEMLINESS
AND INDISCRETION, WHILE OVERCOME BY AN

UNDUE SENSE OF RIGHT

LONDON MDCCCXC
WILLIAM HEINEMANN

Whistler's original title page.

in the body of the book, the introduction had contained some perceptive criticism, particularly the observation that "with a catholic vision and a kindlier impulse" Whistler "might have evoked a wider influence." And it omitted pages of Whistler anecdotes, exhibitions, and antics, culled by the author from newspaper clippings as well as his own submissions to London newspapers and press syndicates.

The little book Ford had begun—in his version of the text—was "the record of some unpleasantness between the Brush and Pen." The ridicule aimed at Whistler in his earlier years was "the common lot when a new force, a personality, makes itself felt. . . . Artists sufficiently original to interpret nature in a new way ever meet with misunderstanding. . . . Those who know Mr. Whistler only through his painting and writing are prone to forget—or never realise—the privations he endured in the attainment of his present position. And it should be set down to the eternal credit of the man that not once during his period of trial—at times approaching starvation—did he waver in his devotion to his art."[9] That Whistler would suppress such encomiums says less for his ego than for the forcefulness of Trixie Whistler, who wanted the proceeds of the book more than its praise of her husband. There would be publicity enough in its reception.

An irony in Ford's introduction which Whistler may have liked less was Ford's observation that Whistler, who "would extinguish the critic" because art needed neither explanation nor translation, in effect became a critic himself through his own recourse to print, "joining the ranks of those whose existence he deplores." Ford was equally peceptive on Whistler as letter-writer, seeing him as "adept in the art of interesting [readers]." He noted Whistler's gift for "wrapping innuendoes in graceful satire" in some cases, while in others forsaking "*finesse*" to indulge in "untempered onslaughts" in which some of his rejoinders had not "the slightest bearing upon the matter at issue." Even so, Ford saw an "uncompromising independence" as the springboard of Whistler's style, and felt that it justified his caprices as they added "to the relish of his existence." Whistler possessed, Ford concluded in his original version of the book, "the sanity of genius" rather than the serenity of the accepted master, and "as long as Art endured, the pen that brings confusion upon pretenders will continue to benefit artists. . . ."

Ford's compilation of praise and blame, a curious package of contradictions which reflected the contrariness in Whistler, was nevertheless as much Ford as it was Whistler, and the Master, while behaving with moral dubiousness, was aesthetically sound in rejecting Ford's interesting but less egocentric compilation. His own version, given his heightened interest in the matter, was also far more eye-catching. As a piece of book design it became a leader in the Art Nouveau movement for the idiosyncratic disposition of black and white on a page, rather than the slavish centering of print, and the combining of simplicity with elegance and taste with economy.

Through the examples of his catalogues and pamphlets, and especially through his *Gentle Art,* Whistler prodded book designers into producing striking effects with the simplest means at the disposal of any print shop. He required only ordinary type and ordinary paper, and inexpensive binding and lettering, but a distinctively unconventional product resulted, and one within the means of the ordinary book buyer—a book to be read as well as looked at.

The *Gentle Art* project was, to Whistler, as much of a work of art as his most ambitious canvas, and the pains he took over each page were paralleled by the time he ostentatiously took over the proof, as befit a literary gentleman. To Frederick Keppel, visiting the studio, he had happily read aloud from the proof sheets for two hours when a servant announced the arrival of a great lady in the English peerage. "Where is she?" "In her carriage at the door, sir." For ten more minutes he continued reading aloud, ignoring the waiting servant, until Keppel, realizing how cold a day in March it was, reminded him of the lady.

"Oh," said Whistler, "let her wait—I'm *mobbed* with these people." Then he read on for fifteen more minutes before ordering the servant to let "her shivering ladyship" in. The book—or the pose—was more important.[10]

Neither Whistler's pose nor his prose could have been deduced from his tranquil *Mother* canvas or the impassive *Carlyle,* the fastidious yet simple later portrait *arrangements,* the evanescent *nocturnes,* the impressionistic etchings, the lyrical pastels. The bitterness of the maker of paradoxes and the belligerence of the maker of enemies materialized in Whistler's art only in the waspish sting in the tail of the butterfly signature. To George Moore the contents of *The Gentle Art* would never have existed had they not been Whistler's "safety-valve by which his strained nerves found relief from the intolerable tension of the masterpiece,"[11] while the public at large probably agreed with the *McClure's Magazine* parody of the sublimely arrogant Whistler who chortled while hurling his scissors through a studio window one morning, "Ha, not yet nine o'clock and another enemy made!" To Max Beerbohm the book was the rare product of a "good talker who could write as well as he talked," and was as cosmopolitan and eccentric as the author:

Read any page of *The Gentle Art of Making Enemies,* and you will hear a voice in it, and see a face in it, and see gestures in it. And none of these is quite like any other known to you. It matters not that you never knew Whistler, never even set eyes on him. You see him and know him here. The voice drawls slowly, quickening to a kind of snap at the end of every sentence, and sometimes rising to a sudden screech of laughter; and, all the while, the fine fierce eyes of the talker are flashing out at you and his long nervous fingers are tracing extravagant arabesques in the air. No! you need never to have seen Whistler to know what he was like. He projected through printed words the clear-cut image and clear-ringing echo of himself. He was a born writer, achieving perfection through pains which must have been infinite for that we see at first sight no trace of them at all. . . . Certainly, the little letters are Whistler's passport among the elect of literature.[12]

G. K. Chesterton could not understand how anyone could think that there was any genuine laughter in the *Gentle Art*. Whistler's wit, he thought shrewdly, "is a torture to him. He twists himself into arabesques of verbal felicity; he is full of a fierce carefulness; he is inspired with the complete seriousness of sincere malice. He hurts himself to hurt his opponent." The paradox Chesterton perceived was that Whistler was not sufficiently objective to be a great satirist, yet his satire survived. "No man," Chesterton wrote, pondering the reason, "ever preached the impersonality of art so well; no man ever preached the impersonality of art so personally."[13] Perhaps in the contradiction lies the success of his satirical writing, although it may still stand as much for its historic value as its histrionic value. The battles Whistler fought, D. B. Wyndham Lewis concluded, were—collectively—not merely Whistler versus the art critics of England but Whistler versus "the Island Race." He was "extremely fortunate in his period" for there was a cultivated, leisured newspaper-reading public and a press which strived to meet its taste without serious concern for the laws of libel:

Living to-day, Whistler would not have seen 5 per cent of his *Gentle Art* letters appearing in the Press; whereas an editor like Edmund Yates ("Atlas") of the *World* not only printed with joy anything Whistler cared to set his pen to, mischievously egging on the merry warrior and pointing out victims he might otherwise have missed as they skulked in the undergrowth, but printed with equal relish Whistler's attacks on the *World's* own critic. . . . The victims whom Whistler scalped with joyous ease and exultant whoops were the solemn dullards, the Tom Taylors ("tough old Tom, the busy City bus, with its heavy jolting and many halts. . . ."), the ineffable "'Arry" Quilters, the Wyke Baylisses ("champion chess-player of Surrey, member of the Diocesan Council of Rochester, Fellow of the Society of Cyclists, and Public Orator of Noviomagus"), the Seymour Hadens, and those critics, metropolitan and provincial, who were to enrich his *catalogues raisonnés*.[14]

Heinemann published *The Gentle Art* late in 1890, a few months after the last pirated version, and Whistler ornamented a pile of presentation copies with inscriptions in the spirit of the book, offering one to George Moore with what was, for the Master, lavish praise for his recipient. "For furtive reading," he wrote, "which means that anything George Moore writes—anything good he writes about painting—was plagiarised from me, James McNeill Whistler."[15] Two years later a second edition appeared, enlarged with more recent missives to the press. Before it emerged Whistler came upon a copy of the first edition in a second hand bookstore. He had given this particular copy to an acquaintance after blandly inscribing, "With the regards of the author." He bought the book, penned in an additional word above the line and sent it back to the ungrateful friend. The amended inscription read, "With the renewed regards of the author."[16] At work as always was the sting in the tail of the butterfly, the animating force behind the collected quarrels; for the butterfly was not born with his sting, but had to develop it and perfect it in self-defense. At the end of his second edition he included an *envoi* to "Atlas"—Edmund Yates. "These things we like to remember, Atlas, you and I," he wrote, "—the bright things, the droll things, the charming things of this pleasant life—and here, too, in this lovely land they are understood—and keenly appreciated. As to those others—alas! I am afraid we have done with them. It was our amusement to convict—though they thought we cared to convince! *Allons!* They have served our wicked purpose—Atlas, we 'collect' no more."

3

Schopenhauerian Compassion, Fictional Structure, and the Reader

The Example of Hardy and Conrad

William J. Scheick

Given Thomas Hardy's and Joseph Conrad's apparent pessimism, the application of the concept of compassion to their work might seem eccentric; indeed, aside from the issue of pessimism, the very juxtaposition of Hardy and Conrad might at first seem odd.[1] A case can be made, however, to support the contention that Hardy's *Jude the Obscure* (1896) and Conrad's *Heart of Darkness* (1902) comprise corresponding artistic expressions of Schopenhauerian compassion.[2] These tentative experiments in Schopenhauerian aesthetics seem to be epitomized in the somewhat similar structures of the two novels,[3] both of which evince a spiral pattern of expanding and diminishing circles within circles. Moreover, as we shall see, this thematically pertinent spiral design potentially implicates the reader in the text in an especially complex manner; it requires the reader to participate in and contribute to the structure of *Jude the Obscure* and that of *Heart of Darkness*.

I

The critical debate concerning Hardy's pessimism is an old one dating from the late nineteenth century, when his novels first appeared. Beyond question Hardy's fiction evinces a dark undercurrent, and the chief problem with the debate on this subject lies in the usually unacknowledged

45

presumption that Hardy never vacillated in mood from work to work or, perhaps, never registered ambivalence in any given work.[4] In fact Hardy's pessimism varies in degree from book to book, with a tendency to darken after 1886 and to include after 1900 some suggestion of social meliorism.[5]

Hardy's pessimism originated from a combination of personal temperament and late nineteenth-century scientific and philosophical thought attractive to this temperament. Hardy's views derive from many sources: the Bible, the Book of Common Prayer, Aeschylus, Sophocles, Darwin, Huxley, Mill, Spencer, Taine, and Swinburne;[6] the works of the Greek tragedians and that of Darwin are particularly gloomy when interpreted simply. Critics generally agree, too, that Schopenhauer's philosophy contributed importantly to Hardy's early dark perspective.

Explicit references to Schopenhauer occur in Hardy's *The Woodlanders* (1887) and later in a passage not in the original version, but appearing in the first edition of *Tess of the D'Urbervilles* (1891). Testimony comes as well from Eden Phillpotts, who discussed Schopenhauer's ideas with Hardy, and from Hardy himself, when he remarked his respect for Schopenhauer's thought.[7] Although Schopenhauer's influence on Hardy is generally accepted by critics,[8] its extensiveness remains open to question, not only in terms of the general difficulties encountered when tracing an author's sources, but also in terms of Hardy's specific attitudes and opinions. Possibly, for instance, Hardy was for a long time familiar only with the most basic principles of Schopenhauer's thought,[9] and much of what he grasped of this thought might have derived from Eduard Van Hartmann, whose Schopenhauerian-influenced *Philosophy of the Unconscious* Hardy read in the third edition (1893).[10] How much of Schopenhauer's philosophy Hardy encountered firsthand or how well he understood what he read are moot issues, but the fact, if not the degree, of the philosopher's effect on his writings is demonstrable well beyond the knowledge that Hardy owned a copy of Schopenhauer's *On the Fourfold Root of the Principle of Sufficient Reason and the Will in Nature* (Engl. trans., 1887).[11] This philosophical presence is greatly evident and least adulterated in *Jude the Obscure*, the most pessimistic of Hardy's novels. The Schopenhauerian authority informing *Jude* was readily remarked in critical commentary on the novel shortly after the turn of the century. Typical are Edward Wright's identification of Jude as Schopenhauer's perfidious lover and Harold Williams's response to the novel: "Not even Schopenhauer has made us feel so forcibly the continuity of human life in its generations."[12] Today, as well, critical discussions of *Jude* sometimes evoke Schopenhauer's presence when, for instance, they speculate on the primary influence on the epic tendencies of the novel.[13]

Hardy's novel is replete with Schopenhauerian echoes. *Jude* emphasizes human "misery and depression."[14] Sue Bridehead tells Jude's son, "All is trouble, adversity and suffering" (p. 406). Life is "Creation's groan," as Jude perceives it, "the grind of stern reality" consisting of, as it were, a hopeless "struggle against malignant stars" (pp. 467, 473, 374). Life is a gin or trap of hereditary and social fate, a Darwinian predestination wherein (Richard Phillotson remarks) "cruelty is the law pervading all nature and society; and we can't get out of it if we would" (p. 389). The malignancy of this fate is not a personal antagonism directed against humanity; rather it consists of the way people, like Jude, feel when facing the utter indifference of fate, especially when they necessarily fail to make rational sense of fate's purpose or of its absence of design. In *Jude* the principle of fate corresponds to Schopenhauer's concept of Will, the aimless force animating all creation and achieving fullest expression in the most evolved of species, mankind.[15]

Underlying the plot of *Jude* is "a blind, amoral natural struggle, with consciousness an evolutionary accident leaving man as a creature who can think and feel and aspire but who is ruled by external and internal forces mostly beyond his control, forces indifferent to his wishes and values."[16] Humanity thinks, has ideas, and within this consciousness lies mankind's greatest source of misery and evil. The advent of human consciousness, according to Schopenhauer and Hardy, brought a painful self-awareness which seems, as Jude senses, "as if [the self-aware person] had awakened in hell. It *was* hell—'the hell of conscious failure'" (p. 176).[17] What necessarily fails are aspirations, hopes and dreams engendered by the ideas of a conscious mind. Consider Sue's experience:

> Vague and quaint imaginings had haunted Sue in the days when her intellect scintillated like a star, that the world resembled a stanza or melody composed in a dream; it was wonderfully excellent to the half-aroused intelligence, but hopelessly absurd to the full waking; that the First Cause worked automatically like a somnambulist, and not reflectively like a sage; that at the framing of the terrestrial conditions there seemed never to have been contemplated such a development of emotional perceptiveness among the creatures subject to these conditions as that reached by thinking and educated humanity (p. 417).

The "full waking" of consciousness consists of the human mind's reflexive scrutiny of itself in the process of thinking. The generation of ideas disguises the aimless, nonrational Will and thereby makes reasoning creatures miserable.[18] Unable to hold on to this latter thought (whereby in the human mind the Will turns against itself),[19] Sue lapses into the hell of conventional ideas.

For Schopenhauer, and Hardy and (as we shall see) Conrad, ideas are an illusion underlying human behavior. Ideas are at once the result and the disguise of "the grind of stern reality" that always dashes these same ideas.

This reflexive pattern comprises the reality behind Jude's life, which is chiefly characterized by the generation and frustration of idea-inspired aspirations. His is a loss by attrition, and near the end of his life he has nothing to replace what has been obliterated:

> I am in a chaos of principles—groping in the dark—acting by instinct and not after example. Eight or nine years ago when I came here [to Christminster] first, I had a neat stock of fixed opinions, but they dropped away one by one; and the further I get the less sure I am (p. 399).

Like Sue, however, Jude never quite arrives at a "full waking," that Schopenhauerian mode of contemplation when the Will is meditatively turned against itself temporarily in the human mind, and when the human mind briefly transcends *Maya* (illusive phenomena).[20] Failing even at the end of his life to realize the malignancy of ideas per se, Jude says, "I felt I could do one thing if I had the opportunity. I could accumulate ideas, and impart them to others" (p. 480). The irony of this remark is bitter, for Jude has indeed accumulated and disseminated ideas, has time and again suffered ideational illusion and disillusionment, in short has to the very end of his miserable life remained both victim and agent of the immanent Will.

Does this authorial distrust of ideas support Jude's belief that "there is something wrong somewhere in our social formulas" (p. 399)? Does Hardy's novel indicate that social reform is possible through human self-control,[21] that (as Arnold Bennett said about the book) social principles are beside the point,[22] or that social progress is at best ambiguous?[23] These are old questions for Hardy's critics. As early as 1918, the issue of social reform figured in critical estimations of Hardy's alleged failure in *Jude*. Specifically, it was argued that the cosmic theory expressed in this novel cannot support the fierce social protest also evident in the work.[24] Twenty-two years later this same ostensible incongruity, viewed in conjunction with related disparities, was said to define "the secret of Hardy's success" as an artist.[25] The debate continues today, and the solution to this apparent incongruity can be found in the concept of Schopenhauerian compassion.

In fact, for Eden Phillpotts Schopenhauerian compassion provides a key to Hardy's fiction:

> What is his [Schopenhauer's] concept of 'Compassion' but an utter-ance of utmost beauty? Not to see all men in ourselves, but ourselves in all men, is an ideal as great as any. . . . Hardy and Schopenhauer share a deep and noble commiseration of his [man's] griefs and disillusionments, his vain expectations and blighted hopes. . . .

Through life's frustrated dreams and desolate realities both great ones point a way of truth and clemency for all labouring under the manifold evils of conscious existence.[26]

Schopenhauerian compassion is a state of mind, a profoundly sympathetic yet non-self-pitying disinterested awareness of the futility of all volition in a life determined by impersonal forces.[27] Schopenhauerian compassion requires a large perspective on life that discerns misery to be (a) intrinsic to human existence (the will to live), (b) meaningless and (c) beyond social reform. But even if social reform offers no hope, it nonetheless is necessary, for Schopenhauerian compassion requires the end of all human strife. So Jude is correct when he observes that something is wrong with social formulas; they presently compound human misery. Their revision will not improve the human lot in any progressive sense, but by curtailing artificially contrived miseries and by at least not adding to the human burden of the manifest evil of conscious existence, social reform can reflect a universal human sympathy.

Renunciation lies at the heart of this compassion. One must resist the demands of personality, especially the principle of individuality.[28] Sue recognizes that the surrender of all ambition results in the most contentedness one can experience in life (p. 383). However, Sue's final declaration of "self-renunciation," of "sacrific[e] . . . on the altar of duty" (pp. 419–20), is grounded on Christian and outdated social ideas; as such her renunciation is ill-conceived, not so much tragic as pathetic. Sue's "renunciation has nothing to resonate *from* but expends its force in a great absorbent emptiness."[29] But if it is too self-centered, Sue's instinctive attraction to renunciation is, in Schopenhauerian terms, nonetheless correct.[30] Furthermore, her example is surpassed by that of Phillotson, who renounces (until the end when Sue insists otherwise) his conjugal rights, according to civil and religious authority, only because he wishes to contribute nothing to Sue's plight. Phillotson approaches the ideal of the compassionate Schopenhauerian saint; he does not speculate about progressive reform, but by his humane behavior of compassionate renunciation implicitly revises social standards.

The issue of conjugal rights is important in the novel, for cardinal to the ideal renunciation of the Schopenhauerian saint is a refusal to procreate. Nothing in *Jude* supports the will to live;[31] everything in this work supports what Eden Phillpotts refers to as Hardy's Schopenhauerian "conviction that it was better not to have lived than face the ordeal of life as a conscious being."[32] In other words, like Jude, every human is "born to ache a good deal before the fall of the curtain upon his unnecessary life" (p. 56). "It seems such a terribly tragic thing to bring beings into the world," Arabella is told by Sue, whose sensitivity to the subject is later exacerbated by Father Time's question about why people have children (pp. 382, 407). The Schopenhauerian ideal of an eventual universal human renunciation of life seems to inform the sense of Jude's comment (apropos his son's murders and suicide) to Sue:

> The doctor says there are such boys springing up amongst us—boys of a sort unknown in the last generation—the outcome of new views of life. They seem to see all its terrors before they are old enough to have staying power to resist them. He says it is the beginning of the coming universal wish not to live (pp. 410–11).[33]

Although neither advocate suicide, Schopenhauer and Hardy regard death as the only release from the misery of consciousness; and they both regard a profound contemplative compassion, beyond religious dogma and social meliorism, as an ideal state of mind anticipating the stillness of death.

Stasis suggests an ideal condition in *Jude,* a novel so marked by incessant character motion that one recent critic complains, "there is too much fussy incident, too many comings and goings, concerning too many different towns."[34] This rebuke is understandable, if aesthetically insensitive; for the reader of *Jude* is indeed exposed to a disconcerting amount of incident and activity, particularly when the protagonist's "nomadic life" (p. 379) is highlighted in the final two parts of the novel. The chief source of Jude's ceaseless motion lies in "the yearning of his heart to find something to anchor on, to cling to" (p. 65), and here too for all humanity is the origin of "the spirit of mental and social restlessness, that makes so many unhappy" (p. 399). Neither nature nor society provides any holdfast; nor does any First Cause behind nature and society become theologically or philosophically manifest to the "full waking" of human reason. The ceaseless motions of nature, paralleled by the biological, social, and ideational motions of human life—motions expressing Will—comprise humanity's subjective reality. These motions end only with death. When he dies, Jude lies "straight as an arrow" in the "motionless and quiet" air (pp. 489, 490). His body has finally achieved peace from the futile ideas of its frustrated mind, and in death his body recalls the arrow Jude carved on a roadside marker: that ironically "static" emblem of the "moving" arrow of his ambition. Outside deceased Jude's bedroom the carnival of life goes on with its nearly frenetic activity.

II

Responding to this pervasive sense of movement in the novel, Ian Gregor remarks how *Jude* proceeds by a sequence of discrete moments having no inherent beginning or end—a processive sequence alien to pattern.[35] In contrast to Gregor's point of view is J. Hillis Miller's appreciation in *Jude* of "a beautiful symmetrical design, structured around harmonious repetitions and neatly patterned convergences."[36] The issue raised by Gregor and Miller—the issue finally of the structure of *Jude*—is a subject on which critics have disagreed as much and for as long as they have pondered Hardy's juxtaposition of universal pessimism and social reform. Aware of Hardy's extensive architectural experience, early critics of *Jude* tended to expect a pronounced structure; and some thought *Jude* well designed, while others did not.[37] Edmund Gosse thought the novel to be a rectilinear puzzle, the mathematical rigidity of which too much determined the characters' lives.[38] In a subsequent letter to Gosse, Hardy admitted that the plot of *Jude* was "almost geometrically constructed," but he insisted upon the *almost* because "beyond a certain point, the characters necessitated it, and [he] simply let it come."[39] In effect, Hardy defended both sides of the debate about the structure of *Jude*, the most peculiar aesthetic feature of which is the suggestion of a rigid pattern of plot (as noted by Gosse and Miller) and at the same time the suggestion of a flow or motion of characters and incident seemingly bereft of any rigid design (as noted by Gregor).

Jude certainly evinces patterns. The novel begins with the birth of Jude's aspiration and ends with the demise of his hopes. Moreover, each of the six parts of the novel repeats this rise-and-fall pattern.[40] This repetitive scheme corresponds to an emphasis in the novel on a parallelism, eventually a reverse parallelism, of events and of characters;[41] even the conclusion of *Jude* consists of an inverted reflection of the beginning of the novel.[42] *Jude* possesses an iterative structure, which becomes most pronounced at the end. Episodes and characters in the novel serve as mirror reflections of each other in a closed Schopenhauerian world in which generation after generation of humanity repeats the same pathetic rise-and-fall process of birth (hope) and death (despair).

This pattern informs Hardy's typology[43]—that is, his adaptation of the medieval biblical system identifying parallels between Old Testament types and New Testament antitypes as well as of the Renaissance modification of this system designating correspondences between the figures of classical mythology and biblical personages. In *Jude,* for instance, allusions to the "tragic doom" of "the house of Atreus" and "the house of Jeroboam" provide a context for "the tragedy of unfulfilled aims" (pp. 350, 39) in the novel; a picture of Samson and Delilah (p. 117) evokes a comparison between these Old Testament figures and Jude and Arabella; and Jude's sense of "what a poor Christ he made" (p. 175) elicits associations between his and Jesus' suffering.[44] *Jude* abounds in such typological allusions because the self-contained mirrorlike reflections they imply reinforce the design of repetitive parallelism demarcating the closed Schopenhauerian world of the novel.

Reader expectations generated by Hardy's system of parallelism, however, are frustrated because no character or event in *Jude* actually completes the typological analogy. Rather, they (like mirror reflections) invert the source of the comparison. In this way something of the typological design is maintained, while at the same time the reader senses a mode of discontinuity, a perception equivalent to the narrator's sense of a "flaw in the terrestrial scheme" (p. 55). This paradoxical appropriation and diminishment of typological design in *Jude* reveals Hardy's ac-knowledgment that in life, as in fiction, we seek, demand, and find design; but in life, as in fiction, the *actual* phenomenal pattern we perceive disguises a still more pervasive *real* principle of animation evincing no system of order or purpose conceivable to the human mind. In the phenomenal world there are indeed natural and social cycles—the hours of the day, the seasons of the year, the episodes of history (including typological recurrences of a sort), the times of celebration in individual human lives (births, weddings, funerals) and in communities (e.g., the Remembrance games)—but these cycles consist of a *perceived* order, a pattern conscious beings discover or, more likely, posit in the closed world of which they are a small, obscure part. Cycles are circular patterns in motion, and as such, Schopenhauer noted,[45] symbolize human experi-ence of *Maya,* the deceit of phenomena.

So *Jude* exhibits an intimated geometry of inverted parallelism. This geometry provides a mirror image of the reader's world, which presuma-bly must be defined by a perceived geometry similar to that of the novel. Whatever is geometric in the design of *Jude* exists in the context of the closed world (the mirrorlike parallelism) of the necessary bounds of the text of the novel; and this context reflects the closed world (the inverted classical and biblical typology) of the necessary limits of the experience of the reader. Between the reader's perception and Jude's perception—that is to say, occurring at the periphery of the characters' world and of the reader's world—is the narrator's voice; and just as the narrative evinces a geometric plot pattern (while inversions challenge the very validity of the design they at once constitute and subvert), so too its narrator mediates between and at the same time separates the reader from Jude.

First, the narrator does not necessarily present Hardy's views. As J. Hillis Miller has noted: "In his fiction [Hardy] speaks not in his own voice but in that of a narrator he has invented" so that "the act of writing has an evasiveness or insulation which [Hardy] seems instinctively to have desired."[46] Second, the narrator is to some extent a character in the novel; he is not always detached, represents no absolute standard of value, shifts moods, becomes ambiguous, and expresses various opinions.[47] Third, it follows that the narrator is unreliable; at the periphery of his narrative,[48] he alternates between detachment from and involvement in Jude's experiences. These facts about the narrator potentially implicate the reader in the narrative process; for without a reliable narrator readers must look to themselves for judgment about and design in the narrative. This experience makes these readers somewhat more detached than the narrator without reducing their share in the narrator's sympathy for Jude. In other words, the dynamic of reader and text interaction in this novel corresponds to the "motion" of natural or social cycles in Jude's life and of the alternation between detachment and sympathy in the narrative voice; this dynamic is cyclic or, to apply a more specifically geometric figure, circular. When the narrator seems detached, the reader tends to rely more on the account of Jude's perceptions; when the narrator seems less objective or seems to coalesce his view with Jude's, the reader looks to himself. As if generating a series of expanding circles, the circumference of Jude's perceptions expands to the circumference of the narrator's viewpoint, which in turn expands to the still more encompassing circumference of the reader's observation. The reader becomes the outermost periphery of the text, as if at the edge of an expanding spiral—a position pertinent to the structure of *Jude*.

The structure of *Jude* is based on the image of a dilating and contracting spiral, a rise and fall in the novel. A spiral suggests both structural rigidity (as remarked by Gosse and Miller) and processive fluidity (as remarked by Gregor). Geometric rigidity defines the limits or the frame of the spiral, a frame which could be likened to an hourglass shape. This hourglass design also informs Hardy's *The Return of the Native* (1878), in which it, at the level of plot or exterior structure, embodies seven reversals or inversions.[49] In *Jude,* Sue and Jude similarly exchange positions. Coming from diverse points—he of Marygreen is religious, she of Christminster is skeptical—their lives intersect and then diverge—she at Marygreen becomes religious, he at Christminster becomes skeptical. Their final position vis-à-vis each other is a mirror reflection of their original positions, a plot pattern represented by an X, or hourglass shape.

The hourglass configuration of the plot of *Jude* represents the limits of Fate, that is to say, of Schopenhauerian Will; as such it functions as a mode of the exterior structure of *Jude*. Within these limits are the rise and fall of time's sand, the motion of all Will-animated phenomenal life. This rise-and-fall rhythm comprises a mode of the inner structure of *Jude,* and it can be diagrammed as contracting and expanding spirals within the hourglass shape. These disparate yet complementary motions (like mirror images) embody the laws of nature so insisted upon in *Jude*. Particularly insisted upon are the laws of "gravitation and germination" (p. 191)—the centripetal force of spiral contraction and the centrifugal force of spiral expansion. Very early in the novel Jude experiences these two forces in a seemingly minor episode adumbrating the pattern of everything to follow in his life. In this scene Jude shirks his duty to frighten birds, which creatures "seemed, like himself, to be living in a world which did not want them"; consequently, he is grabbed and spanked by Farmer Troutham: "'Don't 'ee, sir—please don't 'ee!' cried the whirling child, as helpless under the centrifugal tendency of his person as a hooked fish swinging to land, and beholding . . . [everything] going round and round him in an amazing circular race" (pp. 53, 54). This incident results in Jude's movement (the centrifugal force of germination, growth) away from Marygreen; but it also forecasts Jude's numerous and increasingly wearying returns (the force of gravity, the centripetal force counteracting germination) to Marygreen throughout his life: in effect, "an amazing circular race."

Circularity is the chief image in *Jude*, as in Schopenhauer's works.[50] Circularity informs the cyclic patterns of natural phenomena (e.g., "the planets in their courses" [p. 68]) and of social behavior (e.g., the annual festivity days); it informs the typological repetition of human experience, especially the ceaseless repetition of rising centrifugal hope and falling centripetal despair within the limits of Fate (the hourglass shape of Will). A glimpse of this design occurs in the first chapter, when Jude, dejected over Phillotson's departure from Marygreen, looks into a well. Jude will return to this same well just before his death, and these early and late visits are contrasted to his single encounter with Shaston (at precisely the middle of the novel), the "dream" city situated "on the summit of a steep and imposing scarp" (p. 259). "The well into which he was looking was as ancient as the village itself, and from his present position appeared as a long circular perspective ending in a shining disk of quivering water at a distance of a hundred feet down" (p. 49). Eleven-year-old Jude here stands, as it were, at the periphery of a spiral, or of a circle tapering downward. Pertinently, the well is "nearly in the centre of the little village" and is "the only relic of the local history that remained absolutely unchanged" (p. 50). The well tapering downward symbolizes the spiral of time within the immutable hourglass of Fate or Will. In the well lies, as it were, the water of life from which (in accord with Darwinian theory) all land creatures evolved, and the cycle of drawing life from water (moving the bucket upwardly along what seems to be an expanding circular wall) will eventuate in a return to this water (the fall of Jude's tear downwardly along what seems to be a contracting circular wall, "into the depths of the well" [p. 49]).

The image of Jude at the edge of a spiral appears again a few pages later, in the second chapter, when subsequent to his spanking by Farmer Troutham, Jude ponders life: "As you got older, and felt yourself to be at the centre of your time, and not at a point in its circumference, as you had felt when you were little, you were seized with a sort of shuddering, he perceived. All around you there seemed to be something glaring, garish, rattling, and the noises and glares hit upon the little cell called your life, and shook it, and warped it" (p. 57). This thought, which seems more probably the narrator's than young Jude's, is partially correct; after all, Jude remains obscure, at the periphery of society. Life in the novel sometimes seems to be a centripetal contraction; but the preceding incident with Farmer Troutham, to which this later passage alludes, also indicates that life sometimes seems to be a centrifugal expansion; both laws of nature exert themselves simultaneously and constitute the mutually antithetical, yet complementary modes of intrinsic power (will) governing the motion of all life. That being "at the centre" (in the passage on life in chapter 2) is as horrid as being at the circumference (in the passage on Jude's spanking in chapter 2) suggests the hopelessness of human life. Everyone is (as it were) always off center and always longing for a holdfast "to anchor on, to cling to," even though the experience of being "at the centre" suggests there is no still-point other than death.

Consider Jude's two attempts at suicide that occur in the first and last parts of the novel. The account of the initial attempt, Jude's wish to die at the center of "a large round pond," emphasizes his search for a still-point in the midst of life's circularity:

> Jude put one foot on the edge of the ice, and then the other: it cracked under his weight, but this did not deter him. He ploughed his way inward to the centre, the ice making sharp noises as he went. When just about the middle he looked around him and gave a jump. The cracking repeated itself; but he did not go down. He jumped again, but the cracking had ceased. Jude went back to the edge, and stepped upon the ground (p. 116).

In contrast, Jude's second attempt at the end of the novel is successful. By this time Sue, residing at Marygreen, has remarried Phillotson; and Jude, residing at Christminster, has remarried Arabella. In one last frantic journey, Jude, already ill, goes out into the "deadly chill" of a "driving rain" in which "any sick man would have ventured out to almost certain death" (pp. 467, 471). In this downpour he arrives at "the familiar well at Marygreen" (p. 467); and after a brief, futile interview with Sue he returns to Christminster, where he admits to Arabella the suicidal intent behind his circular trip (p. 472). This episode, which also involves water, parallels

Jude's attempt to die in the frozen pond, to submerge himself in the apparent still-point of "the shining disk of quivering water" of the Marygreen well.

Time and again Jude centripetally returns to Marygreen, the place of his origin, the center of his existence from which his dreams and mistaken impressions of Christminster centrifugally radiate; and if Marygreen is in effect Jude's psychological and social center, then Christminster can be thought of as a place on an imaginary circumference around Marygreen. Ironically Jude does not die at Marygreen, but obscurely at its periphery. Christminster ought to have become a new center for him. Indeed, when he first arrived in Christminster he seemed "to be encircled as it were with the breath and sentiment of the venerable city"; and although "for the present he was outside the gates of everything, colleges included: perhaps some day he would be inside" (pp. 125, 133). Even near the end of his life (as Arabella remarks) Jude believes Christminster to be "a great centre of high and fearless thought" or (as he tells Sue) "the centre of the universe" (pp. 383, 391). Christminster, the reader senses, ought to have become Jude's center, particularly given his eventual skepticism; but in this city he remains off-center, a peripherally displaced and obscure person. Also ironic is Sue's final residence at Marygreen. Sue ought to be the ideal emotional center of Jude's life; but with "unaccountable antipathies" (p. 266), she is as elusive to him as is the still-point in the well. Sue never finds peace at Marygreen (p. 491) because this village lies on an imaginary circumference around Christminster, the place of her physical and intellectual origins.

Jude's and Sue's peripheral displacement leaves the reader off center. That is, so many ironic reversals not only suggest but efface a narrative design intimated by an unreliable narrative voice expressing both sympathy and detachment. These reversals finally abandon the reader on the outermost fringe of the text. The reader is left at the outermost circumference of a narrative of spiral-like expansion from Jude's perspective, through the narrator's, to the reader's. The sympathetic and detached reader's final position at the edge of the text corresponds to Jude's position at the opening of the book, when he tearfully looks down the Marygreen well, and at the end of the book, when he Job-like enduringly looks inward toward rest, death. Throughout the novel the reader's expectations are enticed; just as Jude's hopes have been evoked by Christminster. The reader's attempt to locate a philosophical, social, or aesthetic center or still-point in the novel is continually frustrated by numerous ironic reversals and by an unreliable narrative voice, just as Jude's efforts to make Christminster the center of his life result in futile mirror inversions of everything. Finally the off-center reader is abandoned obscurely at the "phenomenal" edge of the text without any guidance concerning the many ambiguities of the narrative, just as obscure Jude dies at the "phenomenal" periphery of his dream without any definitive insight into the *reality* beneath the ambiguities of human existence. The reader's attention and expectation are centripetally attracted toward identification with Jude as the focal center of the text, only to be (through ironic reversals and unreliable narrative voice) centrifugally forced to the outermost circumference of the novel. In this way the reader becomes implicated in the structure of *Jude*: an aesthetically ambiguous and intimated structure at once externally hourglass-rigid and internally spiral-fluid. This structure exists only in the animating *perception* of the simultaneously sympathetic and detached reader.

Jude abounds in such aesthetic ambiguity. Besides a structure that is externally a geometrically rigid hourglass and internally a geometrically fluid spiral—that is, in another sense, constructed and "deconstructed"— *Jude* emanates and departs from the formula of the *Bildungsroman*. [51] Similarly there is also the much debated issue of whether *Jude* is in a formal sense a tragedy. Hardy speaks of the book as a "tragedy of unfulfilled aims" (p. 39) and has the narrator allude to classical tragedy, particularly Aeschylus's *Oresteia* (p. 350); in fact, the characters as well as the narrator so often use the word *tragedy* that, understandably, early reviews often praised[52] or condemned[53] *Jude* in comparison to Aristotelian standards of tragedy. More recent commentary tends to deflate claims for the novel as tragedy. Typical is D. H. Lawrence's rebuke that the characters in *Jude* are more pathetic than tragic.[54] Actually Hardy combined pathos and tragedy.[55] The characters of *Jude* are tragic insofar as they are *somewhat* divided against themselves and *somewhat* evince an intrinsic dignity of an heroic sort in their struggle for a transcendent centeredness. But they also experience a permanent disjunction with the world. They suffer and (despite Jude's belief that matters might have been better for him had he been born fifty years later [p. 482]) would have suffered at any stage of human history;[56] for in the Schopenhauerian terms of the novel, the ongoing misery of conscious human existence is comprised of an ever-frustrated absurd longing for completion (centeredness) in a cyclically repetitive phenomenal actuality of inversion that always remains an elusively inaccessible and impersonal Other. Herein lies the pathos of *Jude,* the pathos Hardy combines with an intimation of tragedy; and this pathos and tragedy are most notably commingled in the structure of the novel. The rigid hourglass structure suggests the tragedy of missed opportunity at the point of intersection and the rhythmically dilating/contracting spiral suggests the pathos of no potentiality for any other outcome. And just as this total structural effect implicates the reader, who participates at the periphery by perceiving its intimation and effacement, so too with the tragic element in *Jude;* as James Kincaid has aptly noted about the sense of tragedy in this novel: "we are continually being directed toward a pattern of action that is being inverted. It could be said, however, that the novel gains its power only by the discrepancy between these two patterns: the tragic pattern being completed in our minds and the ironic action insisted on by the words on the page. The absence of tragedy thus becomes a presence."[57]

The tragic element, then, remains latent in the text; it is always on the verge of emerging for the reader (at the periphery of the text), whose expectations concerning tragedy have been raised only to be frustrated. This effect gives the reader an experience corresponding to the frustration encountered by Hardy's characters, who time and again seem on the verge of achieving some latent potentiality which finally always eludes them. In this way the reader becomes included in the Schopenhauerian world of the text, the structure of which in effect remains frustratingly potential. Jude's and the reader's mutual reality is *Maya*, the ceaseless motion of phenomena intimating, while diguising a probable absence of, some ultimate design. There is no still-point in the text for the reader or for Jude questing for a holdfast (ironically emblemized on the marker bearing his carved arrow) "to anchor on, to cling to." Because of numerous ironic reversals and an unreliable narrative voice, whatever is centripetally expectant in the reader's attempted closure with the text paradoxically must remain centrifugally detached for the reader abandoned at the outermost circumference of the spiral expansiveness (Jude>narrator>reader) of the text. The mental "motion" in the reader of this simultaneous engagement and disengagement, empathy and detachment, comprises the primary aesthetic effect of Hardy's book: the reader's experience of Schopenhauerian compassion: a profoundly sympathetic yet non-self-pitying, disinterested awareness of the futility of all volition in a life necessarily miserable for all conscious beings and determined by an impersonal and aimless force (Will).[58]

This insight is gained only momentarily in the reader's interaction with (perception of/construction of) the ever-emergent (or potential) structure of *Jude*. Just as this Schopenhauerian compassion is not the product of any system of thought—and Schopenhauer's thought is not systematic—so too Hardy's fiction remains "a series of seemings, or personal impressions" (p. 39); as Hardy says, "a novel is an impression, not an argument."[59] At the periphery of *Jude*, the reader is given a glimpse from the periphery of life, where all conscious beings exist in phenomenal obscurity. Precisely this insight demarcates Schopenhauer's understanding of the aim of art: ideally to make the perceiving mind less aware of itself as an individual entity, be still and, without pleasure or pain, contemplate the what of the world;[60] and in this state, induced by the reader's *perceived* design of art (corresponding to humanity's *perceived* phenomenal patterns), the mind (a) temporarily transcends its limitations as a self; (b) glimpses the absolute (if unknowable) significance beyond any imputed (albeit vehicular) pattern in natural, social and artistic phenomena; and (c) now feels a profound compassion for every fellow human. Herein lies the artistic and humanistic achievement of *Jude the Obscure,* Hardy's outstanding experiment in Schopenhauerian aesthetics.

III

Since Conrad, like Hardy, expressed a variety of moods and viewpoints throughout his literary career, no one of his works can be designated as more or less philosophically typical than another. In fact, reviewed collectively, Conrad's fiction may, as has been argued,[61] reveal three fairly distinct stages in his attitude toward human existence. Similar to the example of Hardy, Conrad tried out ideas, different ideas in the same or in different works, without necessarily endorsing any ideational system. Herein lies a distinct limitation to any discussion of influences on Conrad. Influences are present, but not systematically or with uniform intensity in any given work by Conrad, and not in such a way that they will yield some monolithic measure of all his writings; nor is any given work simply the sum of the influences it evinces. These cautionary notes notwithstanding, *Heart of Darkness* may be approached in the light of Schopenhauerian thought. Even more than *Lord Jim* (1900), composed during the same interval, *Heart* integrates theme, structure and narrative manner through a mode of compassion for which an analogue exists in Schopenhauer's philosophy. Quite possibly *Heart,* like *Jude* in Hardy's canon, is Conrad's most pronounced experiment in Schopenhauerian aesthetics.

The degree of Schopenhauer's effect on Conrad's thought during the turn of the century is as difficult to gauge as it is in Hardy's. As usual, the unresolvable large questions about literary influence remain, difficulties worsened by Conrad's apparent delight in distorting and obscuring his sources.[62] Nevertheless, "of philosophy he had read a good deal," John Galsworthy remarked of Conrad, and "Schopenhauer used to bring him satisfaction."[63] Supporting this testimony by Conrad's acquaintance is a recent argument that the significant presence of Oriental thought in Conrad's writings was transmitted by Schopenhauer,[64] whose work is steeped in Eastern philosophy, especially Buddhism.

Reminiscent of the Schopenhauerian world of *Jude,* existence in *Heart* is a Dantesque hell,[65] "gloomy circle[s] of some Inferno" where "mangroves ... seem ... to writhe" and where people evince "attitudes of pain, abandonment, and despair."⁶⁶ Here resonates a "wail of mournful fear and utter despair," not only from the African aborigines but also (if in different ways) from Kurtz, who as the epitome of civilization, is locked in "an intense and hopeless despair"; and from Marlow, who realizes that his "speech or [his] silence, indeed any action . . . would be a mere futility" (pp. 47, 71, 39).

The phenomenal world of *Heart* is not substantial; it is as dreamlike as the Schopenhauerian world of Hardy's *Jude*. "It seems to me I am trying to tell you a dream," Marlow says, "that commingling of absurdity, surprise, and bewilderment in a tremor of struggling revolt, that notion of being captured by the incredible which is of the very essence of dreams" (pp. 27–28). Living in this dream-reality the characters of *Heart* see as if through a mist, gauze or a veil. The narrator readily compares the "mist on the Essex marshes" to "a gauzy and radiant fabric," and Marlow similarly speaks of human perception as "blurred by a creeping mist" (pp. 4, 13). This prevalent mist is the veil of *Maya*, the Oriental notion adopted by Schopenhauer to describe the illusory nature of all phenomena. In this illusory, dreamlike phenomenal world everyone appears to be an Inferno-esque shadow or shade (p. 78) and everything "seem[s] to belong to some sordid farce acted in front of a sinister back-cloth" (p. 13).

Farcical life is "mere show" (p. 29), Schopenhauer's *Vorstellung*. Since the human participants in this farce perceive each other only in terms of "show," they struggle (like the Company's chief accountant) to keep up appearances (p. 18) and they perpetuate the "sham . . . of all the appearances of success and power" (p. 69). Appearance embodies humanity's social actuality, the mistlike veil behind which lies the isolated self animated by an incomprehensible life principle. This "inner" reality is something "no other man can ever know. They can only see the mere show" (p. 29). And similarly the "inner" reality of the phenomenal world remains unknowable, disguised *Vorstellung*. As Marlow says of his journey up the river, "When you have to attend . . . to the mere incidents of the surface, the reality—the reality, I tell you—fades. The inner truth is hidden" (p. 34). The surface (*Vorstellung*, show) is all we can know of nature and of other humans; our perception is restricted to the mistlike veil of surface phenomena and our actions are limited to the "monkey tricks" or the buffoonery of a "harlequin" (pp. 34, 53)⁶⁷ performing in "some sordid farce acted in front of a sinister back-cloth." Life is a "jig" driving away silence or void (p. 30).

Farce, monkey tricks, jigging, traveling—all suggest that human life is motion, animation, an harlequinesque *danse macabre*, "the merry dance of death and trade" (p. 14).⁶⁸ Observing how the Africans "howled and leaped, and spun, and made horrid faces," Marlow is struck by "their humanity" and by his "kinship with this wild and passionate uproar" (pp.

36–37). Motion comprises the blurry veil which is phenomena; this motion is the essence of *Maya,* the illusion of phenomena animated by Will, not only in the world but particularly in the human mind. The human mind *moves* by the mental activity of conscious thought. Consciousness and the ideas it engenders are, in Schopenhauer's terms, the product of the actualization of Will; for *Vorstellung* means "show" and "idea," and the ideational show of human consciousness constitutes the intrinsic misery of human existence.

Kurtz's anguish arises from his consciousness. He is a man with ideas and with a sense of duty, somewhat like Jude's, to further those ideas (pp. 60–70). In *Heart* ideas are as illusive as are natural and social phenomena, and typically (in Marlow's judgment)[69] the *ideals* of Western civilization, especially when predicated on chimerical *ideas* about progress, are ostensibly "what redeems" Kurtz, as the agent of civilization (p. 7). Assessing his experience of the encounter of the ideas of Western civilization and human behavior in the African jungle, Marlow concludes, "It was as unreal as everything else—as the philanthropic pretence of the whole concern, as their talk, as their government, as their show of work" (p. 25). *Show*: all human activity of mind (talk) and body (work) constitutes *Vorstellung;* and above all else, Marlow suggests, imperialism epitomizes the lie which is *Maya* (life), "that mysterious arrangement of merciless logic for a futile purpose" (p. 71). This latter observation by Marlow itself deceives; for the signified meaning of its words ("merciless logic," "futile purpose") pretends to mean even while in this particular combination they cannot signify, or make sense, to the rational mind. The words of this statement cancel each other as they confront our rational expectations; but, the experience of the process or deceptive phenomenal motion of this statement conveys an insight into the "show" of all human mental and physical activity, insight into the reality that we all "live in the midst of the incomprehensible" (p. 6).

Conscious beings—that is to say, beings partaking of and contributing to the motion of phenomena—can find no refuge from the misery intrinsic to their existence in *Heart.* Even when Marlow dreamily senses that he has returned "to the earliest beginnings of the world," where he has perceived "the edge of a colossal jungle" and, as it were, has "peeped over the edge" of animated phenomena, he discovers a "stillness of life [that] did not in the least resemble a peace. It was the stillness of an implacable force brooding over an inscrutable intention" (pp. 34, 13, 72). Death is the only exit from the inherent frustration and misery of conscious existence, and this is why to Marlow the shrunken heads on poles seem to smile (p. 58).

Short of death, Marlow's example suggests, the best one can do is reduce his or her harlequinesque role in the farce of life's *danse macabre* by attaining an attitude similar to that of a Buddha. The Buddha tableaux, as

William Bysshe Stein has remarked, appears at the beginning, middle and end of *Heart,* an arrangement calling attention to itself. Stein, however, misses the Schopenhauerian analogue for this image. Marlow's lotus posture does not symbolize his "detachment from the conditions, the victories, and the vicissitudes of time"; the novella nowhere intimates that Marlow is "qualified to enter nirvana" but "remains in the world to work for the salvation of all people."[70] On the contrary, Marlow reveals his compulsive attachment to the subject of his narrative, an attachment held in uneasy dialectic with the distancing manner of a somewhat detached narrator. Within the aesthetic phenomena of *Heart* Marlow's disposition simulates what he once glimpsed at the less animated edge of his perception: a "stillness of life [that does] not resemble a peace. It [is] the stillness of an implacable force brooding over an inscrutable intention." In body as in mind, Marlow's "ascetic aspect . . . with arms dropped, the palms of hands outwards" (p. 3), evinces the disposition of the Schopenhauerian saint, whose particular mode of compassion keeps him at the periphery of human existence, at once subjectively involved in and somewhat objectively detached from the misery of conscious life.

Although in his narrative Marlow indicates that he is "not particularly tender" (p. 16), throughout his account he exhibits concern for others, compassion.[71] However hopeless the gesture—and with hindsight Marlow sees the irony—he offers a dying African a biscuit (p. 18). A corresponding sensibility informs his recollection of a deceased helmsman:

> I missed my late helmsman awfully—I missed him even while his body was still lying in the pilot-house. Perhaps you will think it passing strange this regret for a savage who was no more account than a grain of sand in a black Sahara. Well, don't you see, he had done something, he had steered; for months I had him at my back—a help—an instrument. It was a kind of partnership (pp. 51–52).

Here Marlow discloses not only a metaphor for his sense of the absence of any ontological steerage in creation—an echo of his earlier remark that "there was nothing [of Company power] behind" him (p. 28); he also, simply, discloses a compassionate recognition of the essential bond between all humans, at whatever level of social or intellectual development. This sympathetic identity accounts as well for—again however futile it proves to be—his tug on the string of the boat's whistle to disburse the aborigines on the shore before his passengers could get their rifles ready for the "jolly lark" of pointlessly shooting the Africans (p. 69); and it accounts for—however ironic it remains—his "lie" to Kurtz's Intended at the end of the narrative. This "lie"—that Kurtz's final words were her name—is also the truth, for the illusion in which she lives typifies for Marlow "the horror" Kurtz discovers at the heart of illusory civilization,[72] the horror of ontological absence at the core of *Vorstellung*. But the ironic coding of Marlow's reply to Kurtz's fiancée emanates from Marlow's Schopenhauerian compassion; his "lie" does not contribute pointlessly to another's misery and at the same time it does not falsify the truth[73]—in short, it epitomizes the Schopenhauerian saint's Buddhalike engagement in (the compassionate "lie") and detachment from (the ironic truth) human existence.

Marlow's compassion, like the narrator's in Hardy's *Jude*, does not implicitly advocate some ideal of social reform. In *Heart*, as in *Lord Jim*, Marlow's small compassionate actions amount to little more than nothing. Marlow's example simply indicts civilization, especially as manifested in the extension of misery through the imperialistic mission of bringing self-awareness to unself-conscious natives. He indicts civilization as a masquerade of the horror which *is* human consciousness, a masquerade which in the guise of a "civilized" progress augments human misery by implementing a social context always likely to "provoke the most charitable of saints into a kick" (p. 25). Marlow compassionately dissents. With a few minor, feeble efforts to relieve human suffering behind him, Marlow quietly opts for a posture of passivity, a disposition offering him no safety from the world and composed only of a profound detached compassion for humanity.

This compassion informs Marlow's refusal to judge Kurtz, whom he believes to have "suffered too much" (p. 57). Marlow's comments were carefully edited by Conrad with the intention of minimizing, if not completely eliminating a judgmental vocabulary: for example, the *Blackwood's Magazine* version lacks the word *atrocious*, which in Conrad's manuscript Marlow uses to describe the Company manager's thoughts; and the book version lacks the words *of cruelty and greed*, which in the magazine version Marlow uses to refer to Kurtz's "amazing tale."[74] Marlow does not feel superior to anyone in the story, not even to his African helmsman. He does not judge, for he compassionately recognizes the bond between all suffering humanity. But also significantly he is remote. This two-sided disposition characterizes the motivation of his visit to Kurtz's Intended: "Curiosity? Yes; and also some other feeling perhaps" (p. 74). This remark is as deftly worded as is his "lie" to Kurtz's fiancée. Curiosity implies a voyeuristic detachment from her plight, but it also simultaneously suggests Marlow's inability to escape, to become completely detached from life. Just as Jude is immersed in "something glaring, garish, rattling," Marlow is attracted to the glitter of phenomena and the glitter of Kurtz's life, a glitter evident in the eyes of Kurtz's fiancée.[75] The vaguely referred to "other feeling" becomes the opposite of, respectively, detachment and engagement. This combination, as we have seen, precisely defines the nature of Marlow's "lie," that deceiving act (supporting the "show" of life) of truth-telling, detached compassion (hinting at the horror behind *Vorstellung*); and this combination precisely defines Marlow's narrative manner in *Heart*. As he relates his story in the darkness, he sits detachedly still, like a Buddha; but he speaks and so participates in the motion which is *Maya*.[76] Like Kurtz, Marlow is "very little more than a voice" (p. 49). As evidenced in the "lie" he tells Kurtz's Intended and in the hedged explanation he gives his listeners on the *Nellie* (concerning the motivation of his visit to Kurtz's fiancée), Marlow's language is, like Kurtz's, a "pulsating stream of light, or the deceitful flow from the heart of an impenetrable darkness" (p. 48).

IV

Language pulsates. Its motion, similar to the human experience of all phenomena, constitutes its illusory power, *Vorstellung*. Language is the (paradoxically) revealing and deceiving animation of ideas of a conscious mind. As emblemized in Kurtz, who is "little more than a voice," language epitomizes the isolation of each human self ("we live, as we dream—alone" [p. 28]) *and* the unique bond between every isolated self. Time and again Marlow, a detached compassionate voice, indicates that Kurtz was unique, yet paradigmatic. And Marlow's art of story-telling, like Kurtz's music, painting and poetry,[77] emphasizes simultaneously the phenomenal particular and some ultra-abstraction—engagement and detachment. The art of Marlow's narrative does not identify the ultimate reality, for it is beyond human ken and is humanly experienced as an absence or hollowness; his narrative does not celebrate the phenomenal realm of human existence, for it is intrinsically illusory and, given human consciousness, a source of irremediable misery. Marlow's narrative, however, does evince beauty, an aesthetic delight in using the deceptive phenomena of language to hint at the duplicity of all natural, social and ideational phenomena. Marlow uses language, the animation of ideas of a conscious mind, to make the conscious mind of his hearer confront itself as process. This effect accords with what Schopenhauer described as the genuine achievement of art: ideally to make the perceiving mind less aware of itself as an individual entity, be still, and (without pleasure or pain) Buddhalike contemplate the what of the world; in this state, induced by the hearer/reader's *perceived* design of art (corresponding to humanity's *perceived* phenomenal patterns), the mind temporarily transcends its limitation of self; glimpses the absolute (if unknowable and possibly absent) significance beyond any imputed (albeit vehicular) pattern in natural, social and artistic phenomena; and now feels a profound compassion for every fellow human.

Marlow's narrative recalls the manner of the narrator of Hardy's *Jude*: a compassionate employment of a mode of language transcending systematic thought and conveying impressions or "a series of seemings." In *Heart* Marlow's use of this mode is remarked by the narrator: "to him the meaning of an episode was not inside like a kernel but outside, enveloping the tale which brought it out only as a glow brings out a haze, in the likeness of one of those misty halos that sometimes are made visible by the spectral illumination of moonshine" (p. 5).[78] Like the narrator of *Jude*, the narrator of *Heart* hints at a design even while he denies its presence. He appeals to the human demand for pattern in art, in which, as in life, the *actual* phenomenon of perceived design disguises a still more pervasive *real* principle of animation evincing no ordering system conceivable to human intelligence. Like Kurtz and like all human experience, Marlow's account is "hollow at the core" (p. 59). Similar to the glittering phenomena comprising its substance, Marlow's hollow narrative is a misty halo; but it is also hallowed/haloed insofar as its artistry conveys an aesthetic sense of something transcendently Other, although this Other might be nothing. Marlow's art of language, especially well exemplified in his remark about curiosity and his "lie" to Kurtz's fiancée, pulsates illusively into phenomenal existence and at the same time, through ironic reversals defying systematic rationality, evaporates mistlike before our mental scrutiny. It is, in short, all show, *Vorstellung*.

Just as the human experience of the "show" of phenomenal existence conveys an impression of life as "gloomy circle[s] of some Inferno," the reader's encounter with Conrad's phenomenal text evokes an *impression* of halo-like layering about a hollow center. Whatever makes up the plot or outer structure of *Heart* fades before this impression of an emergent inner structure of layers; this impression of design (like the one in *Jude*) exists primarily in the "motion" (the perception) of the reader's search, demand and positing of order in the text, as in life. Marlow's image of experienced facts as "ripple[s] on an unfathomable enigma" (p. 43) is most apt: this image corresponds to that of the circles of hell and of misty halos of layered narrative. The center of *Heart,* recalling the core of the later novels of Henry James, Conrad's mentor,[79] eludes the reader; it is hollow or empty of any anticipated clear social message, even of precise identification of what "the horror" consists. *Heart* remains a text of "folds of eloquence" (p. 69), or expanding narrative layers mimetic of the human experience of the phenomenal realm, around an inscrutable center; for Kurtz's story is encircled by Marlow's narrative, which is encircled by the narrator's account.[80] Although this circular pattern is not exactly the same as the architectonic spiral informing *Jude the Obscure,* it forms an expansive spiral of sorts that certainly implicates the reader in a manner identical to that of the inner structure of Hardy's novel.

Kurtz's frustrated quest for the meaning of what he, like Melville's Ahab,[81] construes to be the inscrutable enigma of existence becomes Marlow's pursuit of the significance of Kurtz's voice; Marlow's pursuit in turn becomes the narrator's search for the kernel-like meaning of Marlow's narrative; the narrator's search in turn becomes the reader's probing of the narrator's account—as it were, a series of layers "in motion" radiating out from some incomprehensible, apparently void center. Reminiscent of the design of *Jude,* the architectonic pattern of *Heart* includes the reader within the Schopenhauerian world of the text; the incomplete structure of this text in effect remains for the reader frustratingly emergent or potential—"ripple[s] on an unfathomable enigma."

Structurally implicated in the text in this manner, the reader is denied any still-point or kernel of meaning. As in *Jude,* the reader is abandoned without guidance (concerning numerous ambiguities) at the outermost periphery of the narrative layers, a position equivalent to the outermost reaches of Kurtz's and Marlow's journey into the Congo. To Marlow "the edge of [the] colossal jungle . . . ran straight, like a ruled line, far, far away along a blue sea whose glitter was blurred by a creeping mist" (p. 13). Marlow's image suggests an hypothetical fringe of glittering phenomena where, as we previously remarked, the motion constituting *Vorstellung* seems to slow and one is, at the margin of perception, on the verge of glimpsing the absolute. At the very fringe of civilization in the Congo jungle—symbolizing an hypothetical verge of the phenomenal realm— Kurtz "stepped over the edge" and Marlow "peeped over the edge" (p. 72). They have glimpsed the Other disguised by phenomenal animation in life and language, the reality of "the stillness of an implacable force brooding with an inscrutable intention." Like Ahab, Kurtz looks directly and goes mad, whereas Marlow looks aslant from the edge and so maintains his "precarious grip on existence" (p. 41). Marlow "peeps" over the edge, and his story brings the narrator, and in turn the narrator brings the reader (at the periphery of the narrative), to the verge of insight into the dark hollow center at the heart of existence and of the text.

Here we have a paradox: the reader must be at the edge in order to glimpse the center; yet being at the fringe distances the reader from the center. This curious stance of engagement and detachment is a Schopenhauerian phenomenological problem inherent to conscious beings, and it has as its correlative in the text itself the fact that Kurtz's departure from the *center* of civilization to penetrate the *outermost* circles of existence results in the metamorphosis of his colonial *frontier* encounters into the *innermost* layer of *Heart*. Similar to the paradox of the simultaneously centripetal and centrifugal spiral of Hardy's *Jude,* Conrad's mirror-work with the notions of *inner* and *outer* exemplifies once more how the language of *Heart* defies systematic reasoning. Equally paradoxical is the fact that language, the unique bond of humanity (Kurtz, Marlow, the narrator, the reader), consists of distancing layers; language at once relates and separates every speaker and hearer, especially Kurtz and the reader.

Made to relate to the narrator, Marlow and Kurtz, and by means of the same language made to become more remote from them, respectively, the reader experiences engagement and detachment. The reader may share Marlow's sympathy for Kurtz and the narrator's interest in Marlow, but the reader is more detached than is the narrator, who is more detached than is Marlow, because of an increasing remoteness from the central events of the narrative. In *Heart* the empathetic "we" and the detached "I" make up the matrix of human consciousness (the edge of perception), and this very situation provides the context for the Schopenhauerian mode of compassion evoked in Conrad's novel. The "motion" or flow of the narrative layers of *Heart* elicits the reader's curiosity, the reader's "motion" of the pursuit of meaning and of the positing of pattern. But the distancing halo-effect of these layers also of necessity insures the reader's remoteness; the greater this sort of distance, given a bond of sympathy, the greater the potentiality for compassion of the Schopenhauerian variety. The meaning of *Heart* lies, as the narrator observed of Marlow's manner, "outside" in the reader "enveloping the tale"; as Marlow tells his listeners, "You fellows see more than I could" (p. 28). To see more with the Buddhalike compassion of the Schopenhauerian saint paradoxically requires greater distance; proximity to the center (engagement) requires remoteness at the edge (disengagement).

As in *Jude,* the combination of these extremes in *Heart* is achieved not systematically in terms of any philosophy but aesthetically within the reader. *Jude* and *Heart* both structurally implicate the reader by inducing in the reader a "misty" consciousness (at the periphery of life and of the text) metamorphosed into an aesthetic experience of Schopenhauerian compassion: a profoundly sympathetic yet non-self-pitying and disinterested awareness of the futility of all volition in a phenomenal realm determined by an impersonal force (aimless Will); the farcical glaring or glittering animation of this phenomenal realm might disguise a "heart of darkness" (nothing) at the core of existence—a place of implacable misery for necessarily "obscure" conscious beings. In this context *Jude* and *Heart* can be described as comparable, and remarkable, experiments in Schopenhauerian aesthetics.

4

Hardy's Interest in the Law

Harold Orel

In March 1894, Thomas Hardy visited some friends in London, and was particularly intrigued by some "*odd* legal experiences" recounted to him by Lord Herschell, the Lord Chancellor.[1] Hardy, who underlined the word "odd" when he recorded it, did not recount any of these anecdotes, although we would enjoy having them in his dry and wittily understated style. Even more disappointing is the fact that he regarded the encounter of insufficient interest to be worthy of retention in his thinly disguised autobiography, and omitted the passage. Nor are there other entries of much concern to us, or to my chosen topic, in the assemblage of deleted paragraphs edited by Richard Taylor in *The Personal Notebooks of Thomas Hardy*. To be sure, there is an allusion to Lady Coleridge, wife of the Lord Chief Justice, who, on June 29, 1889 confided to Hardy that on occasion she had gone on circuit, and sat in court for thirty minutes "to please her husband". If she did not do so, she added, he would say that she took no interest in his duties.[2] One would never guess from what was left out—or, for that matter, what was retained—that Hardy's labors as justice of the peace for the Borough of Dorchester beginning in 1884, and for the County of Dorset beginning in 1894, were serious, deeply committed, and living testimony to his involvement in local affairs. The stereotyped image of Hardy as a recluse in Dorchester who paid little attention to local events because his mind turned continually to national and international developments, or to his relations with publishers, or to a truly massive correspondence with well-wishers, friends, and total strangers, must be modified in the light of our knowledge of a pattern of Hardy's life that can be constructed on the basis of available documents, non-biographical treatments.

Hardy's interest in the law and in the problems created by the administration of human justice was an abiding one, but one would never guess it from reading the two volumes of Robert Gittings's life of Hardy—a work admirable in so many other ways—any more than from the two volumes of Florence Emily's work. The Toucan Press seems not to have identified Hardy's concern with legal problems as significant during his years at Max Gate. Apart from a first-rate piece of research on Hardy's court experiences written up by Edward C. Sampson in the *Colby Library Quarterly* of December 1977, I do not know of any investigation that renders in its true dimensions, and with full consideration of its implications, Hardy's willingness to sit in court at least thirty-eight times as a magistrate and to serve at least sixteen times on grand juries for the Assizes.

This review of some biographical materials considers Hardy's awareness of criminals and cases under adjudication, his friendships with various judges, solicitors, and barristers, his fictionalizations of legal problems that demonstrate rather sophisticated knowledge of courtroom procedure, and his own experiences as a magistrate in the courts of Dorchester.

I will begin with Hardy's knowledge of real criminals and real prison sentences. In 1923—toward the end of his life—Hardy signed a petition for abridging the sentence of a former director of a bank, Walter Crotch, who at the time was serving a jail sentence for fraud. Crotch had already spent almost two years of a four-year sentence behind bars. But Hardy was moved by Crotch's illness and the memory of Crotch's campaign to raise $25,000 to establish a home for blinded soldiers.[3] It would be equally pleasant to report a number of cases in which Hardy, appalled by the harshness of criminal sentences, sought to temper with mercy (or at least to describe with mercy) the fate of various prisoners brought to judgment. What we find instead is a series of narratives, sketches, and notations made for possible future use, in many instances without editorial comment, about men, women, and young people ensnared in the toils of the law.

There is, for example, the well-known story of Martha Brown, the murderess whose execution Hardy witnessed when he was sixteen. The memory of the way in which her "fine figure . . . showed against the sky as she hung in the misty rain, and how the tight black silk gown set off her shape as she wheeled half-round and back" was committed to paper on 20

January 1926 in a letter to Lady Hester Pinney, who had been kind enough to send him some stories relating to the incident.[4] Lady Pinney, as a District Councillor and a Poor Law Guardian, was able to interview old, bed-ridden patients at the Beaminster Infirmary, and she learned of Martha Brown's beauty, as well as of her folly in marrying a man twenty years younger than herself, who apparently had been interested only in her money. Jealous at the sight of another woman sitting on her husband's knee, she hit him on the head with a hatchet. Though she called in a neighbor and claimed that she had found her husband dying at the door from kicks from her horse, "the story was not believed."[5] It is understandable that Hardy's memory of the hanging should have remained vivid for seven decades, but perhaps a little unexpected that he should have felt obliged to apologize to Lady Pinney for having attended the event (". . . my only excuse being that I was but a youth, and had to be in the town at the time for other reasons"). But a note of subdued erotic appreciation, even of prurience, in his description of Martha Brown's body rather startles us, particularly when taken in conjunction with the descriptions of the execution of another woman, Mary Channing, whose sentence for supposedly poisoning her husband in 1705 included both strangulation and burning.

The way in which Mary Channing died, as recounted by Hardy in a notebook entry dated 25 January 1919, as well as in chapter 11 of *The Mayor of Casterbridge,* the poem "The Mock Wife," and an article on Maumbury Ring published in *The Times* on 9 October 1908, was so horrifying that the kindly J. O. Bailey, in annotating the sources of the poem "The Mock Wife," wrote with some dismay, "Some shocking details are here omitted."[6] The point is, at least partly, that *Hardy* did not omit them. Mary Channing was first strangled; the burning of her body revived her; she "writhed and shrieked," and one of the constables, seeking to stop her cries, "thrust a swab into her mouth, . . . & the milk from her bosoms (she had lately given birth to a child) squirted out in their faces 'and made 'em jump back.'"[7] Hardy, who was transcribing these details at the age of seventy-nine, depended for his source on Charles Prideaux, at that time Secretary of the Dorset Field Club, who in turn was remembering what he had been told by "old M—, a direct descendent of one who was a witness of the execution."[8] Hardy was fascinated by this and "other details—(such as the smell of roast meat, etc.)"—and in this account, at least, there is not the faintest indication, as Evelyn Hardy noted, of the existence of either horror or pity "in the heart of the beholder and meditator."[9]

But I am more interested in Hardy's rethinking of the evidence used to convict Mary Channing, for Hardy regarded the case against her as "not proven"—that famous Scottish formulation for equivocating one's point of view. Mary, not yet nineteen when she died, had been married "against her wish by the compulsion of her parents," and the wedding, from the first, had been marked for unhappiness. "The present writer has examined more than once a report of her trial," Hardy wrote in "Maumbury Ring," "and can find no distinct evidence that the thoughtless, pleasure-loving creature committed the crime, while it contains much to suggest that she did not. Nor is any motive discoverable for such an act."[10] As Bailey remarked, Hardy's real feeling lies buried in the phrases "guilty she may not be," and "truly judged, or false," used in the somewhat fictionalized account contained in "The Mock Wife."[11] If Hardy really believed that justice had gone astray in this case, or (what is tantamount to the same thing) that the evidence on which the judicial decision had been based deserved re-examination because it was largely secondhand in nature, and extenuating circumstances had not been taken into account, the horrid details of the execution, recorded faithfully by a soon-to-be octogenarian, underscored the need for officers of the law to move more slowly and majestically before proceeding to a final disposition of a capital judgment. In other words, Hardy's feeling for Mary Channing may have been more susceptible to pity than Evelyn Hardy was willing to concede.

A respectable number of accounts of transgressions against the law turn up in Hardy's nonfictional writings, and these are often linked with the sentences meted out as appropriate punishment. For example, at the British Library, while working on his *Trumpet-Major Notebook,* Hardy recorded with some care an attempt of two soldiers of the York Hussars to desert. They stole a boat, intending to go to France, but by mistake landed at Guernsey; they were captured; and after praying for twenty minutes in the company of two priests, they were "shot at by a guard of 24 men; they dropped instantly, & expired without a groan. The men wheeled in sections, & marched by the bodies in slow time."[12] This incident was to become the basis of the story "The Melancholy Hussar of the German Legion," later collected in *Life's Little Ironies* (1894).

Hardy's probable view, that this punishment exceeded the requirements of justice, may be confirmed by examination of his remarks made on other occasions, as when he noted, after a visit to Chelsea Hospital and Ranelagh Garden on 27 October 1878, that soldiers sentenced to six hundred to nine hundred lashes "if the doctor said it could be borne," would have salt rubbed on their backs "to harden" the flesh. Hardy wrote somberly: "In those days if you only turned your eye you were punished."[13] He was describing a common custom in the same decade in which the German Hussars had been executed.

But if we restrict our attention, for the moment, to Hardy's interest in murders, we find a surprising number of notations on this particular transgression. It is sometimes forgotten that Hardy witnessed a second hanging two or three years after that of Martha Brown.[14] Hardy, remembering that the duly announced carrying-out of the sentence would take place at eight o'clock in the morning, left his breakfast table at Bockhampton, walked hastily to a nearby hill, and clapped to his eye a "big brass telescope that had been handed on in the family," just at the moment that "the white figure dropped downwards, and the faint note of the town clock struck eight." Hardy was appalled by both the suddenness of the event and by his feeling of being alone on the heath with the hanged man. He "crept homeward wishing he had not been so curious."[15]

Hardy's interest in murders may be described as an obsession. On 9 September 1882 a Dr. Brine, over teacups, mentioned that "Jack White's gibbet (near Wincanton) was standing as late as 1835—*i.e.* the oak-post with the iron arm sticking out, and a portion of the cage in which the body had formerly hung." Hardy would doubtless have gone to see it "if some young men had not burnt it down by piling faggots around it" on a Guy Fawkes day.[16]

Hardy carefully recorded the fact that a travelling waxwork proprietor used "heads of murderers . . . as a wholesome lesson to evildoers."[17] On 10 September 1888 he wrote that a T. Voss "used to make casts of heads of executed convicts." A "Dan Pouncy held the heads while it was being done. Voss oiled the faces, and took them in halves, afterwards making casts from the masks. There was a groove where the rope went," and, Hardy added with an historian's love of exactitude, one could see "a little blood" in the case of one murderer, "where the skin had been broken," though not in the case of another.[18] Hardy was fascinated when he learned that the bodies of Lord Frederick Cavendish and of Thomas Henry Burke, the undersecretary in the Irish government, after their murders in Phoenix Park 6 May 1882, had been placed in a room at the Chief Secretary's Lodge. After their removal, the room was not properly cleaned out. Mrs. Lyttelton, Hardy's hostess, told "some gruesome details of the discovery of a roll of bloody clothes under the sofa after the entry of the succeeding secretary."[19] To Hardy all this came as thrilling news; he had personally inspected the scene of the Phoenix Park murders only the day before (23 October 1893). A similar intense emotion came over him when he learned that the plashing of a fountain outside his window at the Hotel de la Paix in Geneva was the very sound heard by the Austrian Empress just before she was murdered by the Italian anarchist, Luigi Luccheni on 10 September 1898. "His accidental nearness in time and place to the spot of her doom," wrote Hardy, "moved him much when he heard of it, since thereby hung a tale. She was a woman whose beauty, as shown in her portraits, had attracted him greatly in his youthful years, and had inspired some of his early verses, the same romantic passion having also produced the outline of a novel upon her, which he never developed." [20] Moreover, Hardy recalled, with some pride of association, that a Dorchester hangman named Davies, who presided over a number of executions in the early part of the nineteenth century, had been a friend of the Hardy family, or so he confided to Rebekah Owen.

Hardy took more than a casual interest in the trial in 1922 of Mrs. Edith Thompson of Ilford and of Frederick Bywaters for the murder of Percy Thompson, Edith's husband. The steady administration of poison over a four-month period, climaxed by a stabbing, as well as Mrs. Thompson's demure and iron-controlled demeanor in the courtroom, led to the printing of sensational headlines, stories, and photographs. Hardy paid special attention to the passionate letters that had passed between Mrs. Thompson and Frederick Bywaters, letters introduced as evidence in the trial. Hardy had no doubt that Mrs. Thompson did what the prosecution maintained she had done. She was no Mary Channing, and her death sentence roused him to no protest (though many Englishmen and women protested in marches and parades at Holloway Prison); but it did inspire one of his most intriguing poems, "On the Portrait of a Woman about to be Hanged," first printed in the *London Mercury* in February 1923, and collected in *Human Shows* (1925).[21] A key element in Hardy's thinking about the case must have been the unwillingness of Percy Thompson to grant his wife a divorce, even though he knew of her adulterous relationship to Bywaters. Hardy's own strong feelings about the necessity for revising England's outdated divorce laws scandalized his wife, invaded his fictions, and became a major concern from the 1890s on. His poem, however, suggests that Mrs. Thompson, so "comely and capable" in a "gown of grace," could not do other than what her destiny necessitated. God, who had brought her into being (Hardy calls God her "Causer"), made her "sound in the germ," but then sent "a worm/To madden Its handiwork." The real question, as Hardy propounded it, was why the It who had made Mrs. Thompson did not choose—on the basis of Its knowledge of what she would become—*not* to have "assayed" her. Why, in brief, did the Causer implant in her a "Clytaemnestra spirit"?

Like many similar rhetorical questions in Hardy's poetry, this one does not find its answer. But Hardy's view on capital punishment for such crimes was once committed to the record, and despite his open doubting of the wisdom of some death sentences, it fairly reflected his lifelong belief. An economist at Stanford University, securing data for a survey on opinions, wrote to Hardy early in the new century, and asked whether Hardy believed in the advisability of abolishing capital punishment in highly civilized communities. Hardy's response is worth quoting in full: "As an acting magistrate I think that Capital Punishment operates as a deterrent from deliberate crimes against life to an extent that no other form of punishment can rival. But the question of the moral right of a community to inflict that punishment is one I cannot enter into in this necessarily brief communication."[22] The striking aspect of this opinion, I believe, is Hardy's pointing to his experience on the bench, where he met with capital offenses. He was conceding that justice might err, and sometimes did; but the existence of capital punishment as a judgment on murderers possessed an intrinsic, and salutary, deterrent effect.

Of lesser crimes Hardy had much to say. Even the most casual reader may observe how vivid a fact of life—both to Dorset history and to Hardy's imagination—smuggling was. Mother Rogers, who carried slung round her hips bullocks' bladders filled with illegal spirits which she sold for cheap prices, was an active smuggler in the early years of the nineteenth century. Hardy's grandfather passed some of his spare time left over from superintending of church music in the storing of some eighty tubs of spirits in a dark closet in his lonely Higher Bockhampton home. "The spirits often smelt all over the house," Hardy wrote in a memoranda book, "being (13) proof, & had to be lowered for drinking."[23] These tubs, brought at night by men on horseback, "slung," or in carts, were taken away the following evening by "groups of dark long-bearded fellows." The smugglers were so bold that they tried delivering the tubs by day, to which Hardy's grandmother objected; but they would not quit until a second house was built about a hundred yards off. For elaboration of this and other smuggling episodes, Hardy invented the story of "The Distracted Preacher" (1879), and even used the real name of a Customs Officer from Weymouth, Will Latimer. Other anecdotes about smuggling he picked up from their landlord at Swanage, "an invalided captain of smacks and ketches." One story turned out so strangely that Hardy wrote it down in full: smugglers were discovered, at sea, by a revenue-cutter; they pretended to fish by rigging bits of tobacco pipe above the shank until lo and behold, they began to haul in mackerel: "The fish had made their deception truth."[24] Hardy devoted four pages to smuggling in *The Trumpet-Major Notebook,* and though these pages contain serio-comic elements, the war between smugglers and customs officers—tilting back and forth without harm to property or life and limb on a number of occasions—at other times (faithfully transcribed by Hardy from his sources) resulted in real deaths. Hardy read books about smuggling, such as Mary Kettle's *Smugglers and Foresters* (London, 1851), and a three-volume work called *The Smugglers* (Edinburgh, 1820). He became interested in the way in which the establishment of coast-guard and preventive stations finally ruined the smuggling trade. And, although Hardy does not editorialize about the claim of the crew of a small smuggling vessel, *Hope of Lymn,* that their captain "was washed overboard the preceding night," [25] the implication that mutiny had taken place on the high seas did not escape his notice.

For a landlubber, Hardy acquired more than a minimal amount of useful information about sailors and the sea (perhaps because he took a muted, but still genuine, pride in the likelihood that Admiral Nelson's Hardy was a descendant, like Hardy's family, from a common ancestor in the remote past); after all, much of the crucial first part of *The Dynasts* takes place at sea, and involves naval personnel. The point I want to make, however, is that Hardy frequently visited law courts in order to acquire background materials for his fiction. His last visit to the Assizes took place in October 1919 when he attended a trial of three men arrested for mutiny "on the high seas which might have happened a hundred or two hundred years before." [26] The threat of the mutineers to hoist the red flag (an act which differentiates them from pirates, who use a black flag with skull and crossbones) did not materialize because a second ship, called in by wireless, came to the rescue; but Hardy, invited to the Assizes by the judge, Mr. Darling, surely remembered his jottings in a comparably sinister case for the *Trumpet-Major Notebook,* largely prepared during the years 1878–79.

The real issue lies not in the frequency with which Hardy recorded, in various contexts and over a period of more than six decades, cases of human behavior that ultimately required the adjudication of law courts, though it is readily apparent that Hardy made notes of far many more cases than he was able to use in his fictions. Rather I am struck by the difficulties inherent in ascertaining Hardy's personal opinion on sinners and sufferers. A number of generalizations, however, may reasonably be made: one, that Hardy preferred to record a well-shaped tale about the workings of justice—one that had an intrinsic point—rather than a number of philosophical musings on the fallibility of justice; two, that he was consistently interested in the basis of a judge's verdict; three, that he believed in the overarching necessity of human laws and human judges, inasmuch as the understanding of why a crime had been committed did not substitute, in his mind, for the forgiving of the crime; four, that social and political conditions in Victorian England guaranteed a hardness of spirit among a very large number of men and women of all social classes; and five, that war between nations was the ultimate crime, for the instigation of which no punishment beyond that of victory in the field had been conceived, and for the punishment of which no tribunal as yet had been devised. Hardy thought more seriously about these matters than most of his novel-writing contemporaries, and his ideas are worth investigating more fully.

I am struck, for example, how often Hardy thought about prisoners. In 1887, on a visit to Rome, he admitted that he had become "obsessed by a vision of a chained file of prisoners plodding wearily along towards Rome, one of the most haggard of whom was to be famous through the ages as a founder of Pauline Christianity."[27] Some of his attentiveness to the rugged conditions under which prisoners moved wearily through their terms of punishment may be traced back to his father, who had told him, on many occasions, of how prisoners were treated in Dorchester. A poignant note in the *Life,* dated 9 September 1888, reads as follows:

> My father says that Dick Facey used to rivet on the fetters of criminals when they were going off by coach (Facey was journeyman for Clare the smith). He was always sent for secretly, that people might not know and congregate at the gaol entrance. They were carried away at night, a stage-coach being specially ordered. One K. of Troytown, on the London Road, a poacher, who was in the great fray at Westwood Barn near Lulworth Castle about 1825, was brought past his own door thus, on his way to transportation: he called to his wife and family; they heard his shout and ran out to bid him good-by as he sat in chains. He was never heard of again by them.[28]

Very early during the Great War, Hardy was fascinated by the thousand German prisoners in and around Weymouth who had acquired enough broken English to cry, "Shoot Kaiser!" and enough knowledge of the melody of "God Save the King" to play it on their concertinas and fiddles: "Whether this is 'meant sarcastic,' as Artemus Ward used to say, I cannot tell," Hardy wrote somewhat wryly in a letter to Edward Clodd (28 August 1914).[29] But Hardy's acquaintance with prisoners was to become more intimate than this somewhat sardonic notation anticipated. By late 1916 a prison camp in Dorchester, including a hospital, held more than five thousand men. Hardy visited sick men in both English hospitals and the German camp, and wrote about these "sufferers" with deep-felt anguish. "One Prussian, in much pain, died whilst I was with him—to my great relief, and his own. Men lie helpless here from wounds: in the hospital a hundred yards off other men, English, lie helpless from wounds—each scene of suffering caused by the other!"[30] Hardy understood that the use of German expressions in Dorset carried a significance that went beyond linguistic peculiarity. In his poem "The Pity of It," published in the *Fortnightly Review* of April 1915, he claimed that the German and the English people were "kin folk kin tongued." As war passions had by this time risen quite high, many objected to Hardy's call for understanding of the blood-ties that war had torn asunder. Hardy responded with some asperity, that those who wrote letters to the editor protesting against his poem were "fussy jingoes," and that "the Germans themselves, with far more commonsense, translated the poem, approved of it, & remarked that when relations did fall out they fought more bitterly than any."[31]

I have written elsewhere about Hardy's views on war, and here I need say only that Hardy believed that England was fighting to save what was best in Germany—not to exterminate it. He sincerely held the conviction that oligarchs, munitions-makers, and warlords had begun the war; common soldiers were mere puppets by contrast, and deserved every man's compassion. It was not just a matter of rhetoric for members of the English intelligentsia. Hardy sent German books to the prisoners, gave food and medicine to them, inquired several times about their welfare, and through his largeness of spirit was directly responsible for letters sent by the prisoners to their families in Germany, and, soon afterwards, for an amelioration of conditions experienced by English prisoners in Germany.

This is recognizably the same Hardy who wrote, on 12 February 1879, a bleak note on the way in which Jack Ketch whipped prisoners by the town pump of Dorchester with lashes of knotted whipcord, so fiercely that "the prisoners' coats were thrown over their bleeding backs" before they were conducted back to prison."[32] He took the time, on a sight-seeing expedition to Paris in June 1888, to visit the Correctional Courts to listen to a number of "trivial cases."[33] But it may not be as widely known that Hardy took the time to write to Charles Carrington, congratulating him for his "extraordinarily powerful" performance as a hangman in a production of The Three Wayfarers in June 1893,[34] which suggests Hardy's capacity to see suffering from two perspectives, that of the prisoner who must pay the penalty for his crime, whatever it may be, and that of the hangman who inflicts the penalty. It explains—it does not wholly extenuate—Hardy's decision not to make a public statement at the time of the re-trial of Captain Dreyfus, when he was requested to do so by the editor of La Vogue and later by the Daily Chronicle. Hardy's ground for remaining silent was that "English interference might do harm" to the Dreyfus cause.[35] But he had no doubt about Dreyfus's innocence.

An intriguing comment was made by Hardy in a letter to Emma, dated 6 November 1900, about a visit he made to the Assizes in a nonofficial capacity. "One of the sons of Dairyman Kingman, whom you knew when he was alive, was sentenced to 5 years penal servitude for nearly killing his wife. He is supposed to be wrong in his head by the family—owing to the kick of a horse in the temple—" and then Hardy adds a characteristic touch—"but the judge did not know this as he ought to have."[36] Here we see combined two elements of Hardy's feelings: obvious sympathy with the Kingman boy, who had been sentenced too harshly in what amounted to a miscarriage of justice; and a more baffling

reticence about the reasons why Hardy, who possessed special information about mitigating circumstances, did not call them to the attention of
the judge.

Nevertheless, Hardy in old age was the same as the young man in
London in the early 1860s who enjoyed seeing the "Judge and Jury" mock
trials at the Cider Cellars and the Coal Hole.[37] Some aspects of Hardy's
attitude toward the law may depress us; it sometimes smacks of the
flippancy of the remark of a young struggling lawyer, made to his friends à
propos of a hanging at the Old Bailey which he wanted to see: "Who
knows: we may be judges some day; and it will be well to have learnt how
the last sentence of the law is carried out."[38] Hardy thought of the law as a
record of investigation, a cumulative documentation, a patient accretion
of small pieces of information. In the late 1880s he noticed, somewhat
dispiritedly, that "the public" at judicial proceedings appeared

> to be mostly represented by grimy gentlemen who had had previous
> experience of the courts from a position in the dock: that there were
> people sitting round an anteroom of the courts as if waiting for the
> doctor; that the character of the witness usually deteriorated under
> cross-examination; and that the magistrate's spectacles as a rule en-
> deavoured to flash out a strictly just manner combined with as much
> generosity as justice would allow.[39]

Nevertheless, the last phrase, "with as much generosity as justice
would allow," resonates, and I take it to be a key to much in Hardy's
thinking. He concerned himself with the problems created by institutional
behavior in a larger sense. In his notes we find information about his
attitude toward those parallel creations of the nineteenth century, the
lunatic asylum and the poorhouse. In May 1891 he paid a visit with his
friend Dr. (later Sir) T. Clifford Allbutt, then a Commissioner in Lunacy,
to "a large private lunatic asylum." The cases proved so fascinating that
Hardy, who had intended to stay only fifteen minutes, "remained the
greater part of the day."[40] There he found a "gentleman who was staying
there of his own will, to expose the devices of the Commissioners"; an old
man who offered snuff to everybody; a "scholar of high literary aims"
who seemed as "sane in his conversation as any of us"; an artist whose
"great trouble was that he could not hear the birds sing," which, he told
Hardy, was "hard" on a man of his temperament; and a number of
fascinating women, some who had been seduced, some who thought
themselves queens (one of them, "who was really a Plantaganet by
descent, perversely insisted on being considered a Stuart"), and all of
whom seemed "prematurely dried, faded, flétries." Hardy was so moved
by the plight of one young woman whose eyes brimmed with reproach as

she inquired when the doctor would let her out, that he appealed for a reexamination of her—"which was done afterwards." (The result of the reexamination was not specified.)

Hardy knew a lot about poorhouses; after all, some had stood in the village of his birth "just at the corner turning down to the dairy." [41] On the occasion of the opening of a clubroom, dedicated as a war memorial in Bockhampton, Hardy reminisced about the buildings in which parish paupers lived before workhouses were built: "In one of them lived an old man who was found one day rolling on the floor, with a lot of pence and halfpence scattered round him. They asked him what was the matter, and he said he had heard of people rolling in money, and he thought that for once in his life he would do it, to see what it was like." But the lightness of the anecdote should not deceive us. Hardy did not think of the population of poorhouses in Dorset as being carefree; he did not yearn for a return to the past. "There is no fuss or foolishness about 'the good old days' in Hardy's picture of the changing world," as R. J. White rightly says in *Thomas Hardy and History*. [42] Hardy believed in the painful, creeping slowness of any changes in human nature that might make poorhouses, lunatic asylums, and wars obsolete; in the words of Lennart Björk, "Hardy did not share Comte's confidence in the Idea of Progress." [43] The Great War permanently destroyed his belief in the gradual ennoblement of man. By 1915, when his "very dear cousin" Frank George, second lieutenant in the Fifth Dorsets, died at Gallipoli, he gloomily withdrew from all movements "of a spiritual or even ethical nature" because his "faith in the good there is in humankind" was so rudely shaken. [44] Björk is correct in his assessment: "Hardy's belief in progress does not, in fact, seem to have been strong at any time . . . and his late claim to 'evolutionary meliorism' in the 'Apology' (1922) is but faintly supported by any public statements." [45]

Space does not permit the exploration of Hardy's laboriously acquired knowledge of an author's rights when dealing with a publisher, and of the encyclopedic mastery of information about royalties, reprints, and copyrights that his correspondence clearly demonstrates. Hardy never wanted less remuneration for his creative labors than the law allowed. Exploited in his earlier years by relatively ungenerous publishers like William Tinsley, Hardy rapidly learned how to play the game, and correctly evaluated his worth in the publishing marketplace. [46]

Hardy's knowledge of the law served him in good stead when he came to write his fiction, as two examples drawn from the history of *Tess of the d'Urbervilles* illustrate. In 1892 the businessman and politician Walter Morrison objected that Angel Clare was "arguably an accessory before, certainly an accessory after the fact of Tess's murder of Alec," and that he "would have got 12 months at least, and so could not have been outside Winchester on the morning of Tess' execution."[47] Hardy pointed out that Angel Clare could not have been an accessory, since he had not believed Tess's story. "If guilty of culpable negligence 3 months wd have been enough—& this wd have elapsed by time of execution—the time he had waited for trial being taken into account in sentence." To another correspondent, the humorist Jerome K. Jerome, Hardy wrote a sharp rebuke to the notion, first promulgated by Andrew Lang, that the hanging of Tess was "rather improbable in this age of halfpenny newspapers and appeals to the British public. The black flag would never have been hoisted."[48] He gave as his evidence to the contrary a statement, made by a Home Secretary, "that he would have seen no reason for interfering with her sentence."

Hardy's knowledge of the ways in which courts operate was used to buttress the probability of actions taken by individual characters. Judges, solicitors, barristers, their clerks, bailiffs, and customs officers turn up in the novels and short stories more frequently than the members of any other profession, including those of architecture and medicine. Here, in alphabetical form, as derived from Frank Pinion's *A Hardy Companion, A Guide to the Works of Thomas Hardy and Their Background,* is a list for reminders: Fred Beaucock of *The Woodlanders,* who informs Melbury about the new divorce law; Mr. Blowbody, the magistrate, whose wife sits next to Lucetta on the occasion of the Royal visit to Casterbridge; Mr. Cecil, Lady Constantine's solicitor in *Two on a Tower;* Mr. Chancerly, the lawyer to whom Lady Petherwin goes when she decides to change her will, after Ethelberta has refused to withdraw her published poems; Charles Downe, a young lawyer in "Fellow Townsmen," *Wessex Tales,* whose wife is drowned when they sail beyond the cliffs; Mr. Grower, the magistrate who attempts to affix responsibility for the skimmington-ride in *The Mayor of Casterbridge;* Hanner and Rawles, the solicitors in *Two on a Tower* who serve Swithin St. Cleeve's paternal great-uncle, Dr. Jocelyn St. Cleeve; Cunningham Haze, the chief constable who on three occasions comes close to arresting Dare in *A Laodicean;* Henry Knight of *A Pair of Blue Eyes,* who, in addition to being a reviewer and essayist, is, of course, a barrister; Will Latimer of "The Distracted Preacher," *Wessex Tales,* the fictional recreation of a real Will Latimer, a Customs officer from Weymouth; Lawyer Long of Casterbridge, in *Far from the Madding Crowd;* Mr. Nyttleton, the solicitor in *Desperate Remedies* who gives Miss Aldclyffe good advice on the appointment of a steward—which she rejects; Pennyways, the bailiff at Weatherbury Upper Farm dismissed by Bathsheba Everdeane for stealing barley, who reenters the story at a critical stage when Troy uses him to reestablish himself at Weatherbury;

Timothy Petrick, a clever lawyer in "Squire Petrick's Lady," *A Group of Noble Dames,* who amasses considerable wealth (the character is based on Peter Walter of Stalbridge House); Charles Bradford Raye, a barrister in "On the Western Circuit," *Life's Little Ironies,* who wins over the servant-girl Anna "body and soul" at Melchester; Stubberd, the constable in *The Mayor of Casterbridge;* Mr. Timms, the Southampton lawyer who, in *Desperate Remedies,* gives advice on the illegal marriage of Manston and Cytherea Graye; and Lord Uplandtowers of "Barbara of the House of Grebe, "*A Group of Noble Dames,* a harsh judge, who cures his wife Barbara of her devotion to her first husband by means that Pinion says are "as sadistic" as they are "effective, and typical of his cynical doggedness." [49]

These characters are, by and large, relatively minor. They do not have the temperaments necessary for the entertaining of large passions, with the possible exception of Henry Knight, or dominate the stage for more than a few moments in any short story or novel. But colorless though they may be, as a class they are professionally competent, and as individuals they are—almost uniformly—worthy of respect; they have earned their rights to a certain degree of complacency; and, as we know from the biographical evidence, Hardy was able to observe them from the very beginning, or at least from the year 1870, when he worked at Mr. Raphael Brandon's office in Clement's Inn, very close to the Royal Courts of Justice (in fact, only a narrow lane separates the office building from the Law Courts). All his life Hardy liked to dine with judges and lord chancellors. On one occasion (17 December 1892) Hardy wrote that their telling stories "old and boring to one another" but "all new" to himself, "delighted" him.[50] He was particularly interested in the details of the Tichborne case, which he followed from its earliest stage to its conclusion. Although he did not view himself as politically committed, he held strong opinions on the inadequacies of some laws, and on the need for reforms. There are, for instance, his strong views on the desirability of liberalizing the divorce laws of England. His preface to *Jude the Obscure* was amplified by a lengthy note dated April 1912, which claimed that he had used the marriage laws "in great part as the tragic machinery of the tale," and that the "general drift [of the novel] on the domestic side" tended "to show that, in Diderot's words, the civil law should be only the enunciation of the law of nature (a statement that requires some qualifications, by the way). . . ."[51] By then he had come some distance from 21 March 1897, when he refused the request of the editor of the *New York Journal* to make public his views, by means of an article for that periodical, on the subject of "such spectacles."[52] But even in that letter he spoke of leaving to others "the consideration of how to right, remedy, or prevent the wrongs which some of them undoubtedly are"; his marriage to Emma, by that time, had dwindled into something less appealing than he had anticipated in the early 1870s. Hardy, as we all know, strongly opposed vivisection, the blinding of birds, the harming of horses and other animals, and, above all, the weakness of the legal machinery that permitted such transgressions against the weak and dumb fellow creatures who inhabit our planet.

I am reviewing, therefore, a pattern of beliefs that rendered almost inevitable Hardy's willingness to assume the duties of a borough magistrate in 1884. According to the *Dorset County Chronicle,* he met the qualifications on 5 April and took his Oath of Allegiance and a Judicial Oath on 23 August. An interviewer found Hardy willing to talk about his playing the role of "Justice Silence with great assiduity, though admitting that the duties of office" kept him "in touch with some sterner facts of existence that are apt to be lost sight of in the dream-world of books." [53] Hardy reviewed a number of cases, not all of them involving legal offenses; many dealt with the licensing of local public houses and excessive school absences by children who had been summoned to court. But he also heard cases of abusive or obscene language, theft, the selling of bad meat, drunkenness, committing a nuisance in "Bollam's Passage," horse theft, violation of swine fever regulations, failure to provide a proper supply of water to a house under the Public Health Water Act, a wife-stabbing by a laborer (he was sentenced to twelve months hard labor, and she received a judicial separation), and even attempted buggery by a laborer with a mare. Hardy shifted his energies from the lower to the higher courts when he began to sit as a grand juror for the Assizes on 1 November 1897. Although these cases included colorful human experiences that were, in general, broader in range than those Hardy had heard while sitting as a magistrate in the Petty Borough Sessions and the County Petty Sessions—"bigamy, indecent and criminal assault on young girls, theft, fraud, incest, forgery, arson, rape, attempted murder, and murder" [54]— all Hardy was expected to do was cast a vote for or against indictment of the defendant in the cases presented to the grand jury. He did not decide guilt or innocence. Nor—if the regular jury decided that the defendant was guilty—did he play any part in the sentencing of a prisoner.

Even so, Hardy's concern for the way in which justice was administered went beyond his active service in the Assizes, which apparently ended in 1916. Hardy returned to the Borough Petty Sessions five more times, to adjudicate cases of food-profiteering between December 1917 and September 1919. One case required a special sitting of the children's court: "A thirteen-year-old boy, charged with trying to steal 9d from 'the automatic lock of a public lavatory,' was given 'six strokes with the birch'." [55]

A brief summary is appropriate at this point. Hardy began his interest in human laws and courts of justice by paying close attention to the lurid and melodramatic tales about smugglers, murderers, and prisoners that were current in the Bockhampton and Dorchester of his youth; he found useable literary materials in the courts (he called it "novel padding")[56] during his years as novelist (as, for instance, in his note of 14 July 1884, that "Witnesses always begin their evidence in sentences containing ornamental words, evidently prepared beforehand, but when they get into the thick of it this breaks down to struggling grammar and lamentably jumbled narrative");[57] and a growing sense of "social feeling"[58] led him to active service as a justice of the peace, both for the Borough of Dorchester and for the County of Dorset.

Hardy's efforts on behalf of the law received their due meed of honor after he died on 11 January 1928. Five days later, on 16 January the Borough Petty Sessions met, and the magistrates stood in silence as a mark of respect. They may have been paying tribute to a fellow magistrate rather than to a world renowned author. At least, I imagine, Hardy would have liked to think so.

And one last note is appropriate: Florence Emily Hardy served as a Borough Magistrate from 1924 on, filling in for her husband, whose age and health had become precarious. She rendered noble service in that position, particularly after the Children's and Young Persons' Act of 1933 was passed. Her work in the juvenile courts, dealing with girl offenders and cases of child welfare, led her to generous interpretations of probationary rules. How deeply she would have become involved in such problems without the prior participation of her husband in Borough and County Petty Sessions, the Quarter Sessions, and the Assizes, may be debated; but her labors as a magistrate for the juvenile court, and later as chairman of the Mill Street Housing Society, when she sought to improve housing conditions in the notorious area called "Mixen Lane" in *The Mayor of Casterbridge,* are still remembered, with gratitude, by many people in Dorchester.[59]

5

The Nature of Things: Hopkins and Scotus

Bernard J. Quint

T he connection between the poetry of Gerard Manley Hopkins and the philosophy of John Duns Scotus is generally accepted. Hopkins does not share Scotus's use of language. The diction of Scotus, the philospher, is dry, subtle, and precise, devoid of poetic expression while Hopkins, a singular poet, uses lush, forceful, and intense language. In philosophy the two agree. The study of Scotus taught Hopkins a view of the nature of things that informed his language and poetry. Although Hopkins was influenced by the philosopher, his poetry did not develop the subtle doctor's philosophical system in a parallel fashion. Hopkins adapted the philosophical system to his poetry because he found in the content of Scotus's philosophy an analysis of nature that was compatible with his own views, that strengthened the objectivity and realism of his poetic vision.

During Hopkins's seminary education he was exposed to the philosophies of both Thomas Aquinas and John Duns Scotus. Although the philosophies developed in the same historical period, they presented two very different ways of looking at the nature of things. The first, that of Aquinas, sharply distinguished essence and existence and gave a thing individuation on the basis of its pure potentiality, or *prima materia*. Scotus denied the distinction of essence and existence, and insisted that the physical nature of an object and its *haecceitas* (thisness), its principles of individuation, are inseparable. The "thisness" of an object cannot exist in any other object because the principles that make the object an individual object belong to it alone. Although the nature of the object and the "thisness" of the object are distinguished formally, the specificity of the object with all that inheres in the object as a subject, cannot be confused with another object or lost in the consideration of the universal. The thing, then, has specificity and a presence that allows it to be known as an object of the intellect in all its ramifications.

Against the Thomistic background, the philosophy of Scotus must have been a release. Although the Thomistic philosophic tradition was penetrating in its analysis, it was coldly logical and deductive about nature and the way nature is known. Thomistic philosophy holds that a person cannot know singular material things directly with the intellect but the knower only knows universals, essences. Because intellect cannot know material objects directly, it knows them through phantasms in which the intellect apprehends the universals, because it has abstracted the intelligible species.[1]

The theory pushes aside the knowledge of the individual material thing. It focuses on the universal element of the individual object which the accidents cannot possibly define. The accidental characteristics of matter, matter possessed only of pure potentiality, follow after the hylomorphic composition of matter and form. Forms, however, arise only in something that actually exists and so could be no more than accidental forms. When being exists, it is finite because it exists, and so existence makes substance a being.[2] Existence, then, is the act by which essence is.[3]

Such a philosophy could not be a help to a poet of Hopkins' propensities. Regardless of the niceties of the arguments and the controversies, the philosophy and method of Aquinas presented a view of nature and the manner of knowing nature that was counter to Hopkins' view. A theory of knowing in which knowledge moves toward the essence of the object rather than toward the nature of the particular, that is, its "thisness," retreats from Scotus's and Hopkins's understanding of reality in an objective manner. If the push is always on the essential abstracted nature to the detriment of what the senses apprehend, objectivity and realism are lost. The thing considered is not "this" so exquisitely present and so close, but it is held at a distance, kept at remove, in order to discover its essence beyond its accidental properties, properties which simply define it as matter signed by quantity. A habit of thought is instilled that keeps material nature at a distance.

Scotus focuses the mind on what makes the being be. To penetrate what makes the being be, that is, to intuit the particular thing as a presently existing subject in which qualities inhere, the thing becomes an object of knowledge in the knowing self which is present to the thing as to the ultimate reality of its being. The knower, Hopkins, comprehends all that inheres in the subject so that the whole is the object of knowledge. What is real about the subject out there inheres in the subject as the object of knowledge. What is known is the thing. In Scotesian philosophy and in Hopkins, then, accidents are not qualities which disturb the search for essence in the abstractive process, but by intuition become necessary to the objective definition of the subject as existent nature actually present in all the powers that make it "this" present to the knower rather than the "what is that" out there that participates in universal abstraction.

The difference between the view of Aquinas and that of Scotus is contrasted in Hopkins's translation of Aquinas's poem, "*Adoro te devote / [supplex]/latens deitas.*"[4] The matter-of-fact language of Aquinas communicates the nature of the event of the cross and the sacrament which, according to his theology, makes it available in the present time.

The matter-of-fact poetry on principal themes is made by Hopkins into a translation which contemplates the event before him. The technical term "*sub his figuris*" of sacramental theology becomes "by these bare shadows" and the poet's presence to the specific personal understanding of and connections with the event resonates in the "lies *here* a heart/Lost," but "lost in wonder" rather than "contemplans."

In verse three the simple statement of the "*Adoro te,*" "*Peto quod petivit latro paenitens*" [I seek what the penitent at the side, sought] becomes "And I pray the prayer of the dying thief." The attitudes of prayer, the identification with the thief at Christ's side as dying rather than just penitent, is not Aquinas's view of that moment. Aquinas looks back into history, into the remote past, and acknowledges that what is known and believed by him is in the figures of the sacrament. Hopkins's view is that the whole event exists here and now because Hopkins and the thief pray the same prayer. Hopkins could have translated the passage more literally and he was certainly capable of doing so. The more important point, however, was to make evident to the reader that the event was to be taken as present. The event, the thing considered, is something so individual that it must stand radically so. Thus, he looks at the same sacrament in the same context as does Aquinas, but he marks it as a distinct incident that cannot be known by abstract and essential statements. The thing would then stand at a distance, less real, less objective.

Hopkins does not take the position of Thomas Aquinas, the official philosopher in the Jesuit seminaries of the time. Having already developed inscape, he was fascinated by the distinctive reality of a given thing or group of things, to know the very essence of them. In 1872 he "found"

Scotus and the subtle theory of knowledge and principle of individuation which fit so well with his inscape and instress.

What mattered was that Scotus asserted that *haecceitas* is the final perfection of the creature and that the knowledge of it is had immediately by the intellect in union with the senses. Such a theory of knowledge about how a thing is known went beyond the rules of rigid deduction. Scotus, "who of all men most sways my spirit to peace; / Of reality the rarest-veined unraveller" solved a problem for Hopkins.[5] He connected the *haecceitas* of Scotus with pitch,[6] that is, the "ultimately simple positive-ness, that by which being differs from and is more than nothing and not-being."[7] It was the philosophy of Scotus that intensified the knowledge of things by forcing the accuracy or objectivity that sets the thing apart from not-being and defines it as being. The person's understanding is intensified because the pitch is raised. Pitch is the function of inscape, the directing energy of pitch.

The proposition may not seem much in the twentieth century, but to Hopkins it must have been something of a release and a revelation, particularly when he was rigorously taught the Thomistic view of the nature of things and the theory of knowledge by which one understands that nature.

The stress of Thomas Aquinas's approach was on the abstract concept when he philosophized about the knowledge of the nature of things. He held that the concept was the means of knowing, but not the object of knowing. The concept is only a likeness of the object which is held in the mind, having been produced by the mind so that the mind can know the object. The concept is that by which the object is understood, not that which is understood.[8]

When Aquinas concluded that all the intellect knows is the essence or the universal, he removed any chance of an intimate connection between singular things and the knower, because the mind could know material things directly or immediately. Scotus, because of his concern with the inviolable connections between essence and existence, claimed that the distinction between the nature of a thing and the "thisness" of a thing was dictated by facts and the need for an objective reference of our concepts. He insisted on the intellectual intuition of a singular object.

Judged by Thomistic standards, the outpourings of "That nature is a Heraclitean Fire and of the Comfort of the Resurrection" are neither objective nor realistic because they are intuitive.[9] "Cloud-puffball, torn tufts, tossed pillows | flaunt forth, then chevy on an air-built thoroughfare: heaven roysterers, in gay gangs | they throng; they glitter in marches./ Down roughcast, down dazzling whitewash, | wherever an elm arches, / Shivelights and shadowtackle in long | lashes lace, lance, and pair" is by

Thomistic understanding a set of accidental conformations that cannot speak of the essence of things nor can it be objective or realistic precisely because it does not deal with the essence. In Thomistic terms Hopkins' understanding of a cloud or clouds is rather the use of the power of imagination. When the image is of the cloud or clouds, an individual thing or group of things is created. It is the image that is known, not the cloud or clouds. The knowledge of the cloud or clouds is only indirect because the conversion to a phantasm is what allows the mind to have any knowledge of the thing. When the imagination converts the thing to an image, the mind knows the thing indirectly only because the image alone is presented to the mind. The conversion of the thing to image is crucial.

For Scotus and Hopkins the apprehension of an object is intense and real. The senses are important to the knowledge, not of the accidents of the thing, but of the thing itself. Although the senses apprehend the thing, the intellect knows intuitively what the senses apprehend.[10] Even though the knowledge of a singular thing is imperfect, it is so because our intellectual operations are imperfect. The imperfection, however, does not prevent the intellectual intuition of a singular thing as existence.[11]

Thus words such as "puffball," "tossed pillows," "chevy on an air-built thoroughfare," and "heaven-roysterers" in one view are simply descriptions of physical outlines, or shapes that are only accidental conformations of the thing. But since this thing or things, here clouds, has a specificity at one moment in time, the attempt to define the thing at that particular moment is to apprehend its "thisness" that marks them essentially. The inscape that holds the apprehension together is marked by the pitch of the "thisness." The result is the immediacy of the intuition of the thing, not only of the poet but also of the reader.

In Scotus's philosophy on the knowledge of things, the role of the senses is important. Although we have intellectual knowledge of the universal and sense experience of the singular thing, he insists that because a singular thing is available to the senses the intellect would know the thing as singular because the senses are a power subordinate to the intellect. What happens is that the higher power intuits the knowledge of the singular thing as existent.[12]

Thus the language about the clouds of the Hopkins' poem is more than a statement of essence abstracted from material things. The instance stands as an example of the way of realistically describing what inheres in the subject, that is, the peculiar "thisness" that belongs to the clouds as those clouds without diminishing their nature as clouds. The emphasis is on the object as present in its actual existence and none other. This is the intuition that focuses sharply on actual existence.[13]

The nature of any one thing is rooted in and necessary for the knowledge of the nature of any one thing. The "accidents," the shape, color, size, etc., are essential to distinguish objects sensibly and intellectually. The *haecceitas* of each remains, sense knowing the individuated thing, and the intellect knowing the universal with intuition always apprehending the present thing as existent. This view protects the objectivity of knowledge, that is, the intellect always abstracts universals from previous knowledge of the singular. [14]

"Pied Beauty," "The Windhover," or "God's Grandeur" are preeminent examples of the philosophical assumptions at work. In "Pied Beauty" the beauty of things, the skies, the earth, the landscape, and all things, praises God. Accepted as a short litany of praise, the abstracted quality of the summary words is stated in much more universal terms. Hopkins is concerned not with a universal, but with the nature of an individual existing thing. "Dappled things, skies, trout, chestnuts, bird wings" are the individual things Hopkins writes of. It is "this" sky, "this" trout, "this" bird wing, at one moment of time caught as each really is. The landscape is *a* field, marked, fenced, ploughed, lying fallow, a particular landscape at a precise moment, the only landscape that can be at that time. The next moment changes it all, but just as really. When the thing exists in the next moment, it is the same and different because it will be known at another time of existence. Thus the beauty that praises God is much like Him: "He fathers-forth whose beauty is past change." The constant essential being and its constant newness with each moment of time shows the constant life of the thing and of God.

The theme of Christ transmuting nature to a spiritual plane is Hopkins' own assessment of the poem "The Windhover." [15] He refers to the "selving" of things, the law of characteristic natural action. The attributes of the falcon, "morning's minion," his "riding" and "rolling," his "striding," the "hurl and gliding" define the nature of the falcon at that moment in time. The falcon has that particular "thisness" about him which tells the reader all about him. The movements, shapes, and color together become more than a conglomeration of attributes, but the definition of the falcon itself. Thus, the precise knowledge of the falcon, this falcon, intuits that the whole is more than its parts. It is the knowledge of the falcon at a given moment, so real and intense that it transcends any attribute to make it "this" falcon and none other. The "selving" transmutes the poet's activity in the completeness of the apprehension:

> Brute beauty and valour and act, oh, air, pride,
>   plume, here
>   Buckle! AND the fire that breaks from thee then,
>   a billion
> Times told lovelier, more dangerous, O my chevalier!

No wonder of it: sheer plod makes plough down
   sillion
Shine, and blue-bleak embers, ah my dear,
   Fall, gall themselves, and gash gold-vermilion.

"God's Grandeur," "The Starlight Night," and "Spring" take up the same themes as do "Pied Beauty" and "The Windhover," "God's Grandeur" is the "fathering-forth" of "Pied Beauty" and the praise is a world charged with His grandeur. In "Spring" it is the "fathering-forth" out of the nature of things Christ the Lord, and in "The Starlight Night" things comprise the home of Christ under the stars. Again and again, it is the intensity with which Hopkins penetrates into the nature of a thing, that it transmutes to another level but only because there is the understanding of the "thisness" of an individual thing as well as the nature of it. Comprehension comes in knowing the singular thing as "this" and not as a part of a single essence.

Hopkins decries the distinction between essence and existence. He opts for the *haecceitas* of Scotus and by it finds the tool that provides him a way of looking at distinctions between the formalities of one and the same object, the formalities which are always part of the nature of the thing.[16]

The physical universe as considered in *itself*, or any physical thing of that universe, or considered to this or that *haecceitas* cannot exist in itself outside the mind and can never be separated from its *haecceitas*. The pitch is intensified because the thing, be it the material universe, or any part or relation of that universe, such as Christ, is always the ultimate reality of the being which is matter or form or a composite thing.[17] Thus, the subtle doctor gave Hopkins a habit of thought that not only allowed intensification of relation with nature in all its forms, but promoted it as a way of comprehending what was realistic and objective, although poetic.

6

A Reconsideration

Confessions of a Young Man as Farce

Robert Langenfeld

*C*onfessions of a Young Man (1888), described by George Moore as "the story of the artistic development of me," has received extensive examination as an autobiography.[1] In addition to using *Confessions* to comprehend Moore's beginning as a writer and his attitudes toward art and literature, readers have used the book to understand more fully the Parisian artistic and literary klatches of the day.[2] As an autobiographical work, it stands in contradistinction to most Victorian autobiography, which works in terms of discourse and reserves a concern for propriety. Moore does not possess the qualms about autobiography, for example, voiced by George Eliot in *Impressions of Theophrastus Such.* Indeed, after its first appearance, one critic termed *Confessions* a book of "the hardest, most audacious, most rigid thinking that our generation has seen."[3] *Confessions* is more akin to *Mlle. De Maupin,* particularly in the tone and subject matter of its famous Preface. Gautier complains about the "great affectation of morality" in his day which "would be very laughable, if it were not very tiresome." He taunts the establishment: "Why, good heavens! worthy preachers, what would you do without vice? You would be reduced to beggary from to-morrow, if people became virtuous to-day." The flamboyant Moore also seems determined not only to taunt but to anger the establishment of his day.

Confessions is adventurous, even temerarious, in its treatment of a wide range of subjects, and of course it is immensely entertaining. This paper does not deny the autobiographical aspects of *Confessions* but reconsiders it in a different light. *Confessions* will be discussed in terms of a specific type of comedy—farce—and placed in a comedic framework to better understand what the book's persona, Edward Dayne, is saying, in his humorous but outrageous fashion, about the society and cultural tastes of the late nineteenth century, as well as what he foresees for the twentieth century.

The unrestrained nature of the book was recognized by Walter Pater, and basic to an understanding of *Confessions* as a farce is a letter from Pater to Moore, first published in the 1904 Preface. The only date given for the letter is 4 March though Moore notes he received it some years before, perhaps shortly after *Confessions'* first publication in February 1888. He characteristically praises Pater as "the last great English writer," and continues: "never forget that Pater's admiration has made this book a sacred book. Never forget that."[4] While Pater's admiration is certainly important to Moore, he does not include the letter simply to verify Pater's accolades for his tenth book. Pater's preoccupation with the satirical and cynical in *Confessions* is important:

> MY DEAR, AUDACIOUS MOORE,—Many thanks for the "Confessions" which I have read with great interest, and admiration for your originality—your delightful criticisms—your Aristophanic joy, or at least enjoyment, in life—your unfailing liveliness. Of course, there are many things in the book I don't agree with. But then, in the case of so satiric a book, I suppose one is hardly expected to agree or disagree. ... And still I wonder how much you may be losing, both for yourself and for your writings, by what, in spite of its gaiety and good-nature and genuine sense of the beauty of many things, I must call a cynical, and therefore exclusive, way of looking at the world [p. 38].

Two ideas are noteworthy: Aristophanic satire and cynicism. Pater is particularly concerned with the harshness of *Confessions*. It is replete with satirical lampoons and cynical comments, but if they are not viewed within the context of a comedic technique, the attacks do seem merely capricious. Intention and meaning appear lost in flamboyance.

Certainly *Confessions* contains satiric elements, but as Ronald Paulson points out, it is not the same thing to say an author wrote satire and to say he wrote *a* satire: "without an article 'satire' refers more to a tone than to a form."[5] Pater rightly calls *Confessions* "so satiric a book," not a satire; Moore's work is not a structured satire. To quote Paulson, "In general the satiric form is anything that will serve to expose a succession of different aspects of a single subject, the object of denunciation."[6] David Worcester echoes the same belief:

Two general principles are useful in deciding whether to call a given piece of writing a satire or a form of pure comedy, such as farce, skit, extravaganza, and so on. First, we should consider the closeness with which the camera pursues the object of satire. If the comic devices are applied to a single object or group of related objects, if a sense of unity is produced by the common bearing of diverse illustrations, we are on the side of satire. If the operations of wit are promiscuous and casual, the presumption is in favor of comedy.[7]

Confessions is quite promiscuous and anything but unified or carefully planned. It is written in the spirit of pure comedy, more pointedly in accordance with the spirit of farce. Moore, imbued with the life of Paris in the 1870s, sets out to attack the stolid convictions of the Victorian attitude in the late ninetenth century. His persona, the dandyish Edward Dayne, gambols along, mocking the vapid cultural tastes and hypocritical social poses of the establishment of his day. His targets are wide-ranging. Social conventions, formal education, the economic conditions of the have–nots, status quo views on art and literature, sex and marriage, and the character of the coming twentieth century are examined in an outrageous manner. In the process of airing his rebellious opinions, Dayne jolts established views and sensibilities by both amusing and offending the reader.

A key to understanding the book as farce is the character of Edwin Dayne. Dayne's claims about his own character are more than whimsical; they make him an iconoclastic clown. An avowed egoist, he enjoys the perversity of experiencing things of even commonplace interest in an intense and totally unusual way. He has an unabated curiosity for its own sake. "Humanity be hanged!" cries Dayne. "Self, and after self a friend; the rest may go to the devil" (p. 185). He delights in aberrant behavior: "I am feminine, morbid, perverse. But above all perverse, almost everything perverse interests, fascinates me" (p. 76). His Parisian days awake "a tense irresponsible curiosity" in the souls of people he hungers to know, but that curiosity is for its own sake. The people he meets are simply "subjects of artistic treatment"; he despises them, indeed thinks them "contemptible" (p. 64).

These characteristics—egoism, perversity, curiosity—are benchmark qualities in farce. As Edith Kern points out, "farce is based on notions of justice quite different from bourgeois standards of morality and ethics. Compared to those standards, such notions often appear immoral, harsh, and cruel."[8] Dayne's character, its petulance and rebelliousness, works against the grain of established values, whether social, artistic, or literary. Morton Gurewitch states that "farce (at its best, to be sure) may promote an exuberant rape of the world's stultified attitudes"; it is "the perfect killer of gravity."[9] Dayne must be an iconoclast, for the "iconoclastic clown—a wild fool tempting us to shun the argument of culture and throw in our lot with the joys of chaos—is the very symbol of gay, gross, instinctual acts of brigandage against the world's custodianship of proper values."[10] His egoism, perversity, and irresponsible curiosity provide a temporary truancy, a saturnalia, from accepted norms. Moore's use of farce by means of the persona, Dayne, "boldly invites us to smash all decency and discipline, all legitimacy and logic, all authority," and embrace "the delectable sins and outrages that the cultural superego plainly denounces."[11]

Equally as important as Dayne's own claims about his character in understanding the basis of farce in *Confessions* are the specific techniques Moore uses to alter established views and to make them suspect. Three kinds of farce are evident: psychic, social, and sexual. Psychic farce, used to characterize Dayne, ridicules stability, the ordered mind and soul. To put it simply, "the essence of psychic farce . . . is zany mental and emotional instability."[12] This kind of farce is expressed through Dayne's capricious attitudes toward himself and others. Dayne the braggart may without notice become Dayne the self-deprecator. The halcyon Dayne may in an instant become the morose Dayne. Dayne the inspired friend may easily become Dayne the conniving Machiavellian. Social farce, on the other hand, slants its barbs toward the absurdities of social conventions, "class stratifications, intimidating institutions, and legislated values. . . . Society is imaged as organized bunk or as a chimera draining the life out of natural man."[13]

Indeed, as Pater keenly observes, *Confessions* is a book not just about art, but about life's potential for liveliness and spontaneity. Dayne's passionate ego is exercised on society. Social farce finds specific but varied targets: established social conventions, the debilitating effects of formal education, the pathetic socio-economic circumstances of the have-nots (Emma in particular), and the art and literature that "society" deems worthwhile. And any book about life is about sex. Sexual farce not only undercuts the hypocrisy of people who supposedly adhere to moral proprieties and in practice do not, but "is an assault on moral prohibitions" themselves.[14] Dayne repeatedly takes aim at sexual relations, pedestrian courtship, and the pieties that cloud marriage. Toward the end of *Confessions*, moreover, Moore stresses a grand theme linked to the various attacks voiced via the three types of farce. Social and cultural darkness will accompany the birth of the twentieth century, a darkness created by the very attitudes and practices Dayne criticizes.

The protagonist is portrayed by means of psychic farce. Edward Dayne's antibourgeois character is evidenced in his dress and in his living quarters. Dayne's foppish demeanor, however, is not original; it is modelled after his artistic friend, Henry Marhall. On first meeting Marshall, Dayne is immediately struck by his sartorial splendors: "my experience had not led me to believe in the marriage of genius and well-cut cloth" (p. 58). Marshall's apartment is a mixture of the bizarre and of the exotic. He examines the great fireplace with "awe" and admires its "artificial bivouac fire." The rest of the studio—"the Turkey carpet, the brass harem lamps, the Japanese screen, the pieces of drapery, the oak chairs covered with red Utrecht velvet" (p. 59)—is a collage of disparate furniture styles and bright colors. Dayne is intrigued and utilizes Marshall's decorating talents, "an imagination that suggested the collaboration of a courtesan of high degree and a fifth-rate artist" (p. 75), for an apartment they later occupy together. Their flat at 76 rue de la Tour des Dames is an iconoclast's paradise: "The drawing-room was in cardinal red, hung from the middle of the ceiling and looped up to give the appearance of a tent. . . . In another room you faced an altar, a Buddhist temple, a statue of the Apollo, and a bust of Shelley" (p. 75). Two final outrages against decorum are a Persian cat and a python that feeds on guinea pigs. Dayne also converts a pair of satin shoes into match boxes and nails them to the wall on either side of the bed.

His dress is an effrontery to convention, too. He usually lounges in a "japanese dressing gown, the ideality of whose tissue delights" him (p. 93). He revels in watching the python, Jack, slowly devour a guinea pig that is tied to "the *tabouret*, pure Louis XV" (p. 93). Dayne's dress and behavior outside his fantastic abode are similarly out of the ordinary. When he and Marshall visit the exposition of the Impressionists, for example, they go "insolent with patent leather shoes and bright kid gloves and armed with all the jargon of the school . . . the boisterous laughter, exaggerated in the hope of giving as much pain as possible" (p. 68).

All the dandyish affections are amusing, but of course beneath the perverse delight is a more serious point: the commonplace dress and conventional quarters of "proper people" are hackneyed, if not dull. The dandy rebels against the pedestrian norms to stimulate spontaneity and interest, to make even the routine in life more lively, or at least less boring. Uncommon exaggeration can best jar the proprieties of decorum. As the fool's outlandish dress, with its bells and bright colors, affords him the license to say the extraordinary and elucidate the foolishness of others, so too does the dandy's grotesque demeanor offer a caveat to the smugness of conventionality. But Moore probes deeper than the dandy's appearance. The zany emotional and intellectual tergiversations of Dayne further complement his zany appearance. The outlandish dress subverts the accepted worth of everyday dress; the capricious opinions and sentiments effectively call into question the seemingly inherent value of psychological stability, order, and logic.

Dayne's psychic character is evident in other ways. He says his entire being is a *tabula rasa*: "I am free from original qualities, defects, tastes, etc. What I have I acquire, or, to speak more exactly, chance bestowed, and still bestows, upon me" (p. 49). But for the whims of chance he might have been a "Pharaoh," an "ostler," a "pimp," or an "archbishop"; he has "felt the good of many impulses" and "hunted many a trail; when one scent failed another was taken up, and pursued with the pertinacity of an instinct, rather than the fervour of a reasoned conviction" (p. 49). Reason has little to do with his psyche. Indeed, the only ostensible guideposts in Dayne's peregrinations through life are what he calls echo-auguries. Moore borrowed the term from DeQuincey; it designates a word that introduces Dayne to a new enthusiasm, and there is no logic to why one word becomes an echo-augury and another does not. This unique aspect of Dayne's character is the stuff of psychic farce. It fosters an improbable and disjointed chain of events that plot a path through a life full of sudden change.

The first echo-augury occurred when he was eleven years old! A woman riding in the same coach with him is discussing an unnamed novel, wherein a murder occurs. A question is posed: "Did Lady Audley murder her husband? Lady Audley! What a beautiful name; and she, who is a slender, pale, fairy-like woman, killed her husband." The boy's imagination is stirred, but when he arrives at his destination Lady Audley "is forgotten in the delight of tearing down fruit trees and killing a cat" (p. 50). After returning home, however, he devours the novel as well as its successors. In the process he comes across a lady who loved Shelley and Byron: "There was magic, there was revelation in the name, and Shelley became my soul's divinity" (p. 50). Dayne carries Shelley's poetry "amid the priests and ignorance of a hateful Roman Catholic college" and believes it "saved me from intellectual savagery" (p. 50). On the mere mention of the name Lady Audley he is moved to read and to love Shelley. By means of a wild and circuitous path, the most rebellious of Romantic poets becomes an appropriate literary hero for the defiant and chaotic Dayne.

A more important turning point in Dayne's life pivots on a conversation with a London painter. He "involuntarily" decides "how jolly it would be to be a painter," not suspecting he had "the slightest gifts, as indeed was the case" (p. 52). He begins to make sketches in the streets and theaters; his father allows him to enter Kensington Museum as an art student, where he "learned nothing" (p. 52). On one occasion his painter-friend muses, "But if you want to be a painter you must go to France— France is the only school of Art" (p. 52). Again, "words heard in an unlooked-for quarter" are catalysts and "without an appeal to our reason, impel belief. . . . Instantly I knew I should, that I would become as a Frenchman. I knew not when nor how, but I knew I should go to France . . ." (p. 53). Dayne, of course, does journey to France. This all-important echo-augury moves him to travel to the center of cultural activity, Paris, in the 1870s. There he meets Degas, Manet, Zola, and other influential artists and writers of the day. After a time in Paris, Dayne's efforts to become a painter are uneven, and he deems himslf unsuccessful; he emphatically comes to the decision to stop painting: "I laid down my charcoal and said, 'I will never draw or paint again.' That vow I have kept" (p. 73). His decision-making process is typically abrupt.

Dayne's third and final echo-augury is as sudden as the previous two. While sitting in a Parisian cafe for breakfast, he reads an essay by Zola in the magazine *Voltaire*. The words "*Naturalisme, la vérité, la science*" are repeated several times: "Hardly able to believe my eyes, I read that you should write, with as little imagination as possible, that plot in a novel or in a play was illiterate and puerile. . . ." He orders coffee and stirs in the sugar, "a little dizzy, like one who has received a violent blow on the head. . . . And now for a third time I experienced the pain and joy of a sudden inward light . . . above all the phrase 'the new art', impressed me as with a sudden sense of light" (p. 94). This inordinate praise of Zola's influence is not unexpected, yet constancy is an anathema to Dayne. He later reproaches Zola because "he has no style. . . . He seeks immortality in an exact description of a linenshop; if the shop conferred immortality it should be upon the linendrapers who created the shop, and not on the novelist who described it" (p. 110). Dayne's unpredictability is the basis of his farcical character. He becomes a lover of Shelley at the mention of the words "Lady Audley"; he becomes an artist and moves to Paris at the mention of the word "France"; he gives up painting with similar suddenness; he becomes a Zola votary at the turn of the phrase "the new art," yet later rebukes his once cherished literary mentor as facilely as he first embraces him. Woven through the abrupt turns of mind are mocking comments, directed not only toward others but toward himself: trademarks of the consummate jester, the farcical fool.

Instability is the hallmark of his friendship with Marshall. Dayne does not view friendship in a conventional sense. Even friends are to be used to one's advantage. A useless friend is no friend at all. Marshall advises him on many points, from clothes to the arrangement of his rooms: "I strove to copy his manner of speech and his general bearing; and yet I knew very well indeed that mine was a rarer nature. . . . I used him without shame, without stint. . . . I never had useless friends hanging about me" (p. 61). Dayne admits that the "thoughtless reader" will probably judge him "rapacious, egotistical, false, fawning and mendacious" and indeed he "may be all this and more" (p. 61). Still, the reader will misunderstand because he will assume Dayne is taking advantage of Marshall when in fact he is simply allowing him to "contribute something towards my well-being" (p. 62). Chance is instrumental in providing useful friends. "How," says Dayne, "we may tear to shreds our past lives in search of—what? Of the Chance that made us" (p. 62). Dayne claims he can explain how chance might give him Marshall and not someone else:

> Chance, or the conditions of life under which we live, sent, of course thousands of creatures across my way who were powerless to benefit me; but then an instinct of which I knew nothing, of which I was not even conscious, withdrew me from them, and I was attracted to others. Have you not seen a horse suddenly leave a corner of a field to seek pasturage further away? (p. 62)

Yet chance may give and take away. Even though Dayne asserts he is "very sincere in my friendship, and very loyal in my admiration" for Marshall, he makes a break in the relationship. It is a characteristic inconsistency that the man who praises the usefulness of friendship is tortured because Marshall makes him "feel that I was only a means for the moment, a serviceable thing enough, but one that would be very soon discarded and passed over" (pp. 73–74). It all becomes unbearable, and though the dissolution of the friendship, "a dastardly action," causes Marshall "grave and cruel difficulties," in "ridding himself of him," says Dayne, "I felt as if a world of misery were being lifted from me" (p. 74).

Naturally the rift between Dayne and Marshall is not permanent; permanence is a serious affliction to Dayne's mind. He manages a reconciliation with Marshall, but one not based on logical, thoughtful emotions. He sees Marshall in an admirably cut overcoat perfectly suited to his figure, "and I remembered that if I had not broken with him I should have been able to ask him some essential questions concerning it. Of such trifles as this the sincerest friendships are made; he was as necessary to me as I to him . . ." (p. 75). The basis of the reconciliation, trifling and bizarre as it is, seems appropriate for Dayne.

The element of psychic farce, then, is dominant in Dayne's character. His precipitate decisions undercut stability and order; his lack of methodology and his disdain for agonizing over a choice in life subvert the conventional wisdom which says to obtain the best results in life people should ruminate on a course of action before pursuing it. The case cannot really be made that Dayne would have been happier, more fulfilled, or more intelligent if he were more reasonable. His views on friendship, moreover, challenge the generally accepted beliefs on what friendship is and how one should conduct oneself in it. Many people use their friends or become miffed because of jealousy, real or imagined. Unlike Dayne, though, such a "friend" often couches his sentiments in rationalizations and justifications and then proceeds to become less of a true friend than the callous Dayne. Many a friendship has risen or fallen on something just as trivial as the cut of a coat, though few would admit it.

A final point needs to be made about the psychic character of Dayne. As Jean C. Noël has asserted, some critics are uncomfortable with what they see as the inchoate structure of *Confessions*. He correctly notes this is intentional on Moore's part, for he wants to insure multiplicity and ambiguity in the book.[15] The lack of order and structure in *Confessions*, furthermore, is a perfect reflection of the mind of the first-person narrator. The desultory movement from one subject to another mirrors the element of psychic farce that is fundamental to Dayne's character. A man who is attempting to question, if not mock, the inherent value of reason and order does not write a reasonable, well-ordered book.

It should not be surprising that Dayne, who is unreceptive to stability and reason, finds bourgeois mores and respectability loathsome. Social farce is employed by the blithe dandy, who ridicules the absurdities of social conventions, unjustified class snobbery, self-important institutions, and values by fiat. His chief vehicle for unleashing a scintillating attack on bourgeois respectability is the extended comparison of the Club (or suburban villa) versus the Tavern.

The Tavern can offer "the world of Villon and Marlowe" (p. 138). It is a place where the mind is imbued with passion, new ideas, and lively conversation: it breeds "enthusiasm and devil-may-careism; and the very aspect of the tavern is a snort of defiance at the hearth" (p. 138). The growing influence of fashionable domesticity, of the hearth and home, makes it "impossible for the husband to tell his wife that he was going to the tavern; everyone can go to the tavern, and no place in England where everyone can go is considered respectable" (p. 138). The rise of respectability and home virtues spells the demise of the rebellious, life-oriented environs of the Tavern. This respectability is "the genesis of the Club— out of the Housewife by Respectability. Nowadays every one is respectable—jockeys, betting men, actors, and even actresses." Dayne's sardonic tone continues:

> Did any one ever see a gay club room? Can anyone imagine such a thing? You can't have a club room without mahogany tables, you can't have mahogany tables without magazines . . . a dullness that's worth a thousand a year. (p. 138)

The horror of the Club, or the suburban villa with its "piano in the drawing room" and dinner at home, Dayne concludes, is its lack of "intensity of feeling, fervour of mind" (p. 138).

The growing influence of the Club is emblematic of a more serious danger—that is, of respectability "sweeping the picturesque out of life" (p. 139). William Morris's conception of democratic art in a socialistic world terrifies Dayne. Universality, whether in dress or cultural taste, is smothering superior individuality. National costumes are rarely worn; even the Japanese vie for respectability by becoming Christians: "To-day our plight is pitiable enough—the duke, the jockey-boy, and the artist are exactly alike; they are dressed by the same tailor, they dine at the same clubs, they swear the same oaths, they speak equally bad English, they love the same women" (pp. 139–40). All this inevitably makes for a "period of decadence" which grows steadily more acute. Everyone, unfortunately, is susceptible to the pervasive powers and manifestations of respectability: "no man is, after all, so immeasurably superior to the age he lives in as to be able to resist it wholly" (p. 141). It is as though the great flood is creeping into every quarter of society. The pressures on the individual are "as water upon the diver; and sooner or later he grows fatigued and comes to the surface to breathe; he is as a flying-fish pursued by sharks below and cruel birds above; and he neither dives as deeply nor flies as high as his freer and stronger ancestry" (p. 141). The monster respectability is strangling society like an "octopus," transforming art, science, and politics to suit its requirements.

There is, however, one lone figure who represents some hope in the dark seas of respectability, the snob. While the "old gods" are disappearing there is little to which one may lift his heart, but at least "snobbery is left to us, thank heaven, deeply graven in the English heart; the snob is now the ark that floats triumphant over the democratic wave" (p. 140). Dayne himself, of course, is a snob; this affords him the vantage point from which to criticize polite society. His disdain for people who sit in Clubs pleased with their self-importance is provoked not because they are egotistical. Dayne is an avowed egotist. His contempt is for the basis of the self-importance; the convention of being "proper" and frequenting the "correct" place has become an end in itself. Dayne would not argue with artificiality, but he cannot abide the worship and continued support for lifeless and unimaginative respectability. The jester cannot resist taking aim at the commonplace in society, especially when it becomes so oppressive and threatens to crowd out spontaneity and individuality. In a sense, Moore expresses through Dayne the same fear that John Stuart Mill and others had: democracy, the Great Leveler, can reduce almost everything to the prosaic, if taken to an extreme. Moore's comic spirit refuses to surrender and accept the status quo as inevitable when the life and culture of the era is clearly losing its richness of diversity and nuance.

One villain responsible for fomenting the respectability Dayne dreads so much is formal education. On a number of occasions, he mocks the sacred institution and in the process chides people who have a mindless confidence in its glories and beneficial influences. For Dayne, the dichotomy is clear. There is the "natural man, who educates himself, who allows his mind to grow and ripen under the sun and wind of modern life, in contradistinction to the University man, who is fed upon the dust of ages, and after a formula which has been composed to suit the requirements of the average human being" (p. 53). Again, society inculcates young minds with knowledge designed on the basis of "formulas" and "requirements" to produce just an "average human being"; all of this inhibits the potential for the unusual mind, the unique viewpoint, which may allow people to know themselves and their time more clearly. Formal training, to Dayne's mind, is also fatal for art. Education should be limited to "clerks, and even them it drives to drink" (p. 111). He denies the vaunted belief that there is a "recipe" for the beautiful. In the end, "education destroys individuality" (p. 112).

Dayne reserves his most delicious outrages, however, for the "unimaginable dreariness" of Universal Education:

> The spectres of famine, of the plague, of war, etc., are mild and gracious symbols compared with that menacing figure, Universal Education. . . . The cruelties of Nero, of Caligula, what were they?—a few crunched limbs in the amphitheatre; but thine, O Education, are the yearning of souls sick of life, of maddening discontent, of all the fearsome and fathomless sufferings of the mind. (p. 140)

In the past, the fires of formal enlightenment could be extinguished by barbarians, but they are gone. The time will come when edicts must be written so "that not more than one child in a hundred shall be taught to read, and no more than one in ten thousand shall learn the piano" (p. 140). Dayne's humorous exaggeration evinces a fear that formal education, instruction by common consent, will create a generation of educational clones, whose interests and talents are all-too-similar. Society and culture should value individuality and allow a place for the unusual or iconoclastic person.

In addition to the attacks on respectability and education, Moore uses social farce to treat the socioeconomic conditions of the have-nots, concentrated particularly in the characterization of the pathetic servant, Emma. Dayne's rendering of Emma is darkly sardonic, gallows humor, but quite serious. Her limited knowledge and extremely mundane interests, or for that matter lack of any interest besides work, make her sadly comic. Emma is not by any stretch of the imagination intelligent. Dayne explains the routine for breakfast:

A knocking at the door, "Nine o'clock, sir; 'ot water sir; what will you have for breakfast?" "What can I have?" "Anything you like, sir. You can have bacon and eggs, or—" "Anything else?" —Pause— "Well, sir, you can have eggs and bacon, or—" "Well, I'll have eggs and bacon" [p. 137].

She works many hours a day scouring, cooking, tending wretchedly rude children of the house, carrying coals up flights of stairs. She is, says Dayne, "very nearly an animal," her "temperament and intelligence . . . that of a dog that has picked up a master, but makeshift master who may turn it out at any moment" (p. 134). She appears neither young nor old, since work has obliterated any "delicate markings" that might give a sense of age. Emma cannot, of course, read. Her drudgery allows no time for such luxury. She has no firm notion of God; indeed she admits she has not even heard of God. Even Emma's brother is indifferent to her plight. When told she has been given a half-day holiday, he retorts "you might as well give a mule a holiday" (p. 135). Dayne acknowledges that the phrase is brutal but descriptive; she is "a beast of burden, a drudge too horrible for anything but work . . ." (p. 135). Dayne's portrayal of Emma's harsh life is not so much an indictment of people in her unfortunate position, but of those social reformers, the falsely sympathetic do-gooders, who know little of the fearful lives of the have-nots. The reforms have not affected the Emmas of London. She is "one of the facts of civilization" that people either "sentimentalize or laugh over" (p. 134).

Dayne's position on the art and literature that "society" deems valuable is similarly harsh—rebellious. Naturally his opinions are not static, which is in accordance with the psychic nature of his farcical character. Initially he and Marshall find the Impressionists absurd, but later Dayne ridicules both his and Marshall's ignorance and insensitivity: "we stood and screamed at Monet, that most exquisite painter of blonde light. We stood before the 'Turkeys,' and seriously we wondered if 'it was serious work'. . . . 'Just look at the house! why, the turkeys couldn't walk in at the door. The perspective is all wrong'. Then followed other remarks of an educational kind" (p. 70). They do not understand the Impressionists, opines Dayne, because they were educated with the "grammar of art, perspective, anatomy, and la jambe qui porte; and we found all this in Julien's studio" (p. 71). He learns to love the Impressionists, after realizing that art is "mere emotion, right or wrong only in proportion to its intensity" (p. 71). Marshall, however, never understands or appreciates this school of painting. He ignores Degas and Manet and speaks of Jules Lefebvre and Bouguereau, generally showing himself "incapable of any higher education" (p. 128).

The idea of formally teaching painting becomes repulsive to Dayne, particularly the idea of teaching a "correct" method of painting, as though one sort is better than all others: "Art is not mathematics, it is individuality. It does not matter how badly you paint, so long as you don't paint badly like other people" (p. 112). The genesis of the grave misconception is the idea of "Democratic art!" (p. 112). A democracy like Athens with a few thousand citizens and many thousands of slaves—"call that democracy!" says Dayne. The masses of modern democracy, in fact, can only appreciate "*naive* emotions, puerile prettiness, above all conventionalities," the Lefebvres and Bouguereaus. The desire for conventional form is even seen in the destruction of the crafts. While some men will always sacrifice their lives to paint good pictures and write good literature, the decorative arts depend upon the general taste of many. Reflecting the taste of the majority is the demise of the decorative arts: "I'll give you five thousand, ten thousand francs to buy a beautiful clock that is not a copy and is not ancient; and you can't do it. Such a thing does not exist" (p. 113). The republican nature of governments has contaminated art and the crafts.

Dayne's assaults on what he sees as the conventional and lifeless in literature are also evident throughout *Confessions*. His ruminations on writers and their works are labyrinthian, to say the least. To people of his day, whether English or French, literature is but "idiotic stories of the *Petit Journal*" (p. 112). The conventional story-line novelist deserves contempt, as does the painter who adheres to the grammar of art. Hardy's work, for example, is "unilluminated by a ray of genius, it is slow and sodden. It reminds one of an excellent family coach. . . ." His writings read "more like a report, yes, a report,—a conscientious, well-done report, executed by a thoroughly efficient writer sent down by one of the daily papers" (p. 156). Robert Buchanan, "a type of artist that every age produces unfailingly" (p. 160), is much more commonplace than Hardy. Buchanan "has written a novel, the less said about which the better—he has attacked men whose shoe-strings he is not fit to tie, and having failed to injure them, he retracted all he said, and launched forth into slimy benedictions" (p. 160). Edmond de Goncourt is "puerile" and has written on "*bric-a-brac.*" Unlike Goncourt, Dayne contends a true writer "does not trouble himself about immortality, about everything he hears, feels and says; he treats ideas and sensations as so much clay wherewith to create" (p. 114).

A source responsible for the "vulgarism" (p. 143) in English literature is the circulating library.[16] The constricting effect of the suburban villa, on which Dayne exercised his wrath, helped to hatch the censorious circulating library. English fiction under its auspices became "pure, and the garlic and assafoetida with which Byron, Fielding, and Ben Jonson so liberally seasoned their works . . . disappeared" from English literature (p. 144). Dayne relishes the opportunity, however, to illustrate the hypocrisy of censoring the bawdy and the life-oriented in literature. Humans have always liked what the circulating library calls dirty stories; it can be called an incurable disease, but even if driven inward it will break out again, "with redoubled virulence" (p. 144). Ironically, while the English public goes to church, appears "good and chaste" (p. 145), and turns away from books like *Mlle. de Maupin* and *L'Assommoir,* the newspapers are at the same time sensationalizing an infamous divorce case, printing detailed accounts of adultery.[17] The public devours the sordid facts, and it is clear, say Dayne, that human nature has once again intervened: "poor human nature! when you pinch it in one place it bulges out in another, after the fashion of a lady's figure" (p. 144). The painstaking rendition of the Colin Campbell scandal erupts like a volcano: "the burning cinders of fornication and the blinding and suffocating smoke of adultery were poured upon and hung over the land" (p. 145). Dayne reproves strong-armed attempts to censor literature, particularly when the public so obviously craves the salacious. "I wonder why," muses Dayne, "murder is considered less immoral than fornication in literature" (p. 173). In the circulating library, the "powers that be" are singularly ignorant of human nature, and so the Charles Edward Mudies and W. H. Smiths of the literary establishment eliminate the spicy ingredients, the "garlic and assafoetida," which give delight and evidence an affinity with the human. The vapid moralizing of the circulating library is neither desirable nor necessary, and Dayne offers a lively explanation of what literature should strive to be, as he did in discussing art.

Dayne uses Gautier, Baudelaire, Verlaine, Balzac, and the Elizabethan dramatists as a group to illustrate what authors should attempt to write— after their own fashion of course. In Gautier he finds refreshment from the tiresome glorification of spiritual passion, so common to the literature of his day. Gautier provides the "great exaltation of the body above the soul. . . . This plain scorn of a world as exemplified in lacerated saints and a crucified Redeemer opened up to me illimitable prospects of fresh beliefs, and therefore new joys, in things and new revolts against all that had come to form part and parcel of the commonality of mankind" (p. 78). He finds it invigorating to look "without shame" and accept the "love of the flesh" (p. 78). Baudelaire, with the "clean shaven face of the mock priest, the slow, cold eyes and the sharp, cunning sneer of the cynical libertine" (p. 80), also offers new stimulation, as he records "his unbelief in goodness and truth and his hatred of life" (p. 87). Verlaine, however, becomes his poet, for "hate is to him as commonplace as love, unfaith as vulgar as faith" (p. 87). Dayne admits to becoming "a sensualist in literature," that "there are affinities in literature corresponding to, and very analogous to, sexual affinities—the same unreasoned attractions, the same pleasures, the same lassitudes" (p. 99).

His passion for Balzac is complete: "Upon that rock I built my church, and his great and valid talent saved me from the shoaling waters of new aestheticism, the putrid mud of naturalism, and the faint and sickly surf of the symbolist." Balzac's "intense and penetrating sympathy for human life and all that concerns it enabled him to surround the humblest subjects with awe and crown them with the light of tragedy" (p. 100). And with his study of the Elizabethan dramatists, "the real literature of my race" (p. 166), Dayne claims to purge himself of the triteness of the literature in his time.

Two common threads weave their way through these exemplars: a rebellious stance against what is generally believed to be good or evil, beautiful or ugly, and a close affinity for what is human and life-oriented in literature. "Contact with the world," declares Dayne, "is in me the generating force; without it what invention I have is thin and sterile, and it grows thinner and rapidly, until it dies away utterly . . ." (p. 101). The authors he cites with affection run counter to the simpleminded literature of the *Petit Journals,* the moralizing of a Buchanan, the censorious posturings of circulating libraries. He emphasizes the kind of writing that defies moral and ethical preconceptions. The human body, the passions and the emotions associated with it, is the stuff of art for Dayne. The praise for subjects concerned with life and rebellious natures are perfectly akin, moreover, to the mind of the comedian. There is a radicalism that is related to comedy, which Dayne clearly embraces.[18] Comedy, too, stresses an affinity with life and not rarefied concepts; its common denominator is a "pure sense of life."[19]

The social farce in *Confessions,* then, embellishes several central themes. The vacillating character of Dayne is a means of rebellion against so-called correct attitudes and orderly character. Specific attacks are directed against what people commonly agree is proper social conduct. The Tavern is an affront to the fixed manners and thinking of the Club or the quiescent suburban villa. Club respectability must be questioned, for to be responsive to change demands not blind acceptance of the status quo, but the willingness and the ability to re-evaluate attitudes and mores that seem acceptable. Because the establishment—that amorphous but influential power—deems a certain approach to education in the best interest of a culture does not necessarily mean it should be forever perpetuated. There should be, says Moore, an alternative to the university mentality, an avenue toward self-knowledge that admits more flexibility, subtle distinction, and personal identity. The potential even of the peculiar mind should be given the opportunity to grow and to come to fruition by whatever means it judges congenial. The unfortunate, moreover, should not be fodder for callous amusement, sentimentality, or careless, superficially interested reformers who lack a real understanding of what it is to be an ignorant have-not. And the same values that rule these social issues should not be applied to art and literature. Such stultifying estimations contaminate the world of culture. These themes are sounded in various places throughout *Confessions,* and no pattern organizes their appearance. The reader's values or lack of sensitivity to such issues are jarred by the whimsicalities of the farcical clown. Exaggeration is employed to outrage, to amuse, and thus to understand the heart, in the hope of forcing the reader to reconsider his convictions.

Moore uses sexual farce to comment on sex, marriage, and the passion for unobtainable ideal love. All are of the same cloth. The interrelationship among the three is not often recognized, especially by men. Dayne is amused, not surprised, to discover married women seeking the affections of men other than their husbands. Both men and women pursue the mysterious and unobtainable. Dayne's three-month retreat to "a sweet seaside resort," after his first break with Marshall, proves a playground, "where unoccupied men and ladies whose husbands are abroad happily congregate" (p. 75). Women enjoy the hunt for what they cannot find in marriage, but Dayne asserts they are not overly sentimental or rudely disappointed when the sought-after passion is transitory or unfilled.

Unrefined men, however, are particularly susceptible to the delusion that ideal love can be permanently secured and continually satisfying. Thus Dayne presents an exaggerated sentimental reverie on the ideal woman and undermines it with pointed comments that set forth the true nature of the sex-marriage-ideal love triangle as he sees it. He does admit, though, that some men do not simply seek the gratification of sexual need. An elite number realize "that sense of sex which is so subtle a mental pleasure." The charms of the women in Julien's studio—"the gowns, the hair lifted, showing the neck; the earrings, the sleeves open at the elbow" (p. 57)—can arouse a man's interest in women. For too many men, however, the "sense of sex" leads them to seek foolishly the ideal woman, the perfect relationship.

The embodiment of the ideal for many unwary men is "the woman of thirty." A man courts delusion in his preoccupation with her; "he longs for mystery, deep and endless, and he is tempted with a foolish little illusion—white dresses, water colour drawings, and popular music" (p. 89). He sees the young girl as pretty, but her "prettiness is vague and uncertain"; she "suggests nothing" and thus cannot touch the imagination: "no past lies hidden in those translucid eyes, no story of hate, disappointment, or sin" (p. 90). Only the woman of thirty seems to be the ultimate ideal—tall, stately, filled with mysterious aspirations a young man longs to see revealed. Such a man is a knave, says Dayne: "he dreams of Pleasure, and he is offered Duty; for do not think that sylph-like waist does not suggest to him a yard of apron string, cries of children, and that most odious word, 'Papa'" (pp. 89–90).

Marriage, especially the marriage of the woman of thirty, is a "riddle that no Oedipus will ever come to unravel" (p. 91). And all the striving for the ideal woman is, says Dayne, a "terrible malady" (p. 92). It evokes a beauty but is nevertheless a "disease." Dayne's view of the sex-marriage-ideal love triumvirate is perhaps overly harsh, but the highly idealized portrait of the woman of thirty is sketched to mock those who are too sentimental about love as well as those who embrace illusions—those who allow "that sense of sex which is so subtle a mental pleasure" to overwhelm them and make the beauty of the ideal pedestrian. Marriage and the ideal are totally incompatible: "Marriage—what an abomination! Love—yes, but not marriage. Love cannot exist in marriage, because love is an ideal; that is to say, something not quite understood—transparencies, colour, light, a sense of the unreal" (p. 1 1 1).

In addition to the attacks on social mores, formal education, the conditions of the have-nots, art and literature, sex and marriage, Dayne emphatically accentuates one grand theme germane to all he discusses in *Confessions*: the coming darkness of the twentieth century. The world has been ceaselessly drifting toward bourgeois tastes and comforts. History has continued in this direction "since the coming of the pale socialist of Galilee" (p. 123), but worse lies ahead, "the coming night of pity and justice which is imminent, which is the twentieth century" (p. 124). On the surface this century will be consumed with perpetuating the ideals of established justice, and those questionable ideals will be hypocritically pursued with an unthinking, unquestioning fervor. People will have no sense of subtle distinction; they will fail to realize that

> Every immortal deed was an act of fearful injustice; the world of grandeur, of triumph, of courage, of lofty aspiration, was built up on injustice. . . . What care I that some millions of wretched Israelites died under the Pharaoh's lash or Egypt's sun? It was well that they died that I might have the pyramids to look on, or to fill a musing hour with wonderment. Is there one amongst us who would exchange them for the lives of ignominious slaves that died [pp. 124–25]?

The coming age will forget this and lapse into "barbarism." Indeed, the "old world of heroes is over now. The skies above us are dark with sentimentalism, the sand beneath us is shoaling fast. . . ." There is need for the paganism of the "antique world, its plain passion, its plain joys in the sea, where the Triton blew a plaintive blast. . . . There, there is real joy in the flesh; our statues are naked, but we are ashamed, and our nakedness is indecency . . ." (pp. 125–26). For Dayne, however, the continuing predominance of machinery over human beings will be perhaps more ominous still. "The world," he says, "is dying of machinery: that is the great disease, that is the plague that will sweep away and destroy civiliza-tion" (p. 113). The very plates his book are made from are indication enough of the coming dark shadows that machinery will cast over the individual. The great revolution will occur when mankind revolts and smashes machines. There is in Dayne's words a fear, if not a realization, that a worthy *weltanschauung* and a passionate lifestyle, a concern for the individual's particular talent or craft, will be lost in a new century and a new age which will possess vastly different values than those of the past, whether Christian or pagan.

The final pages of *Confessions* seem the peroration of the farce-clown Dayne. He boldly, if not brutally, taunts the reader, and in the process reveals the purpose of his rambling discourse: to implore the reader to look not just at Dayne's character and views, but at his own attitudes and values. He tells the reader, "O hypocritical friend," not to deceive himself, for he will leave the world no better than he found it: "Look back upon your life, examine it, probe it, weigh it, philosophise on it, and then say, if you dare, that it has not been a very futile and foolish affair" (p. 179). The unthinking reader will dismiss Dayne's ideas as those of a madman, of no merit; he will see himself superior to Dayne. Everyone's "eternal and immutable delight" is to think he is better than his neighbor. "This is why," says Dayne, "I wrote this book and this is why it is affording you so much pleasure . . . because it helps you to the belief that you are not too bad after all" (p. 180). Despite an air of mistaken superiority, Dayne contends the reader must admit an interest in Dayne's wickedness; had the reader money and health he too would lead "a fast life." Only an "ingrained sense of propriety" and fear make the reader chary: "you would sell your wretched soul for what I would not give the parings of my finger-nails for—paragraphs in a society paper" (p. 185). The average citizen takes refuge in humanitarianism and lauds himself with self-righteous praise. Dayne reverses the generally held view on the nature of man and jars bourgeois complacency with a diapason of scorn:

Humanity is a pigsty, where liars, hypocrites, and the obscene in spirit congregate; it has been so since the great Jew conceived it, and it will be so till the end. Far better the blithe modern pagan in his white tie

and evening clothes, and facile philosophy. He says, "I don't care how
the poor live; my only regret is that they live at all;" and gives the
beggar a shilling [p. 186].

Dayne believes the honest reader should not think "too hardly" of him.
His confessions are spirited probings into the human heart and conscience:
"in telling you of my vices I am only telling you of your own. . . . in
showing you my soul I am showing you your own" (p. 190).

It is fitting to conclude this discussion of *Confessions* with an important
constituent in its genesis, Pater's letter. Pater's comments on the acrid
satire and harsh cynicism in the book are certainly justified. And no doubt
readers today find much to disagree with in Dayne's vitriolic attacks, but
then as Pater says, "in the case of so satiric a book, I suppose one is hardly
expected to agree or disagree." Surely one cannot agree with everything
Dayne asserts in *Confessions*. His comments on Hardy, for example,
appear rather ludicrous today. (Moore of course was prone to wax almost
hateful on Hardy's work, and in later years thought Conrad's position in
English letters equally overrated.) Still, when *Confessions* is understood in
terms of farce, the harshness and extended exaggeration seem assuaged by
one principal goal in the composition of the book: to question the
worthiness of established viewpoint, whether in the social or the artistic
realms. The questioning itself, regardless of whether the implied conclu-
sions are correct or not, is interesting and worthy of consideration.

In a sense the immodest Dayne's assaults on the complacency and
ostensible modesty people of the day pretend to are the reverse of the
"modest" narrator's musing in Swift's "A Modest Proposal." Unlike
Swift, however, Moore uses a different literary tactic. His far-ranging
subject matter is more suited to the flexibility inherent in the comedy of
farce. Dayne can be gay and raucous as well as darkly satirical in tone,
depending on the object of his attack. The topicality of both works is
overshadowed by the mutual desire to pose fundamental questions about
issues common to the human experience, to utilize humor to attain a
clearer sense of values and self-knowledge.

While not a "great book," *Confessions* is entertaining and thought-
provoking. It delightfully probes topics worth considering in the late
twentieth century, just as it did in the late nineteenth century. And
Confessions admittedly has some prophetic moments. The fears of universal culture overwhelming the richness of diversity is evident today in the
mindless worship of mass-produced pop culture. The loss of unique
individuality Dayne dreaded finds its parallel in the rush by so many
people to mimic the latest vogue, whether in dress, in leisure, or in cultural

activity. The restriction of the craftsman's singular talent by automation and the predominance of machinery now threatens the individual's ability to exercise meaningful control over his destiny. Such restrictions appear to be extrapolations of the growing democratization of society Dayne criticizes. In view of the farcical tempests generated in *Confessions,* one can only imagine how exercised Edwin Dayne would be at conditions in the late twentieth century if he could speak his mind today.

7

In Excelsis

Wilde's Epistolary Relationship with Lord Alfred Douglas

David B. Eakin

A ny study of Oscar Wilde's letters to Lord Alfred Douglas is necessarily frustrated by the regrettable gaps in their surviving correspondence. Wilde's arrest and conviction in 1895 incited numerous correspondents to destroy their letters from Wilde, often out of moral indignation but just as frequently for fear of legal reprisals. It was not, however, until many years after the trials that Douglas, by his own admission, burned some 150 letters, leaving only 33 known to exist. "Nothing," Douglas wrote in 1929, "could more serve to rehabilitate Wilde, from a moral point of view, than (if it were only possible) the publication of every single letter he ever wrote to me and every single letter that I ever wrote to him. As it is, just those few selected as damaging to us (first by my father and then by Robert Ross) have been produced. Those published would not amount to more than five per cent of the whole lot we wrote to each other."[1] Douglas's sporadic fits of moral indignation and self-righteousness in the last half of his life throw serious doubt on his claim that the destroyed letters would reveal an Oscar Wilde not already apparent in the 33 published letters. Certainly the extant letters, covering a five-year period, reflect an adherence to an epistolary technique very much in line with Wilde's aesthetics. Epistolary performance was the manner and the method by which his mood or passion could be given form that was at once aesthetically pleasing and emotionally cogent. Wilde's attitude toward Douglas underwent numerous changes, some more fleeting than others, but what seems like inconsistency of attitude or opinion in the letters is merely fidelity to mood, that ephemeral emotional state he praised so highly in his early dialogues. Throughout the letters Wilde's inconsistency is one of matter, his consistency one of manner.

With the exception of *De Profundis*, none of the letters to Douglas was written with noticeable deliberation. But the very lack of deliberation makes the letters all the more appealing because they reflect the genius Wilde claimed, in his famous remark reported by André Gide, that he had put in his life rather than his works.[2] Since the reputed brilliance of Wilde's conversations can only be reconstructed by memoirists and biographers, the letters, with their note of spontaneity and conversational tone, are the closest we can come to Wilde as the flesh-and-blood performer. And nowhere in his epistolary corpus is his performance more brilliant than in his letters to Douglas, for in these letters Wilde is not only interested in expressing his own realized personality but in recreating Douglas along aesthetically pleasing lines.

The most salient feature of Wilde's letters to Douglas is the "jeweled style" of the prose. Flashy and flamboyant, the letters, even when they are about such mundane subjects as money, rarely falter from the grandiloquence to which they aspire. Thus there is relentless, even egregious, use of alliteration and assonance, personification, metaphor and simile, all designed to glorify the recipient, even when Wilde is half-heartedly trying to reprimand the young Douglas for his incontinent behavior. More than once is Douglas addressed as the "gay, gilt and gracious lad."[3] Perhaps most noticeable is the personification of the letter writer's various emotional states, most often a reflection of his current attitude toward Douglas. In a note of reconciliation written in late 1893, apparently after a minor altercation, Wilde clothes his love for Douglas in regal apparel: "I am happy in the knowledge that we are friends again, and that our love has passed through the shadow and the night of estrangement and sorrow and come out rose-crowned as of old" (pp. 347–48). Appropriate enough for the Mauve Decade or the Yellow Nineties, Wilde rarely fails to provide his letters with a color motif, generally using purple prose for his own purple passions and bright gold for his "gilt lad." In his first surviving letter to Douglas, Wilde boldly suggests that the two of them go off somewhere "hot and coloured" ([? November 1892], p. 322). Those places to which Wilde would most like to accompany "the honey-haired boy" are painted with various auric hues, both to suggest the material opulence of "gold coins . . . dropping from heaven to gladden me" ([ca. 16 April 1894],

p. 3 54) and to brighten the golden halo over Douglas's head. The primary colors are commonly reserved for the baser elements of life. Significantly, Queensberry, Douglas's belligerent father and Wilde's nemesis, is the "Scarlet Marquis."

Befitting the letters' flowery language, Wilde's favorite metaphors are drawn from the floral world. Thus in one letter alone, written during the trials, Douglas is referred to as "my sweet rose, my delicate flower, my lily of lilies" ([20 May 1895], p. 397). In the same letter, Wilde expands his horticultural analogies and places his garden in the midst of his newly found desert:

> my life is a desert fanned by the delicious breeze of your breath, and whose cool springs are your eyes; the imprint of your little feet makes valleys of shade for me, the odour of your hair is like myrrh, and wherever you go you exhale the perfumes of the cassia tree (p. 398).

Whatever literary device Wilde uses, he intends his prose to well reflect the language of sensuality and seduction, as appropriate to the love letter as to the Elizabethan sonnet. Some will complain that the epistles are little more than love letters relying exclusively on the hyperbole of passion, but Wilde's hyperbole is quite conscious and lies at the heart of his aesthetic. What Wilde most favors in his letters and his works is an imaginative mendacity that at once exaggerates and selects: "Art itself," he says in "The Decay of Lying," is "really a form of exaggeration; and selection, which is the very spirit of art, is nothing more than an intensified mode of over-emphasis."[4] It is this overemphasis which is at the heart of the liar's temperament; it is the basis for an artful mendacity which at once obscures and reveals—obscures because it shuns the accuracy of facticity; reveals because it allows the participant to behold prismatic images imperceptible without the artist's vision, without the liar's exaggeration.

It is in his epistolary language Wilde wished to extol, if not reproduce, the beauty he peceived in Douglas, beauty which must be at once divine and visible. Wilde believed that in order for abstractions and ideas to be aesthetically apprehended they must be poetically and cogently expressed or, in the case of love, made incarnate. Persistently in his letters Wilde saw Douglas as the incarnation of that love which he as artist was able to experience, if not create. "You are," he writes to Douglas about August 1894, "the atmosphere of beauty through which I see life; you are the incarnation of all lovely things" (p. 363). And on 20 May 1895 he writes, "What wisdom is to the philosopher, what God is to the saint, you are to me" (p. 398). Wilde found that truth in art is rendered by Beauty made apparent by "the unity of a thing with itself: the outward rendered expressive of the inward: the soul made incarnate: the body instinct with spirit" (*De Profundis*, p. 473). He found, further, that his inwardly felt love for Douglas could be given expression, and Douglas himself—poeticized and recreated by the vision of the artist—became for Wilde the outward expression of that love. By projecting his own primal emotions, glossed in the letters with hyperbolic metaphor, onto the Hyacinthus of his dreams, Wilde imagined an artifact of flesh and dangerously played with that most unstable union of life and art.

If Wilde had titled the group of letters written to Douglas before *De Profundis,* he might well have called them "In Excelsis," so glorifying were they of Douglas and his influence on him. In light of what Wilde reveals in *De Profundis* about the storminess of their relationship before 1895, replete with ugly scenes of verbal vituperation and unbecoming excesses of all varieties, one is tempted to conclude that just as he had refuted Arnold's famed dictum with its reversal ("to see the object as in itself it really is not" [5]), so he wrote his letters with a mind to see the beloved as he really is not. Witness one of the two infamous letters read aloud during the trials and evidently written just after one of their more heated quarrels:

> Your letter was delightful, red and yellow wine to me; but I am sad and out of sorts. Bosie, you must not make scenes with me. They kill me, they wreck the loveliness of life. I cannot see you, so Greek and gracious, distorted with passion. I cannot listen to your curved lips saying hideous things to me. I would sooner be blackmailed by every renter [i.e., male homosexual] in London than have you bitter, unjust, hating. I must see you soon. You are the divine thing I want, the thing of grace and beauty ([March 1893], pp. 336–37).

The other letter read in court was defended by Wilde's solicitor, Sir Edward Clark, as a "prose sonnet." [6] Passionately and willfully, Wilde apotheosizes the all-too-human Douglas:

> My Own Boy, Your sonnet is quite lovely, and it is a marvel that those red rose-leaf lips of yours should have been made no less for music of song than for madness of kisses. Your slim gilt soul walks between passion and poetry. I know Hyacinthus, whom Apollo loved so madly, was you in Greek days ([? January 1893], p. 326).

At the trial, Wilde himself insisted the letter was a "prose poem." [7] Two years later, as he sat in Reading Prison composing the long letter which would be published posthumously as *De Profundis,* he continued to defend these early letters. In specific reference to the "prose poem," he makes vivid the living nightmare when artistic motive is sullied in the mire of social prejudices and devastating legalities:

You send me a very nice poem, of the undergraduate school of verse, for my approval: I reply by a letter of fantastic literary conceits: I compare you to Hylas, or Hyacinth, Jonquil or Narcisse, or someone whom the great god of Poetry favoured, and honoured with his love. The letter is like a passage from one of Shakespeare's sonnets, transposed to a minor key. It can only be understood by those who have read the *Symposium* of Plato, or caught the spirit of a certain grave mood made beautiful for us in Greek marbles. It was, let me say frankly, the sort of letter I would, in a happy if wilful moment, have written to any graceful young man of either University who had sent me a poem of his own making, certain that he would have sufficient wit or culture to interpret rightly its fantastic phrases. Look at the history of that letter! It passes from you into the hands of a loathsome companion: from him to a gang of blackmailers: copies of it are sent about London to my friends, and to the manager of the theatre where my work is being performed: every construction but the right one is put on it: Society is thrilled with the absurd rumours that I have had to pay a huge sum of money for having written an infamous letter to you: this forms the basis of your father's worst attack: I produce the original letter myself in Court to show what it really is: it is denounced by your father's Counsel as a revolting and insidious attempt to corrupt Innocence: ultimately it forms part of a criminal charge: the Crown takes it up: the Judge sums up on it with little learning and much morality: I go to prison for it at last. That is the result of writing you a charming letter (*De Profundis*, pp. 440–41).

Most of Wilde's early letters were, of course, neither stolen nor used for blackmail, but most of them were written with the intensity of a sonneteer. Even the letters that are chiefly news or gossip often contain a suggestive line or two. In a letter of about May 1893, really little more than a dinner invitation, Wilde first notes that he has spoken to Prince Pierre Troubetzkoy, a Russian-American portrait painter, and then insists, "You really must be painted, and also have an ivory statue executed" (p. 341). In early 1894 while Douglas was in Florence, Wilde made sure that his friend was informed of the "sonnet-like allusions" their mutual acquaintances were supposedly making to Douglas's "gilt silk hair" ([? 20 April 1894], p. 355). Two months later, Wilde was more explicit in his fondness for Douglas:

I want to see you. It is really absurd. *I can't live without you.* You are so dear, so wonderful. I think of you all day long, and miss your grace, your boyish beauty, the bright sword-play of your wit, the delicate fancy of your genius, so surprising always in its sudden swallow-flights towards north or south, towards sun or moon—and, above all, you yourself ([? July 1894], p. 358).

Ineluctably Douglas is the divine but pagan icon whom Wilde fashions and beholds. Love becomes the link between Life and Art because it partakes of that "dreadful universal thing called human nature"[8] and because it is stylized and given more appealing expression by the artificial.

Wilde was arrested on 5 April 1895, charged the following day, and imprisoned at Holloway Prison until his first trial began on 29 April 1895. There are three surviving letters written before his conviction[9] which together form an interesting prelude to the complex and paradoxical *De Profundis*, written almost two years later. Certainly the hallmark style is still apparent, but the dominant note, perhaps expectedly, is one of desperation. Indeed, after Wilde had lost his case against Queensberry and faced prosecution by the Crown, he was by no means as confident that the social prejudices against him, grotesquely manifested by the hounding Queensberry, would be redressed. It was more specifically the doubts of Wilde's lawyers that convinced Douglas to leave the country on the eve of the first trial. Certainly the three letters of this period do not evince the bitterness toward Douglas that is so prominent in *De Profundis*. Rather Wilde sees his love for Douglas as the one thing that will give him the stamina to endure the humiliation and pain of his predicament. In one letter he contemplates the possibility of abjuring their relationship, but he quickly foresees the unacceptable consequences:

> Now I see that that would have mutilated my life, ruined my art, broken the musical chords which make a perfect soul. Even covered with mud I shall praise you, from the deepest abysses I shall cry to you ([20 May 1895], p. 397).

Suffering, Wilde came to believe, imbued his love for Douglas with an almost religious purity, a purity that nonetheless still found the beloved, now with a "Christ-like heart," dwelling "on that high hill where beautiful things are transfigured" (p. 398). And while Wilde raised Douglas's mortal status, he began to reevaluate his own stature, intimating the tragic role he would later play in *De Profundis*:

> Every great love has its tragedy, and ours has too, but to have known and loved you with such profound devotion, to have had you for a part of my life, the only part I now consider beautiful, is enough for me. My passion is at a loss for words, but you can understand me, you alone. Our souls were made for one another, and by knowing yours through love, mine has transcended many evils, understood perfection, and entered into the divine essence of things ([May 1895], p. 397).

Wilde also entered Pentonville Prison shortly after his conviction on 25 May 1895, and his correspondence came to an abrupt stop. In fact, there are no surviving letters to anyone that were written during his stays at Pentonville and Wandsworth. Initially, he was allowed to write only one letter every three months. Hart-Davis stresses that the first ones "were certainly" to his wife Constance and her lawyers (p. 398). All the surviving twenty-four prison letters, including the four petitions to the Home Secretary, were written from Reading, where Wilde was transferred on 20 November 1895. Only one of these was written to Douglas, and there is no evidence that there may have been others written to him during the eighteen months Wilde was in Reading. The prison letters are interesting if only because they provide the only account of Wilde's emotional and intellectual state during this time. In *De Profundis* Wilde refers occasionally to his "development" in prison, yet the letters to his other friends, particularly Robert Ross, provide better evidence that the fidelity to moods, which he had praised so often before, was just as important in prison. Indeed, Wilde seems to have found that prison moods could be made even more intense and that the realization of such emotionally induced attitudes as despair could be perfected through the poetry of pain. All the while at Reading, Wilde fluctuated between hope and despair, and he was wont to tell Ross his latest mood as if it were the last. He emphasized the poeticized mood, the mood which was made more intense by its poetic expression.

De Profundis was written during the first three months of 1897, after Wilde had served three quarters of his two-year sentence. The circumstances of composition were anything but favorable. Each day Wilde was issued one folio sheet of four pages of blue ruled prison paper which was withdrawn each evening. Originally Wilde intended that the letter be sent to Robert Ross, who, after having a copy made, would send the original to Lord Alfred Douglas. Prison officials denied Wilde's request and agreed only to hand over the manuscript on the day of his release, which action initiated a series of events that gave the letter a very complex history.[10] In fact, a full and accurate version of the text was not published until Hart-Davis included it in his 1962 volume of Wilde's letters.

Numerous studies of the letter, in its various published forms, have been made in the last seventy-five years. Many of these studies have seen the letter as a formal piece of literature, a view to which Wilde would not have objected since he wrote it just as much for posterity as he did for Douglas. To Robert Ross he describes the letter as "the only document that really gives any explanation of my extraordinary behavior with regard to Queensberry and Alfred Douglas" (1 April 1897, p. 513). To More Adey he confides, "It is the most important letter of my life, as it will deal ultimately with my future mental attitude towards life, with the way in which I desire to meet the world again, with the development of my character, with what I have lost, what I have learned, and what I hope to arrive at" (18 February 1897, p. 419).

The marked difference in attitude toward Douglas is attributable to the simple fact that Wilde had reason to doubt the validity of Douglas's love, that "divine essence" which he had hoped would palliate his sufferings. He had been assured by Douglas and his family, desirous of ridding themselves of their unstable patriarch, that they would offer all the help and encouragement they could, including payment of all legal costs. Until the eve of Wilde's first trial, Douglas remained a loyal friend, paying daily visits to his unfortunate friend in Holloway. When, however, Douglas withdrew to France, Wilde's troubles went from bad to worse. His own sources of income all but ceased with the closing of the two plays which were then on the boards, *An Ideal Husband* and *The Importance of Being Earnest,* and the striking out of his books on publishers' lists. In addition, creditors had auctioned off the entire contents of his house at 16 Tite Street under what H. Montgomery Hyde describes as "scandalous conditions." [11] Neither Douglas nor his family at any time helped to defray Wilde's expenses, even after the first months of his prison term when he was brought before the Bankruptcy Court. But the most devastating blow to Wilde was that he did not once hear directly from Douglas during his entire sentence. It was this situation that made Wilde doubt Douglas's love, and he concluded that Douglas's hatred of his father far outweighed his love for Wilde (p. 445). That the great love of his life should so heartlessly abandon him made paramount a reassessment of his role in the romance he had written for his life.

A second circumstance that prompted Wilde's reassessment can be described most generally as his loss of position. Not only did he find himself in prison on moral charges, but his inevitable bankruptcy, a formal estrangement from his wife and two sons, and the loss of his literary rights in England spelled nothing but another form of ostracism on his release. To know that the position, both in literature and in society, for which he had always worked and to which he had grown accustomed, was forever lost, made his fall much harder than it otherwise might have been. The consequences of his loss of position Wilde summed up best not in *De Profundis,* but in a letter to Ross written after his release:

> I used to rely on my personality: now I know that my personality really rested on the fiction of *position.* Having lost position, I find my personality of no avail. . . . I feel very humble, besides feeling very indignant: the former being my intellectual realisation of my position, the latter an emotion that is a "survival" of old conditions ([29 March 1899], p. 791).

The rude and sudden awareness that his stature was irrevocably lost and that the love in which he had invested so much energy, both personally and artistically, was called into doubt made the Oscar Wilde of *De Profundis* interested in recreating a personality suitable to his new conditions and appropriate to his artistic temperament. So he set about not to excuse his past behavior but to explain his new role. The personality that emerges from *De Profundis* is not so very different from his former personality, dressed though it is in different trappings and subjected to different circumstances. He continued to believe that Art was "the great primal note by which I had revealed, first myself to myself, and then myself to the world" (p. 447). He believed, as before, that Art was "the supreme reality, and life . . . a mere mode of fiction" (p. 466). Treated as a mode of fiction, life could offer a deper intensification of experience. For Wilde the goal of existence was never in doubt:

> Nothing seems to me of the smallest value except what one gets out of oneself. My nature is seeking a fresh mode of self-realisation. That is all I am concerned with (p. 467).

Throughout the letter Wilde reminds Douglas of the worst vice and the best virtue: "The supreme vice is shallowness. Everything that is realised is right" (p. 425). Only by intensifying experience and by intensifying personality can one realize one's potential. Wilde complains, with characteristic exaggeration, that his habit of catering to Douglas's whims and tantrums had thwarted his growth as a realized individual: "it had stereotyped my temperament to one permanent and fatal mood" (p. 430). Further, he believed that the subjugation of his own will power to the unintellectual appetites of Douglas had arrested a development, which in prison he had begun to realize. In prison he had arrived at an "intensity of individualism" which set him apart from the common banality of the populace: "Most people are other people. Their thoughts are someone else's opinions, their life a mimicry, their passions a quotation" (p. 479).

Wilde also developed the theme of suffering he had raised in the Holloway letters:

> Suffering—curious as it may sound to you—is the means by which we exist, because it is the only means by which we become conscious of existing; and the remembrance of suffering in the past is necessary to us as the warrant, the evidence, of our continued identity (p. 435).

It was his own crucifixion by the very society which had deified him that turned Wilde's thoughts to Christ as the "supreme Individualist" (p. 479). The value of Christ for Wilde rested on two cardinal points. First, just as an artist conceives life as expression, Christ "took the entire world of the inarticulate, the voiceless world of pain, as his kingdom, and made of himself its eternal mouthpiece" (p. 481). Second, Christ himself was an expression of sorrow made beautiful. It was, for the incarcerated Wilde, sorrow which gave one identity, and when that sorrow was given poetic form, as Christ had given it, it became even more revealing:

> I now see that sorrow, being the supreme emotion of which man is capable, is at once the type and test of all great Art. What the artist is always looking for is that mode of existence in which soul and body are one and indivisible: in which the outward is expressive of the inward: in which Form reveals (p. 473).

Wilde could "realize" sorrow because he could understand it—not, that is, merely rail against social injustice or Douglas' betrayal—and because he could express it, give it form, and set it next to Beauty. Sorrow became for Wilde a truth colored by passion, that indisputable criterion for any truth. His mask of Sorrow, worn at all times in the writing of De Profundis, was cast by the most intensified and longest lasting mood of his life. He made noble his sorrow by imbuing it with Christian metaphor.

Wilde hoped that his long letter would clear up some of the mystery surrounding his relationship with Douglas. Certainly the letter has biographical interest in its detailing of the many turbulences in their life together before 1895, but it does not deal with Douglas much differently than his early epistles. However filled with scorn and vituperation, the letter rests on two pivotal concerns: Wilde's reassessment of his own role as artist-lover, and his abiding infatuation with Douglas. Absence having made the heart grow skeptical, Wilde wrote with a view to expunge his doubts and his bitterness. The "golden" days long gone, Wilde could no longer perceive his beloved through the same veil of art. Eighteen months of silence had convinced him that the innocent Hyacinthus had been ruthless and pitiless in his betrayal. But discovery of Douglas's weaknesses by no means prompted Wilde to forgo their relationship, In fact, at the beginning of De Profundis Wilde emphatically, and at length, insists that Douglas read his epistola for its cathartic value:

> I have no doubt that in this letter in which I have to write of your life and of mine, of the past and of the future, of sweet things changed to bitterness and of bitter things that may be turned into joy, there will be much that will wound your vanity to the quick. If it prove so, read the letter over and over again till it kills your vanity. If you find in it something of which you feel that you are unjustly accused, remember that one should be thankful that there is any fault of which one can be unjustly accused. If there be in it one single passage that brings tears to your eyes, weep as we weep in prison where the day no less than the night is set apart for tears. It is the only thing that can save you (pp. 424–25).

Wilde's clear intention was to refashion his relationship with Douglas, not to abort it. By the end of the fifty-thousand-word letter he suggests that they see each other again one month after his release. But he clearly wants to see a different Douglas, one remolded along the moral caveats of his missive. Insisting on the value of suffering and always remembering the purity of Christ, he wishes to draw Douglas away from mere appetites and inculcate in him a sense of intellectual motive. The "gilt lad" of those days of pleasure must become the refined companion in the years of pain.

It might thus be expected in the post-prison letters that a new figure would emerge. But when Wilde was released from prison in May 1897, he quickly supplanted sorrow with hope, and the intentions of De Profundis were all but forgotten. As for Douglas, he dubiously claimed never to have received the letter and never to have discussed it with Wilde.[12] At any rate, it seems clear that the letter had no discernible effect on their relationship, epistolary or personal, during the three remaining years of Wilde's life.

The ten surviving letters written after Wilde's release are all dated in the summer of 1897, while he was living in Berneval-sur-Mer. Eight of the ten letters were written in June, and internal references suggest that the two were in almost daily communication. Initially, it is clear that Wilde thought their lives must remain "irreparably severed, as far as meeting goes" (4 June, p. 595); but by the middle of the month plans had been made for Douglas to visit Wilde at Berneval. Days later, however, Wilde insisted that the plans be abandoned because he feared the interference of Queensberry. The language of the June letters echoes that of the early letters. Douglas is once again the "honey-sweet boy," and Wilde's suggestion for his assumed identity is "Jonquil du Vallon." He insists that theirs must be an epistolary affair:

> So simply we must write to each other: about the things we love, about poetry and the coloured arts of our age, and that passage of ideas into images that is the intellectual history of art. I think of you always, and love you always, but chasms of moonless night divide us. We cannot cross it without hideous and nameless peril (17 June, p. 613).

Late in the summer Wilde made the decision to risk the "nameless peril." His last surviving letter to Douglas well epitomizes Douglas's influence on his aesthetic sensibilities, or at least the influence Wilde was wont to herald. It is both a plea for artistic rejuvenation and a reaffirmation of the power of that fleshly beauty he had poetically enhanced in his letters:

> I feel that my only hope of again doing beautiful work in art is being with you. . . . you can really recreate in me that energy and sense of joyous power on which art depends. . . . Do remake my ruined life for me, and then our friendship and love will have a different meaning to the world ([? 31 August 1897], p. 637).

Thus it was with the intensity of the lover and the artifice of the aesthete that Wilde was reunited with Douglas. In September 1897 the two moved into the Villa Giudice at Posilippo, just outside Naples. The action immediately brought protest from virtually all his friends, but Wilde persisted in his belief, writing to Ross that his return to Douglas was "psychologically inevitable. . . . I cannot live without the atmosphere of Love. . . . I must love and be loved, whatever price I pay for it" (21 September 1897, p. 644). That he found with Douglas a means to recreate his life there can be little doubt. Certainly the only piece of literature he wrote after his release—"The Ballad of Reading Gaol"—was composed at Posilippo with Douglas at his side. Quite consciously Wilde was trying to reorder his "maimed and mutilated" life. Had he been allowed to stay indefinitely with Douglas, he might well have remade his life on his own terms and kept alive the artistic temperament which demanded an atmosphere of love and beauty. But financial circumstances forced Wilde and Douglas to forego their idyllic life together at Posilippo. In early 1898 Wilde returned to Paris a defeated man and a broken artist. In a letter postmarked 9 March 1898 to Carlos Blacker, he confides, "I don't think I shall ever write again: *la joie de vivre* is gone, and that, with will-power, is the basis of art" (p. 715).

After his return to Paris, Wilde made no serious or sustained effort to revitalize his life or personality. Deprived of Douglas's love, he sought pleasure from a host of boulevard boys and in a letter to Ross in May 1898, likened his life to a "'Circle of the Boulevard', one of the worst in the Inferno" (p. 737). His friends' generosity he repaid with profligacy, drinking absinthe, and smoking Turkish cigarettes. His health deteriorated as quickly as his resolves. He complains to Ross 16 April 1900 that he is overcome by a "mode of paralysis—a *cacoethes tacendi*," a craving for silence which seven months later was satisfied when he died in the Hotel d'Alsace, on 30 November 1900.

In many of his letters, and especially in the letters to Douglas, Wilde wished to poeticize the human experience. All art, including the art of the personal letter, was for Wilde "a mode of acting, an attempt to realize one's own personality on some imaginative plane out of reach of the trammelling accidents and limitations of real life."[13] In his epistolary relationship with the young and handsome Douglas, "real life" played a small part indeed. Even the menacing threats of Queensberry did not long keep Wilde from lifting his eyes toward Parnassus. Though given more to excess than excellence, he never lost sight of what he hoped to realize in his letters. The letters were written at times *de amicitia,* at times *de profundis,* at times *in excelsis,* but they were always written in a homage to Art that bespeaks a curious combination of discipline and license.

8

Oscar Wilde's *Salome*, the Salome Theme in Late European Art, and a Problem of Method in Cultural History

Robert C. Schweik

O ne problem which the emergence of modernist art poses for cultural historians has been vividly described by Carl Schorske, who notes that at the end of the nineteenth century

> European high culture entered a whirl of infinite innovation, with each field proclaiming independence of the whole, each part in turn falling into parts. Into the ruthless centrifuge of change were drawn the very concepts by which cultural phenomena might be fixed in thought. Not only the producers of culture, but also its analysts and critics fell victim to the fragmentation. The many categories devised to define or govern any one of the trends of post-Nietzchean culture—irrationalism, subjectivism, abstractionism, anxiety, technologism—neither possessed the surface virtue of lending themselves to generalization nor allowed any convincing dialectical integration into the historical process as previously understood. Every search for a plausible equivalent for the twentieth century to such sweeping but heuristically indispensable categories as "the Enlightenment" seemed doomed to founder on the heterogeneity of the cultural substance it was supposed to cover.[1]

"What," Schorske asked, "was the historian to do in the face of this confusion?" His own response was that brilliant series of studies which went to make up his *Fin-de-siècle Vienna: Politics and Culture,* where he adopted the strategy of doing a series of synchronic studies in depth, within the specific context of Viennese social and political life, which enabled him to point out some cultural forces that powerfully influenced Freud's thought, Klimt's art, and Schoenberg's music. Such a methodology of course avoids the problem Schorske so aptly described, but it is not a strategy for dealing directly with it. My own concern here is to explore the possibility of using the very multiplicity of analytic categories available to the historian to characterize more precisely the cultural "place" of complex works of art; in effect, I wish to suggest an appropriate strategy for historians undertaking diachronic studies of late nineteenth- and early twentieth-century European culture. Specific consideration of Wilde's *Salome* and its relationship to certain other treatments of the Salome theme in European art from 1840 to 1940 will be followed by generalizations upon the methodology implicit in the adopted procedure.

In creating his play *Salome,* Oscar Wilde linked himself with a wide array of nineteenth- and twentieth-century artists ranging from Heinrich Heine to Evan John, from Henri Regnault to Pablo Picasso, and from Jules Massenet to Paul Hindemith, all of whom produced some work of art based at least in part on the Salome-Herodias legend. The treatments of that legend are as diverse as the artists are many, and the complex history of the Salome theme in art has been the specific subject of at least four separate studies and the partial subject of many others.[2] I have no intention of ignoring that rich artistic context of Wilde's play—I intend to consider it explicitly later—but I wish first to examine Wilde's *Salome* in connection with a very limited number of works of art which are all related as either possible influences on or as derivatives of Wilde's play and which, on further examination, appear to have an enigmatic irrationality notably absent from many other treatments of the Salome theme in art both before and after Wilde's work. The following works will be central to the study: Stéphane Mallarmé's "Hérodiade" (specifically the part titled "Scène" first published in 1869 in *Le Parnasse Contemporain*); Gustave Moreau's oil painting, *Salome Dancing Before Herod* (1876); Oscar Wilde's *Salome* (French, 1893; English, 1894); Aubrey Beardsley's drawings for the English version of Wilde's play (1894); Richard Strauss's opera *Salome* (1905); and Gustav Klimt's *Judith II,* commonly called "Salome" (1909).

The purpose of segregating such a limited set of works which, despite their common subject, differ so in medium, technique, and effect, is to enable me to concentrate primarily on pointing out one common analytic category into which they fall and one line of development they appear to share. Doing so should demonstrate that Wilde's play is one of a group of works which incorporates in its treatment of the Salome theme a distinctive irrational element[3] which links it to that "irrationalism" which Schorske described as one of the "categories devised to define . . . the trends of post-Nietzschean culture"; that the works comprising this group differ radically from another set of treatments of the Salome-Herodias theme created over the same range of time and including works by artists so diverse as Arthur O'Shaughnessy, Jules Massenet, and Pablo Picasso; and that from a consideration of the peculiarly independent relationships which the similarities and differences of these groups have to one another, and of similarly independent relationships which appear when Wilde's play is considered in terms of other analytical categories applicable to it, some suggestions can be made about a method which cultural historians might employ to use multiple analytic categories as a means of characterizing more precisely the complex relationships among the bewilderingly varied works of high art that began to emerge so prominently in fin-de-siècle Europe.

Mallarmé and Moreau

Let me begin, then, by first considering Mallarmé's "Hérodiade" and Moreau's *Salome Dancing Before Herod*. When Mallarmé published "Scène" in 1869, he had already gone far to shake off the Baudelarian influences that appear in his earlier work and had begun his long search for a more "pure" mode of communication—and it is a truism that the result was a poetic style characterized by a remarkable discontinuousness, so that individual words and images resonate against others in ways that leave the reader confronted with abrupt and confusing shifts of sense. I do not wish to seem to dismiss Mallarmé's style as simply idiosyncratic—it is one manifestation of a development in modernist art which later shows up in such diverse writers as the Russian Futurist poet Kruchenykh, and the self-proclaimed "cubist" poet, Gertrude Stein—but I am more concerned here with Mallarmé's treatment of the drama of "Scène" in which he creates a sharp disconnectedness between Hérodiade's actions and motives, between the intensity of her responses and the acts she responds to, and between various elements of her character, some of which have marked parallels in Wilde's play. The nurse's three efforts to minister to Hérodiade, for example, are repulsed with such extreme emotion in language so violently strong that it is scarcely related to the nurse's intended acts. Thus, when the nurse attempts to adjust her hair, Hérodiade responds:

Stop in thy crime
Which chills my blood to its source, and repress
That gesture, famous impiety: ah! tell me
What sure demon throws on thee this sinister emotion. . . .

Yet, later in the poem, Hérodiade speaks as if, having been unharmed in the lion's den, she fears no touch:

But who will touch me, by lions respected?[4]

It is this well known feature of "Scène" I wish to recall here, for throughout the poem Mallarmé presents Hérodiade in precisely such contradictory extremes—vulnerability and invulnerability, passion and virginity, fire and ice. Of course readers sometimes attempt to resolve this incoherence by interpreting the action as psychologically symbolic, with the nurse as a representative of the adult sexual world which Hérodiade is alternately frightened of and defensively hostile toward; but such resolutions are contrived from elements which themselves retain a kind of defiantly inconsistent irrationality.

To turn from the poetry of Mallarmé to the painting of Moreau is to shift not only from one medium to another but to a kind of art which in many respects is far more conservative. Yet, although Moreau's style has much in it that testifies to his eclectic conservatism—to the influence of such diverse artists as Michelangelo and Carpaccio; Poussin, Ingres and David; Delacroix and Chasseriau—his Salome pictures and other works both before and after those reveal a willingness to introduce into his painting enigmatically conflicting elements very much as Mallarmé did in his "Hérodiade." This willingness is certainly in part the result of Moreau's commitment to include in his paintings a mysterious "beauty of inertia" and, in addition, a "necessary richness"; both are notable in *Salome Dancing Before Herod,* and the complex symbolism which resulted from this combination of principles[5] carries such radically disjointed implications that its contradictory elements seem to stand in a state of unresolved suspension. On the one hand, Moreau included a host of details intended—as his notebook entry makes clear—to suggest the powerful sexual force of the eternal feminine, destructive to men in her search for a vague sensual idea: Salome's waist is girdled with the trophy-like heads of men; she carries a lotus flower, the Indian symbol of female sensuality; before her crouches a panther, which, in legend, lures men to destruction with its sweet breath; and in the background, above and around Herod's throne, there are innumerable sphynx figures as well as fertility symbols in the form of statues of Diana of Ephesus and of Mithras.[6]

But we know that Moreau also intended to present Salome as a very different kind of religious object—as a sibyl whose costume contains her divinity like a reliquary[7]—and this kind of counter-symbolism is particularly notable in his curiously inert disposition of the human figures in the painting. Salome herself is rendered in a pose that is rigidly static and far from evoking any sense of powerful sensuality; rather, she is made almost ethereal: anatomical detail is largely suppressed by the *richesse* of her costume, and she is poised in a highly unnatural stance, on the very points of her toes, so that she almost floats, as a portion of her robe does mysteriously float behind her. Just how ambiguous and enigmatic Salome's stance is, is made clearer, I think, by the fact that in his related watercolor titled *The Apparition,* Moreau presents Salome in very nearly the same posture, though in this picture she presumably stands in horrified terror as the head of John the Baptist rises in the air before her. In short, in exploiting a conflicting symbolism and a static "mysteriousness" in his Salome painting, Moreau sought to incorporate in it what Julius Kaplan has called a distinctive "irrational" element[8]—comparable to what Mallarmé did in his "Hérodiade."

Wilde's Salome

It is possible that Wilde knew Mallarmé's "Scène" and Moreau's Salome pictures directly; it is certain he knew them through the distorting lens of Huysmans's *A Rebours.*[9] But whether or not these may have influenced Wilde, his *Salome* is also notable for a similar vein of irrationality. This appears most strikingly in what Alan Bird has called Salome's "paradoxical lust for Iokanaan, whose body is as virginal as her own" and which simultaneously repels and attracts her.[10] But it is more than a matter of paradox: Wilde dramatizes Salome's reactions to Iokanaan in a way which powerfully emphasizes the wholly arbitrary and irrational character of her acts. In having his Salome love the Baptist, Wilde may have been influenced by the precedent of Massenet's *Hérodiade* (the libretto, of course, was by Paul Millet, but was approved by Massenet). Salome, abandoned as a child, has been helped and kindly treated by John; she plausibly falls in love with him and remains so while being gently urged by John to love him only in a spiritual way. By contrast, in Wilde's play, Salome, a princess who is virginal and withdrawn, suddenly is totally consumed with lust for Iokanaan, and their dialogue abruptly takes the following (greatly abridged) form:

Salome: I am amorous of thy body, Iokanaan! Thy body is white, like the lilies of a field that the mower hath never mowed. . . . There is nothing in the world so white as thy body. Suffer me to touch thy body.

Iokanaan: Back! daughter of Babylon! By woman came evil into the world. Speak not to me.

Salome: Thy body is hideous. It is like the body of a leper. It is like a plastered wall, where vipers have crawled; like a plastered wall where the scorpions have made their nest. . . . It is of thy hair that I am enamoured, Iokanaan. Thy hair is like clusters of grapes, like clusters of black grapes. . . . Suffer me to touch thy hair.

Iokanaan: Back, daughter of Sodom. Touch me not. Profane not the temple of the Lord God.

Salome: Thy hair is horrible. It is covered with mire and dust. It is like a crown of thorns placed on thy head. . . . It is thy mouth that I desire, Iokanaan. Thy mouth is like a band of scarlet on a tower of ivory. It is like a pomegranate. . . .[11]

Even granting Wilde the convention of sudden lust, this kind of arbitrary and erratic behavior is so bizarre that it goes well beyond any recognizable dramatic convention and constitutes, rather, an extreme instance of enigmatic, motiveless irrationality.

Wilde's willingness to introduce into his play such irrational elements is notable, too, in the peculiar meaninglessness of what might be supposed to be the most explicit symbolism of the play. The moon, for example, is made the subject of a series of parallel speeches which seem to be leading to some significant point: the page sees it as a dead woman, the Syrian as a dancing princess, Salome as a virgin, Herod as a naked drunken woman, and the skeptical Herodias sees it simply as the moon. These recurring moon references culminate in Iokanaan's prophecy:

In that day the sun shall become black like sackcloth of hair, and the moon shall become like blood, and the stars of the heaven shall fall upon the earth like unripe figs that fall from the fig-tree, and the kings of the earth shall be afraid (p. 155).

What, one wonders, is the relationship of this prophetic assertion to the elaborately developed set of references to the moon made earlier? Possibly, for example, those might have been developed so as to establish the prophet's vision as the true or proper one—but no: when Herod notes that the moon has become red and Iokanaan's prophecy has come true, the cynical Herodias undercuts the point with a prompt rejoinder in which she notes that Iokanaan's prophecy has not come true and that Herod is simply frightened and foolish:

Oh, yes, I see it well, and the stars are falling like unripe figs, are they not? And the sun is becoming black like sackcloth of hair, and the kings of the earth are afraid. That at least one can see. The prophet is justified of his words in that at least, for truly the kings of the earth are afraid. . . . Let us go within. You are sick. They will say at Rome that you are mad (p. 166).

But even a character like Herodias, who is so often given the role of a pragmatic cynic, can be involved in dialogues which have that crazy kind of inconsequence so characteristic of Wilde's later comedies. Consider, for example, the following, in which Herodias acts out a role which brings to mind Lady Bracknell. The Jews are talking about rumors that the Messiah has come:

> First Nazarene: He hath come, and everywhere He worketh miracles!
> Herodias: Ho! ho! miracles! I do not believe in miracles. I have seen too many. [*To the Page.*] My fan.
> First Nazarene: This Man worketh true miracles. . . . He healed two lepers that were seated before the Gate of Capernaum simply by touching them.
> Second Nazarene: Nay; it was two blind men that He healed at Capernaum.
> First Nazarene: Nay; they were lepers. But He hath healed blind people also, and He was seen on a mountain talking with angels.
> A Sadducee: Angels do not exist.
> A Pharisee: Angels exist, but I do not believe that this Man has talked with them.
> First Nazarene: He was seen by a great multitude of people talking with angels.
> Herodias: How these men weary me! They are ridiculous! They are altogether ridiculous! [*To the Page.*] Well! My fan? [*The Page gives her the fan.*] You have a dreamer's look. You must not dream. It is only sick people who dream. [*She strikes the Page with her fan.*]

In short, although Keven Sullivan's comment that Wilde's *Salome* is "an all but flawless piece of nonsense" [12] is wide of the mark for the play as a whole, it is certainly true for some of its most prominent elements.

Beardsley's Drawings

I wish to focus here on only one limited aspect of Beardsley's very complex art—specifically, those elements in Beardsley's *Salome* drawings which have that peculiarly defiant irrationality about them that I have been tracing in the other works I have considered so far. These are not difficult to identify. First of all, there is the way so many of Beardsley's illustrations are either singularly irrelevant to or even at odds with the spirit of Wilde's play. Such, for example, is that array of bizarre figures which stand out prominently in Beardsley's illustrations but not at all in Wilde's work.

What is one to make of that grumpy-looking, aged fetus who holds Herodias's cloak in "Enter Herodias" and reappears, inexplicably, as a figurine in one suppressed version of "The Toilette of Salome"?[13] Or of the bald and masked Pierrot-like figure who attends to Salome's toilette and later reappears, supplied with a frizzy ring of hair, to assist a bearded satyr prepare to lower the naked body of the dead Salome into a gigantic powder-puff box in the drawing which served as the end-piece to the series? Of course nothing like these appear in Wilde's play at all.

And then, too, there are the queer and pointless shifts in appearance and costume the characters undergo. Salome's hair, for example, changes inexplicably from drawing to drawing, as does her dress: in one illustration she is in a sweeping Whistlerian "Peacock Skirt" while in another she appears in no more than a simple loose draped gown which bares one of her breasts; in yet another, titled "The Black Cape," she is pictured in a modish end-of-the-century cape-coat, with narrow waist and sweeping skirt. This last, of course, is only one of Beardsley's many outrageous anachronisms: his "The Toilette of Salome," for example, is set in a room equipped with venetian blinds and modern dressing table stocked with copies of *Manon Lescaut* and works by de Sade and Zola! Or, again, there are the gratuitously malicious allusions to Wilde, Whistler, and others which appear unmistakably in many of the illustrations. Small wonder, then, that one reviewer described Beardsley's *Salome* drawings as a vast prank and exclaimed, "But what a fantastic way of illustrating a Biblical tragedy!"[14] Of course Beardsley's *Salome* illustrations are very much more than a prank; yet, unquestionably, they include elements of the fantastic and irrational even more extreme than those of the play they illustrate.

Strauss and Klimt

The complex relationship which exists between Wilde's *Salome* and Strauss's operatic version of it has been extensively analyzed elsewhere;[15] my concern here is limited to a brief consideration of how Strauss is known to have captured the "irrational" elements I have pointed to in Wilde's play and the way that his opera is a link between Wilde and Klimt. The libretto Lachmann provided for Strauss retained, of course, many of those elements, but omitted some features of Wilde's play which, if not compensated for by Strauss's music, would have greatly altered the impact of the work. Lachmann, for example, deleted much of the repetitiousness of Wilde's script—perhaps as much as forty percent—and the resulting text no longer has so much of that repetitive dialogue and Maeterlincklike inertia that play such an important part in the effect Wilde sought for his drama. But what Hedwig Lachmann deleted Strauss restored musically—and in doing so, often reinforced the sense of motiveless irrationality which Wilde had originally created by repetitions. Strauss himself called his opera a scherzo with a fatal conclusion, but it is a scherzo whose music is so nervous and perverse that when, shortly before his father's death, Strauss played a portion of his *Salome* for him, the old man exclaimed: "Oh God, what nervous music. It is exactly as if one had one's trousers full of maybugs!"[16] The technical means Strauss employed to achieve this musical equivalent of the perverse and irrational malaise in Wilde's *Salome* have been brilliantly discussed by Gary Schmidgall in his *Literature as Opera;* I need only point here, then, to one major conclusion which Schmidgall reached:

> Salome is a score of loose ends, or more specifically, exposed nerve-ends. Its orchestral underworld is thus like the mental underworld—full of false starts, shards of malicious desire, an ill-fitting mosaic of psychic bits whose conscious (i.e. audible) life represents but a brief foray out of the oblivion of the subconscious. This sense of shattered and truncated musical development is probably what led Bellaigue to the perceptive though ill-meant observation that *Salome* is "composed of nothings, nothings in the plural, innumerable nothings, but nothings nevertheless."[17]

It is in this operatic form, then, that Wilde's play had whatever impact it did on Gustav Klimt's *Judith II* ("Salome").

The extraordinary range of cultural influences which went to shape Klimt's very complex art have been traced elsewhere;[18] here I will be concerned largely with pointing to the irrational elements in Klimt's treatments of those paintings of his which have come to be associated with the Salome theme. Of course, irrational elements were notably present in Klimt's earlier work—in his University Hall paintings, for example, which aroused complaints so strong and so persistent that in the end Klimt was prompted to buy his pictures back. It is not surprising, then, that Klimt's "Salome" paintings should involve irrational elements as well; but it is worth noting the extremes to which Klimt carried them.

His first "Salome" painting is usually called *Judith I;* it was completed in 1901 and now hangs in the Österreichische Galerie in Vienna. What is striking about *Judith I* is that Klimt presented the dutiful Jewish heroine as a barebreasted Gibson girl whose half-closed eyes and parted lips create the impression that she is at the moment of orgasm while holding the decapitated head of Holofernes. The clash between the title of the work and its manifest content is so obvious that, although Klimt painted the title *Judith and Holofernes* on the canvas itself, it was sometimes listed in catalogues and other descriptions with the title "Salome,"[19] and at its earliest showings, in Allesandra Comini's words, it "stunned and enthralled Viennese critics with its blatant decadence and terrifying invocation of the irrational."[20]

Klimt did not return to the subject which would again become known as "Salome" until after Strauss's controversial opera had had its Vienna premiere in 1907. Of course he had a number of reasons to take a special interest in that premiere: earlier there had been a sharp conflict between his friend Gustav Mahler and the Viennese censor who had refused Mahler permission to stage the world premiere in Vienna, and the set for the Vienna production was designed by another of Klimt's close friends, Alfred Roller. But, above all, it is likely that Klimt was impressed by Fanchette Verhunk's performance in the role of Salome, for her face bears a considerable resemblance to the face of the woman Klimt portrayed in the second Judith picture he completed in 1909.[21] But whether or not Klimt's *Judith II* was influenced by Fanchette Verhunk's performance, it is clear that he intended to go far beyond his earlier work in creating an effect of extreme self-contradictory irrationality. Of course by the time Klimt painted *Judith II* he had already fully developed that strange symbolic-ornamental style which characterizes those oils and mixed-media works—for example, *Fulfillment*—which he created between 1905 and 1909. Hence, predictably, the spaces in *Judith II* are filled with Klimt's swirls, curlicues, and other ornamental designs which constituted his private symbolism. But it is in his treatment of the subject itself that Klimt most startlingly exploited the engimatic and irrational. Again there is a picture of a woman holding the severed head, and the title Klimt gave his work, *Judith II*, identifies it as a second version of the story of Judith and Holofernes he had first portrayed in 1901. But now what a Judith! In place of the Gibson girl beauty of *Judith I*, the viewer is confronted by a woman with a hard and pitiless face and with skin of such deathly gray that it nearly matches that of the head she carries. Her cheeks and lips are rouged, her nose thin and aquiline, and she leans forward with a menacing expression and with claw-like hands. The effect of this figure is thoroughly sinister and repulsive. Not surprisingly, Klimt's *Judith II* often appears in modern catalogues of his work with the designation "Salome" in parentheses after the title Klimt assigned to it.[22] That modern scholars would be driven to this odd double-titling itself conveys precisely the point I wish to emphasize. The opposition between what the picture is stated by its title to represent—the beautiful widow, Judith, who with pious courage saved her people in obedience to God's will—and the death-like hideousness and wickedly cruel pitilessness which in fact it does portray—amount to a nearly irreconcilable contradiction. Unlike some of his contemporaries, Klimt is not usually called a pre-Dadaist, but in *Judith II* he approached the kind of extreme Dadaist contradictory irrationality epitomized in Man Ray's flatiron with tacks welded to its soleplate.

Conclusion

I have reached a point, now, when I can consider Wilde's *Salome,* and the special element of irrationality it shares with the other works I have discussed, in the larger context of the history of late nineteenth- and early twentieth-century art. First of all, what is clear about Wilde's play and the other treatments of the Salome-Herodias legend I have analyzed is that, with respect to the element of distinct irrationality they share, they constitute a special subset of a much larger body of art based on the Salome-Herodias story. Consider, for example, two such works: Heine's *Atta Troll* (German, 1841; French, 1847) and Flaubert's "Hérodias" from his *Trois Contes* (1877); both have been cited as possible influences on Wilde's *Salome,* [23] but, with respect to the irrational element I have been considering, they are sharply different. Heine's work, like those I have already discussed, contains, in its treatment of Herodias, a distinctly irrational quality. In *Atta Troll* Heine transforms the folk tradition of the "condemned hunt" into a delightful romp in which Herodias (whose motive for demanding the head of the Baptist was, Heine says, unrequited love for him) lovingly kisses his severed head and laughingly throws it in the air like a ball—all of which prompts the narrator to confess he has fallen inexplicably in love with her!

> Yes, I love you! I can tell it
> By the trembling of my soul.
> Love me, and be my beloved,
> Beautiful woman, Herodias!   ·
>
> Love me, and be my beloved!
> Throw away that bloody dumbhead
> Together with the charger, and enjoy
> The taste of a better dish.
> I'm exactly the knight
>
> You need—it makes little difference to me
> That you are dead and wholly damned—
> I'm not prejudiced— [24]

By contrast, Flaubert's story, "Hérodias," is wholly devoid of such perverse irrationality and depends, rather, upon the carefully researched and minutely realistic social detail that is one of Flaubert's characteristic achievements in fiction. And, indeed, many works of art share the

Salome-Herodias theme, both before and after Wilde's play, which similarly lack that distinctly irrational element: these include works so diverse in time, style, and medium as J. C. Heywood's *Herodias* and *Salome* (dramatic poems, 1862 and 1887 respectively); Henri Regnault's *Salomé* (oil on canvas, 1869); Theodore de Banville's "Hérodiade" (poem, 1870); Arthur O'Shaughnessy's "The Daughter of Herodias" and "Salome" (poems, 1870); Henri-Léopold Lévy's *Hérodias* (oil on canvas, 1872); Jules Massenet's *Hérodiade* (opera, 1881); Jean Lorrain's "Hérodiade" (poem, 1883); Pablo Picasso's *Salome* (drypoint, 1905); Henry Matisse's *Hérodiade* (line drawing, 1932); and Paul Hindemith's *Hérodiade* (tone poem, 1944).

Many of the works cited so far also constitute a subset of a still larger category of works of art embodying some aspect of the "fatal woman" theme and the "dancer" motif which attracted so many artists in the nineteenth and early twentieth centuries,[25] and Wilde's *Salome* is among those. Thus, in its embodiment of the "fatal woman" theme, Wilde's *Salome* is linked to works so diverse as Ivan Gilkin's "Amour d'Hôpital" and Richard Le Gallienne's "Beauty Accursed," while its irrational elements connect it to that widespread tendency toward an increasing preoccupation with enigmatic and motiveless irrationality which culminated in twentieth-century art movements like Dadaism, Surrealism, and Theatre of the Absurd. What I particularly wish to emphasize here is that Wilde's *Salome,* and, in fact, any other similarly complex work of nineteenth- and twentieth-century high art which is related to other works by virtue of falling into some common category with them, may be related only in that special way, while having many other distinctive features which it shares with entirely different sets of works comprising altogether different lines of development in the history of art.

Apart from that element of the enigmatic and irrational which links it with the other works already discussed, are a number of distinctive features of Wilde's *Salome* which might have been singled out instead. First, in its repetitiveness, Wilde's play has no special connection with any of the other treatments of the Salome theme cited—but this repetitiveness in Wilde's play links it to another development in the arts—to one which involves predecessors such as Maeterlinck's *La Princesse Maleine* and subsequent works of artists like Beckett and Warhol. Second, in its relatively more explicit depiction of Salome's aberrant sexuality, Wilde's play is related to a long succession of works of nineteenth- and twentieth-century artists who attempted to explore with increasing explicitness the varieties of human sexual experience—a succession which extends from Manet, Baudelaire, and Swinburne through Hardy, Klinger, Lawrence, and others. And, finally, there is the conclusion of Wilde's drama which provides a crude but conventional kind of poetic justice that links it to one predominant convention for closure in nineteenth century literature and art but *not* to a notable tendency in some late nineteenth- and twentieth-century art toward endings which provide a less well-defined sense of resolution—endings such as those in Hardy's *Jude the Obscure,* Forster's *A Passage to India,* and Shaw's *Heartbreak House*—or, to again take examples from a different art form, the conclusion of Stravinsky's first version of *Petrushka* and, as an extreme instance, the circular, unended form of Karlheinz Stockhausen's *Zyklus.*

These different features of Wilde's *Salome* are relatively independent of one another in the sense that they are associated with distinctly different developments in the arts. For example, that preoccupation with the Salome-Herodias story and with the larger theme of the "fatal woman" is a phenomenon which had its strongest manifestation in the nineteenth century; on the other hand, the "irrationalism" notable in the works I have discussed earlier is related to a larger movement toward the absurd in art which began to peak just after World War I. And, like Wilde's *Salome,* any complex work of high art in the nineteenth and twentieth centuries in Europe is likely to combine similarly various features which can be associated with independent developments in the arts.

This phenomenon is certainly not unique in the history of art; but it is particularly important to keep in mind when dealing with the art at the end of the nineteenth century and after in Europe because of the extraordinary speed and nearly chaotic complexity of the cultural fragmentation which begins to take place then, and the multiplicity of analytic categories to which that fragmentation has led. Much of the confusion which results from the availability of so many categories comes about because they are so often seen as competing umbrella terms of fully adequate descriptors when, in fact, they are really most helpful in the far more modest task of pointing to individual threads in the warp and woof of an exceedingly complex cultural web. In fact, this very multiplicity of available analytic categories can provide a useful method for characterizing the cultural "place" of works of art. Implicit in this procedure are studies which would devote themselves to the difficult problem of clarifying and refining the existing categories used to describe developments in the arts in modern Europe, with special emphasis on those which cut across different media and different countries—on the assumption that such developments are most likely to reflect more profoundly felt and far-reaching cultural changes.

It would be a vain hope that full and complete agreement would ever be reached as to what categories would be most revealing and informative; but, rather than waste time in a futile effort to create some umbrella term or terms to describe the post-Nietzschean world of art, a more modest effort to sort out the existing confusions in the multiple categories that already exist would be of great value.[26] An array of well-defined categories identifying specific lines of development could then be used to characterize the cultural "place" of a given work by making it possible for a historian to specify what particular subselection of categories it combines in its most distinctive features. The results would be particularly useful for what they could reveal about the patterns which individual lines of development make as they combine to create the waves of change in the arts which began to sweep across Europe at the end of the nineteenth century—and they would, I believe, make it easier to pinpoint what particular cultural forces were making the waves.

9

The Publication of *The Private Life of Henry Maitland*

A Literary Event

Pierre Coustillas

Anyone who has more than a casual acquaintance with the life and work of George Gissing is aware of the existence of a highly controversial biography of him published in the guise of a *roman à clé* by his former fellow-student and close friend Morley Roberts, *The Private Life of Henry Maitland*. When the book first appeared in 1912 no full biography was available, and the only serious attempt at a biographical sketch was the now well-known (and largely unreliable) entry, patiently compiled by Thomas Seccombe, in the *Dictionary of National Biography*.[1] The revelations made by Roberts created a scandal, and for months English and American newspapers bubbled over with comments ranging from glowing approval to downright slating. Public controversy in the press was naturally attended by a good deal of private quarrelling, verbal and epistolary. While the major critics of the day expressed their divergent views on the book, Gissing's friends and relatives on both sides of the Channel passed sharp strictures on the offensive yet vividly suggestive volume. It is now more than seventy years since Morley Roberts was deafened by the outcry he consciously raised, and his book has been reprinted several times. Doubtless much material of fleeting interest has perished during these seven decades, but time has also allowed many documents connected with the book to emerge, and it therefore seems worth trying to reconstruct the whole controversy in the hope that this will lead to a scholarly revaluation of a piece of work which, if judiciously used, is sure to remain a major source for the study of Gissing's life.

That Morley Roberts was one of the best potential biographers of Gissing no one doubted in 1912. The two men, born in 1857, had known each other since Roberts's entrance at Owens College in 1873, a period of thirty busy years, with a short interruption from 1876 to 1880. In particular Roberts was familiar with Gissing's unhappy domestic life, and few contemporaries had followed his literary career more closely since the days young George wrote verse and articles for the *Owens College Union Magazine*. In December 1903 Roberts had travelled all the way from London to the Spanish frontier to see his friend on his deathbed at Ispoure and had been the only English man of letters to attend his funeral. Not only had he read all Gissing's books, including the posthumous fiction, but he had discussed with him the contents and artistic aims of all those published up to the early 1890s. On several occasions critical estimates from his pen had appeared in magazines and journals: they might have been more laudatory had not Gissing repeatedly warned his friend against the dangers of logrolling.[2] Early in 1904 Roberts had bravely vindicated Gissing's memory when the *Church Times* had irresponsibly declared that the novelist (a consistent agnostic to the end) had died in "the Catholic faith,"[3] and in the following December he had celebrated in his own way the first anniversary of the writer's death in an article entitled "The Exile of George Gissing."[4]

Further prolegomena to *The Private Life of Henry Maitland* should be recalled. Roberts could claim that, in addition to first-rate knowledge of his subject, he had secured permission from him to be his biographer if, as proved to be the case, Gissing predeceased him. This was probably an ill-advised decision on Gissing's part since he had complained several times that Roberts had only a poor understanding of his work, but it was a solid asset should the dead novelist's family show signs of hostility. Besides, three times at least, Roberts had in his own fiction depicted characters openly modelled on his friend. In his first novel, *In Low Relief* (1890), John Torrington is a striking likeness of the author of *New Grub Street*. *The Degradation of Geoffrey Alwith* (1895) has a minor character, Will Curgenven, "writer, teacher and general apostle of culture," in whom Gissing was invited to recognize himself.[5] (Curgenven is first seen writing an essay on Greek metres in his dingy Baker Street flat, quoting Porson on "the nature of things.") "I take it rather as an honour than otherwise to be put into your book," he wrote to his friend on 31 January 1895,[6] an encouragement which Roberts must have remembered at the time he was writing *Henry Maitland*. Once again, after Gissing's death, he introduced him into one of his stories, "Tritt," which is based on the adventures, artistic and sentimental, of Plitt, the German pseudo-artist who accompanied Gissing on his first trip to Naples. This time fiction was closer than ever to reality, as can be seen by comparing the plot of the story with some entries in Gissing's diary, and Gissing himself is transparently called Ryecroft.[7]

I

The biographical project which was to become *Henry Maitland* began to take shape while the quarrel about the publication of Gissing's post-humous historical novel *Veranilda* (1904) was raging.[8] H. G. Wells's preface to the novel, though rejected by the family, appeared as an article in the *Monthly Review* for August, and was thought so offensive that Clara Collet, co-executrix with Algernon Gissing of the novelist's will, declared her wish that Wells's errors be corrected and his innuendoes repudiated. Walter and Alfred, the novelist's sons, were still under age and they had to be protected, she thought, against all possible unpleasant revelations concerning their father—his first marriage to a street-walker he vainly tried to redeem, the short term of imprisonment he had served after his expulsion from Owens College, his disastrous second marriage to a lower-class girl who developed into a shrew and went insane, and his free union with his translator Gabrielle Fleury.

As early as 28 September 1904 Miss Collet encouraged Roberts to write the authoritative biography of their late friend, but she was desirous to protect Gabrielle's reputation: "Although I am most anxious that George's friends should keep out of all newspaper controversy I am equally anxious that you should do as you suggested and write of him as you knew him—not for publication at present. And above all I wish that you would give some idea of the later years of his life with Mme Gissing; so that people may understand that it was in every true sense of the word a marriage."[9] The next day Roberts replied that he had written "a lot about Gissing, most of it only for private circulation among a very few, and among those not A[lgernon] G[issing]," George's brother, whom everyone in his own circle regarded as a weakling. He was, he said, "doing G. just as I knew him, from the beginning, without any concealment of anything; for only then can one judge what an awful tragedy his life was. . . . I want you to see what I'm doing about G. among the first."

Clara Collet refrained from giving Gabrielle too many particulars. All three were to meet in the Basque country for the anniversary of Gissing's death, in late December 1904. Shortly before the gathering took place, while she was already staying with Gabrielle at the Pension Larréa in Ciboure, she warned Roberts that Gabrielle objected to the idea of his publishing a biography within the next few years. Only two or three close friends were aware that she had not been legally married to Gissing; she was confronted in daily life with petty material difficulties resulting from her double identity and she dreaded the reactions of her many straitlaced relatives and upper-class friends. Clara Collet was doing her best to reconcile Roberts's desire to publish an oft-requested biography of George with Gabrielle's anxious wish to see her eminent part in the writer's life acknowledged without her social position being damaged by the revelation. "I do not think you ought to publish it until both the boys are old enough to be consenting parties to the publication," she wrote to Roberts before his arrival.[10] But the boys, she knew, were under the jealous care of Margaret and Ellen Gissing, the novelist's sisters in Wakefield, whose strict conventionality was an obstacle to the publication of anything personal about George.

The question of the biography was discussed at length by Roberts and the two women at the end of the year. He was then seeking contacts with George's friends and relatives, but Gabrielle saw difficulties in many quarters. She begged Miss Collet to warn him not to ask Eduard Bertz, who had known George since 1878, for any letters. Bertz, she thought, would be envious of anyone claiming to know Gissing better than he did. As for the relatives in Yorkshire, they looked askance at all George's friends—these belonged to a world the Wakefield ladies could neither understand nor approve of. Meanwhile, however, it was being rumored in London that Roberts was at work on the biography and that Bertz was contemplating publication of the impressive number of letters he had received from Gissing. In a letter of 12 January 1905, Roberts told Clara Collet that William Robertson Nicoll, who was an influential member of Hodder & Stoughton and editor of the *Bookman*, had made him "an offer for a book about George." C. K. Shorter, editor of the *Sphere,* and, like Nicoll, a former acquaintance of Gissing, was also urging Roberts to proceed with his project. As for Clara Collet, the correspondence of the period makes it clear that she egged him on to write the book with as much energy as she fought the idea of publication in the near future. "It is expecting from you," she observed, "a great deal of self-denial to undergo all the pains of authorship without allowing you to reap the artist's reward for twelve years perhaps. I know that and realize it fully."[11] Were he willing to wait, she pleaded, he would have an opportunity to do a much more complete work, and to consult Gissing's diary when his elder son Walter was of age. Gabrielle concurred with all this: "There is no doubt whatever that it is most desirable that this Life sh[oul]d be written by a true friend of his and someone who has known him so long and so intimately." [12]

However, as Roberts carried on a friendly correspondence with both women and as they both expressed themselves candidly on the Gissings, he came to realize early in 1905 that his task bristled with difficulties. A letter from him to Clara Collet of 18 February shows that he was despairing: "After reading your last letter I made up my mind to proceed no further with my book about George. I should only make trouble for myself and get myself disliked, after all. I certainly shall do nothing for 12 years ahead." He promised to inform Gabrielle and Robertson Nicoll of his decision. At this point, fearing that Roberts might also have been put off by the financial aspect of the question, Gabrielle and Miss Collet offered to buy his manuscript when completed. But Roberts refused to take any money; he no longer wanted to write the book. "I foresee nothing but danger and difficulty and hornets' nests all about me," he wrote to Clara Collet on 21 April 1905. "I should be damned on all hands when it was published." Still he was conscious of the interest of what he had written and he proposed to arrange for Miss Collet to have it all if he predeceased her. "I should like *you* to tell Gabrielle that I have given up the idea of the book, at any rate for some years." In the following June he was still hesitating; he had shown Gabrielle part of what he had written about George. Perhaps, after all, he would some day sell his manuscript to his two women friends if they were of the same opinion and would act together.

No serious progress was made until 1912, the year *Henry Maitland* was actually written and published, but a letter from Clara Collet to Roberts about the projected edition of Gissing's letters to Bertz in late 1907 reveals at once her own illusions and the odium Roberts would incur when he chose to publish his life of Gissing: "I am quite sure that the letters ought not to be published but I know that Bertz is anxious to show that he was George's only real friend by giving every intimate particular he can. . . . With the exception of yourself I don't expect a single person connected with George to sacrifice personal interests out of consideration for him or his chidren to the extent of twenty shillings." [13] The danger, however, was only temporary. Bertz, as Arthur Young relates in his edition of the remaining letters, gave up his project and destroyed all those which, prior to 1888, referred to Gissing's first wife. But Roberts was less disinterested and certainly not prepared to sacrifice his chance of bringing out his biography of Gissing. What prompted him to brave public criticism and private fury was the news that a young novelist of twenty-six, Frank Swinnerton, was preparing a critical study of Gissing's works for Martin Secker. Naturally Swinnerton tried to obtain biographical information from the author's friends: "I applied for help concerning Gissing's boyhood to his lifelong friend, Morley Roberts," he wrote in the preface to the third edition of his book in 1966. "But Roberts, being then, he afterwards told me, distracted by domestic grief [his wife died in September 1911] returned a dusty answer for which he afterwards felt self-reproach. He proposed to use his unique knowledge, he said, either later, in a formal biography, or at once in a fictional narrative." [14]

Roberts was now determined to carry out his plan as quickly as possible and not to let himself be forestalled by Swinnerton. The last letter he received from Clara Collet, written on 2 June 1912, five months before *Henry Maitland* came out, was in answer to specific questions and contained an invitation to show him Gissing's correspondence with her on the following Sunday. The end of the letter conveyed the strained relations among Gissing's friends. After making some alterations in a portion of the manuscript Roberts had submitted to her, Miss Collet openly confessed her embarrassment: "If I seem to be lacking in cordiality in this matter don't attribute it to any want of sympathy with you. It is the consciousness of pain which any record however finely and unselfishly written, must cause to his sons and sisters. . . . I am not attempting to deter you. George Gissing was sent into hell for the purpose of saving souls. Perhaps it is a necessary thing that his story should be written by all sorts of people from their different points of view. But I am responsible to his sons, not to society, and I feel as though I were walking on smashing glass." Still, she assured him that her sympathy with him was "warm and real, even if I come into collision with you in this matter, or in others."

II

The *Private Life of Henry Maitland* appeared in England late in October 1912 under the imprint of Eveleigh Nash. The title page declared it to be "A record dictated by J. H. Revised and edited by Morley Roberts." The volume was inscribed to the memory of Mrs. Roberts and a controversial preface expounded the author's purpose. "In the whole book, which cannot be published now," Roberts said, "there are things worth waiting for. I have cut and retrenched with pain, for I wanted to risk the whole, but no writer or editor is his own master in England." A Note to the Preface was clearly intended to thicken the atmosphere of mystery: "The full manuscript, which may possibly be published after some years, is, in the meantime, placed in safe custody." Roberts was behaving cautiously. Not only did he endeavour to propitiate adverse opinion in his Preface, but he made slight alterations throughout his narrative when quoting from letters and other documents or referring to Gissing's friends. Doubtless he was trying to protect himself should any judicial proceedings be brought against him. Thus, though he had taken the trouble to obtain an official certificate for Gissing's second marriage, he deliberately gave a date which was wrong by about a month; or, again, when he quoted in Chapter I from Clara Collet's letter of 2 June 1912 he changed "deter" to "dissuade" and willfully misreported her occupation.

The publisher, for his part, spared no effort to promote the sales of the book. The announcements were uncommonly large for those days; they advertised "a literary sensation." If Gissing's name was not mentioned, some suggestive excerpts from reviews clearly indicated that the volume contained six shillings' worth of scandal. A passage quoted from the *Daily Telegraph* proved most useful to the publisher: "No one . . . will fail to recognize the portrait . . . a very true book, very poignant and very impressive." [15] An announcement in the *Daily Mail* declared: "This book is now one of the topics of conversation in cultured circles, and has had splendid reviews in the press." [16]

Whether or not this was the case must have been very much a matter of opinion six months later, after the controversy had spread to America and Australia, and after a crowd of reviewers, authors and newspaper readers inspired by the subject had aired their contradictory views on biography in the guise of fiction. Virtually all reviewers identified Gissing. The earliest, C. Lewis Hind, who as editor of the *Academy* from 1896 to 1903 had been in touch with the novelist, wrote with the greatest candor in the *Daily Chronicle:* "It is no secret. The secret is revealed on every page. This remarkable book, as sincere as it is sorrowful, bald and bold, sympathetic and intuitive, tells the life of George Gissing." [17] Nobody complained about Hind's procedure, as he himself recalled ten years later in *More Authors and I*, but the next day the *Daily Telegraph,* in an exceedingly courteous review which refrained from lifting the thin veil of disguise, asked a few questions which were to be at the core of the debate: since the pseudonyms were transparent, "would it not have been franker and more satisfactory to publish the book openly as a biography?" Some contemporaries were sure not to relish the figures they cut in the book. The true Maitland was there for the first time, but "whether anyone, including the subject of the biography himself, is better off for the revelation, is a question which Mr. Morley Roberts must settle with his own literary conscience." [18]

It was James Douglas who set the house on fire, first in the *Star* and three days later in the *Daily News.* He pitied Gissing and inveighed against the Owens College authorities for having sent him as a youth to prison— "prison for Gissing meant that he was blighted for life"—and he turned against Roberts for having butchered a soul in order to point a moral. "It is simply a question of the posthumous sacredness of the soul. The pain or the privilege of looking into the deeps of a man's anguish is for his friends, not for the crowd." [19] Douglas waxed downright angry in the *Daily News,* where his violent condemnation of fiction as a vehicle for biography was melodramatically entitled "The Grave-worm." "The time has come," he began, "to state a case in the Court of Letters against the degradation of the English novel into a scandalous chronicle of private affairs." If such practices as Roberts's went on, it would be necessary to organize drastic measures in the Society of Authors, in the Publishers' Association, and in the press. "At all costs the plague must be stamped out." [20] This triggered a flow of correspondence in which a number of literary men took part—W. L. George, "a friend of Mrs. Gissing" (who was almost certainly Alice Ward, the Paris correspondent of the Society of Authors and a friend of Gabrielle), May Sinclair (who had corresponded with Gissing in 1897), W. J. Locke, R. Ellis Roberts, Thomas Hardy and A. St. John Adcock. [21] On 7 November William Robertson Nicoll devoted three and a half columns of his *British Weekly* to the book. [22] He had known Gissing, talked at large about his private life [23] and was evidently delighted to let his pen twinkle without restraint. He cursorily condemned the thefts committed at College by young Gissing in his fits of idealism—for Nicoll did not forget he was editor of a Nonconformist journal—and dwelt at length on the novelist's misfortune. In the *Sphere,* C. K. Shorter, the ubiquitous editor, was all too glad to remind the world that he had known Gissing personally and published many stories of his. With him, reviewing was apt to lapse into self-praise. He took Roberts to task for his inaccuracies and for making his subject more gloomy than he was, that is when Shorter himself had happened to see him, mostly on festive occasions. True, he said, there was the man who had painfully mismanaged his life, but there was also the "man of handsome genial presence and kindly nature and a great genius for friendship, whose clever work in fiction is destined to live and whose memory to those who knew him—less intimately than Mr. Roberts, I admit—is of a man of singularly charming and upright character." [24]

As days passed the controversy spread apace, drew in new personalities and degenerated into journalistic bickering. If the *Sunday Times* and the *Globe* [25] deliberately eschewed the aggressive note, Shorter gleefully pointed out the contradictions between James Douglas's reviews in the *Star* and the *Daily News,* denouncing the commercial aspect of Douglas's campaign. [26] These early reviews were relatively mild, but beginning in mid-November, Roberts suffered several attacks. The *Nation* rightly observed: "He has failed to respond to the finest fibres of friendship by the tone of comments now over-blunt, now hard, now slightly tinged with patronage."[27] Was Roberts a real friend of Gissing? The novelist's other friends would decide, and indeed, as we shall see, they did— negatively and privately, with the exception of H. G. Wells, who trumpeted abroad his hostility. The *Pall Mall Gazette* attacked Roberts's method—conducive to "an appearance of muddle and unreality"[28]—and the *Christian Commonwealth,* turning against Gissing, poured scorn upon "the tragedy of a moral weakling,"[29] while the *Spectator* expressed its poor opinion of Roberts as a biographer. "At times he is extraordinarily incoherent, and he talks far too much about himself and his own writings. . . . If the record had to be made public, it would surely have lost nothing in reticence, but would have gained something in frankness, by being freed from these absurd trappings of anonymity."[30] Perhaps the severest anonymous attack came from the *Evening Standard,* which styled Roberts's note at the end of the preface "puny and puerile." "Must a biographer . . . pry into every folly and misdemeanour of his subject? Must he rake up the sins of youth, exhibit the errors of middle age in a high light, and not let go of the wretched fellow till every man or woman who can read has been provided with a seat in the confessional to listen to the secrets that might have remained secret and gloat over the spectacle of their brother's torture? If this is what biography should be, Mr. Roberts has written a masterpiece."[31]

With the publication of the December monthlies several more members of the Gissing circle entered the fray: Austin Harrison (Gissing's former pupil) quietly in his own journal, the *English Review;*[32] Swinnerton with more than unexpected fairness to Roberts;[33] and H. G. Wells with a bull's determination to tear *Henry Maitland* to pieces. Wells and Roberts had become estranged after a futile quarrel; jealousy now spurred him on. He lavished inordinate praise on Frank Swinnerton's book—which, like a few other critics, he reviewed concurrently with *Henry Maitland*—and, largely out of an inveterate taste for polemics, he trampled Roberts's in the mire. To him *The Private Life of Henry Maitland* was "downright bad, careless in statement, squalid in effect, poor as criticism, weakly planned and entirely without any literary distinction."[34] It must have cost Roberts some effort to refrain from replying to Wells's four-page attack, but he had promised Shorter he would not fly at his critics and he duly abstained. And fortunately there were critics like the reviewer in the *Westminster Gazette*[35] and Holbrook Jackson in *T. P.'s Weekly,*[36] who did not enjoy polemics and could see beyond the causes of the quarrel. Rather than be unduly hard on Roberts, whose performance he little relished, Jackson preferred to stress the considerable amount of interest in Gissing's works that had been manifested since the publication of Swinnerton's critical study in mid-

November. Now, he noted, had come the time and opportunity for a sufficiently enterprising publisher to make arrangements for a complete and definitive edition.[37]

III

By the end of December the controversy shifted to America, where Doran published the book. Judging by certain reviews, the lengthy appreciations which had filled the columns of the London press had not been overlooked by American critics. Besides, the publication in America of Swinnerton's critical study, whose effect on Gissing's reputation was to be certainly more damaging than that of *Henry Maitland,* added zest to the affair, as the book, quite independently of the fictionalized biography, roused much adverse criticism. On the whole, it was felt that Swinnerton, bent on proving with superfluous zeal that a new broom sweeps clean, had written an all-too-able deprecation of his subject. Fewer people had known Gissing in the United States than in England, and those who had, had actually known him as a struggling youth in Boston and Chicago, but he had plenty of admirers in the New World. At all events the two volumes were, for different reasons, of the kind to excite much ill feeling, and the passions were fanned by the reprinting of some English articles, Wells's for instance, in American papers. Those readers who treasured Gissing's books and sensed behind them a fascinating personality had good reasons for rejecting a biography that asserted that he should never have written fiction, and a critical study that claimed that "to write of Gissing is to write of one who failed." [38]

The *Literary Digest* for 21 December 1912 imported the quarrel hot and spicy into the American press with a provocative title, "Body-snatching in Fiction," allusions to personalities who had already taken part in the wrangle (Thomas Hardy among them), some startling details about Gissing's life, and a good portrait with this comment: "The most autobiographical of modern English novelists. The things he left untold about his life are now published in a novel by his most intimate friend, and reprobated by many." [39] In quick succession the *Boston Evening Transcript* of 11 January 1913 reproduced a substantial part of Wells's vituperative review and the *New York Times Review of Books* of 12 January the whole of it.[40]

As in England, reactions to the book varied, sometimes with the same paper. The editor of the New York *Sun* seemed fascinated by Roberts's book. He began by printing a noncommittal review on 25 January, went on with a prominent recapitulation of the whole controversy on 15

March, and concluded with a sharply critical assessment on 12 April, in which Roberts's anecdotes on Greek metres and food, as well as his refutation of Gissing's so-called Christian death, were somewhat futilely censured.[41] A more appropriate and careful attack came from the pen of Edwin Francis Edgett, a genuine admirer of Gissing, in the *Boston Evening Transcript*. Edgett complained that, since the story of Gissing's life had been known to many people for some twenty years, what was needed was "a straightforward biography . . . without subterfuges, without pretence," altogether devoid of the "pitiful machinery of literary humbug" that had been used in *Henry Maitland*. This turned out to be the most serious, the most perceptive attack of the many levelled at a highly vulnerable book. "In its egotism, its self-sufficiency, its aggressive complacency, *The Private Life of Henry Maitland* is unequalled. . . . Throughout [Roberts] plays the role of judge and censor, and he approves or disapproves of Gissing's conduct and ideas as if he were the one and only man competent to express an opinion upon them."[42] Whereupon Edgett pilloried Roberts's disrespect for Gissing's hatred of militarism together with his patronizing comments on his friend's short-lived adhesion to Positivism and harrowing domestic difficulties.

Simultaneously George Middleton scored one more protest in the American *Bookman* against the fictional form which would forever deprive Roberts's book of its potential authority. He was content to sum up the main phases of Gissing's life and to offer a broad, congenial analysis of his contribution to the English novel.[43] So did the earnest-minded conservative critic Paul Elmer More in the New York *Nation*. His oft-quoted dirgelike words might serve as an epigraph to a study of Gissing's reputation for the next fifty years: "Unfortunate in his life, it seems as if Gissing were destined to be unfortunate also in his death." Like Edgett, More deplored Roberts's patronizing and unsavory tone and the tenuous guise of fiction: "The procedure is a bit offensive. If Mr. Roberts could not relate the facts as frank biography, he should have kept silence; to approach them in this oblique fashion gives the impression that he is ashamed of the man whose friend he proclaims himself to be."[44]

To the end, the reviewers' appraisals of the book remained very much a matter of personal sensibility, knowledge of the subject and editorial policy of the journal in which the reviews appeared. *Current Opinion* elected not to take sides and offered a conspectus of the conflicting opinions roused by Roberts's biography.[45] The *Independent* read it as a key to "the atmosphere of unmitigated gloom that pervades all of Gissing's works"[46] and the *Literary Digest*, transcending the controversy that had been raging for over a half year, viewed the book as a study of a human soul, commenting that "one would have to look far to find a more enthralling narrative."[47] As the storm raised in England was dying out on the American shore, the reprint of Upton Sinclair's New York *Sun* article in the London *Academy* — an article which was largely a disenchanted plea for tolerance — elicited an ultimate sour note from one of the hostile reviewers of the book, H. G. Wells. Since Wells had objected to so many things in Roberts's picture of Gissing, Sinclair urged him to write another biography of Gissing: "In this way we shall see Gissing from two angles; he will become a figure of three dimensions, instead of two."[48] But when in his own autobiography Wells wrote at some length on Gissing, he did so with a dose of egotism which was on a par with Roberts's.

The Private Life of Henry Maitland prompted journalistic comments wherever English books were reviewed, especially in Australia. There H. H. Champion, who had known Gissing and Roberts personally and had done much to promote Gissing's works through his successive journals, refrained from all criticism. He turned his *Book Lover* review into an opportunity to relate at some length his occasional contacts with Gissing and to quote from letters he had received from him.[49] The other Australian reviews also systematically avoided the polemical note — distance, relative unconcern, and perhaps a different moral climate doubtless accounted for the more peaceful reaction.[50]

But in England, where the controversy had been at its highest, a new and final conflagration burst out in Manchester when the University authorities proposed to raise a memorial to Gissing. The appeal,[51] which was supported by a committee including a number of influential names, some of them former friends of the novelist (but, for whatever reasons, not Morley Roberts), was fought for a whole month by the *Manchester City News* in a campaign of abject philistinism.[52] That the English press, national or local, greeted this outburst of self-righteousness with silence proved that public opinion had begun to swing back. The memorial was created, and the Gissing scholarship associated with it is still being awarded every year in memory of his academic triumphs and — to those who happen to know — irreparable disaster.

IV

The private reception of *Henry Maitland* was, if anything, even less cordial than that of the press. The book embarrassed Roberts's friends, some of whom were more attached to Gissing than he was. W. H. Hudson's thoughtful response, which would be worth quoting in full, shows how shocked he was: "I have just read it nearly all through with intense and painful interest. There are things in it which make one feel very bad and which, when I come to them, make me wish you had never attempted this thing." Hudson was not quite sure he could forgive Roberts. "The bitter thing is that those who are related to him will never . . . believe that it was best to have it all out about the man, and they will hate and curse you for it."[53] Edward Clodd, whom Gissing had liked so much, and whose diaries give ample evidence that their affection was mutual, deliberately avoided a verbal conflict with Roberts: "All that I felt was that where the veil of anonymity was necessarily thin the employment of fictitious names, titles and places was needless. Let it stand at that."[54] Clodd was obviously worried, though there were things in *Henry Maitland*, such as Roberts's brave defence of Gissing as a consistent thinker to the end, that pleased him. He swore to himself that he would find a more straightforward manner to pay homage to his dead friend, and he did so by publishing letters from Gissing on three occasions, notably in his *Memories* where he passed an urbanely censorious comment on the superfluous trappings of Roberts's book.

Nor was Henry Hick, a former schoolfellow of Gissing's who had renewed his acquaintance with him in 1895, much satisfied with Roberts's performance. Better than any friend of the novelist he could realize how painful the revelations made in the book would be to the Gissings in Yorkshire. But Hick was no sentimentalist. A letter from him to Roberts dated 26 July 1912 shows that Roberts had sought his assistance while at work on his manuscript, so that he may have been aware that the biography would actually appear in the guise of fiction. He notified Roberts of various slips—it was in Manchester, not at Wakefield that Gissing recited German to him; he had come straight to Wells's, not to Hick's on his 1901 visit to England; the whole affair of Gissing's gluttony was a purely verbal phenomenon.[55] As for Wells, as soon as he had read *Henry Maitland*, he sent Roberts a letter amounting to a declaration of war: the facts given in the book were blazingly inaccurate, Roberts's estimate of Gabrielle Fleury was ridiculous, the book was neither planned nor written, but shied onto paper. An infrequent user of euphemisms, Wells said he could not praise it.[56]

With no one was the breach more abrupt than with the two wo-men—Clara Collet and Gabrielle Fleury—in whose good books he had been. Although Roberts, encouraged by all and sundry to write a life of his friend, had kept Clara Collet posted on his plans, he had not told her that, combining sensationalism and fecklessness, he was actually writing a *roman à clé*. Miss Collet, who liked straightforward dealings, had, as she repeated, to think of the Gissing children's interests; she must also remember her promise to George, when he and Gabrielle had opted for life in common that, as long as she was alive, Gabrielle would have a friend in

England. She therefore had to choose between two friends—and did not hesitate. Chancing upon Roberts in a London street she cut him dead, and it would seem that no reconciliation between them ever took place. The many long-winded, passionate letters of Gabrielle to Miss Collet—unpublished with one exception—throw superabundant light on her own violent reactions to Roberts's book while enabling us to infer those of Clara Collet. Both women had trusted him to an extent they now bitterly regretted. In the years immediately after George's death, Gabrielle often referred to Roberts amicably, expressing her confidence and admiration; she saw him as a "true friend" of George. As her letters to Miss Collet testify, she met him several times in the south of France, she read with interest some of his books, and there is evidence that he courted her—in vain.

When *Henry Maitland* appeared in late October 1912 Gabrielle's first reaction was not one of surprise: "My feeling is that *I,* or *you,* s[hou]ld say *nothing,* so long as no direct question or explanation is asked," she wrote to Clara Collet on 31 October. She predicted her French relatives would break with her; if she nursed any regret, she said, it was only on account of her mother, now two years dead. Still, in the emotional, chaotic, ungrammatical torrent of comment on the volume that poured from her pen in the next six or eight months, she more than once expressed her resentment at George's having left her in such a socially vulnerable position, even though loyalty and pride invariably had the upper hand. She lived again with great intensity the years she had spent with him:

> So much did poor G. feel himself that he had not done for me what he ought and might have done, that in the summer before his death, he was constantly preoccupied with the idea, the wish to rewrite his will, and wanted to go soon to London for that purpose. Of course there was no *money* question about it; but the feeling that he had to put me in a morally recognized position, in so far as it could *never* allow *anyone* to be able to assert—judging only from the appearances—that our union was a mere ordinary *liaison,* which might have been broken any day.[57]

She managed to keep her temper till the end of the year because until then she abstained from reading the book in which she and George were discussed at such length. Echoes of it reached her mainly through Miss Collet and Miss Ward, a staunch friend of hers who dabbled in journalism and was then writing a memoir of Gissing to serve as a counterblast to *Henry Maitland.* But the manuscript, rejected by several publishers, was never printed, and its surviving pages reveal a weakness incompatible with commercial publication.[58] Since consolation could no longer be expected from that quarter, Gabrielle eventually immersed herself in Roberts's volume. Because she appeared in it in disguise, she could only see it in the light of scandal, systematically placing the worst interpretation on any statement concerning George, herself, and her family. If only, she sighed in vain, Gissing had found time to write the second collection of essays in the Ryecroft manner that was to celebrate his life with her! With the stubbornness of passion, she was now convinced that Roberts had published *Henry Maitland* to revenge himself upon her for having rejected his attentions.

Reading the book put her in a rage. She thought of suing Roberts for libel, dreamt of having a member of her family "horsewhip that man," dreaded that one of her acquaintances in Saint-Jean de Luz, Stuart-Menteath, should be offended by an awkward reference to him in one of Gissing's letters Roberts had cited. She loudly complained that her life with George was grossly misrepresented, that the eminent role she had played in his later life was constantly played down, and she denounced with some indignation a number of erroneous factual details which she laboriously set out to correct for Miss Collet's benefit.[59] Roberts's deliberate alterations of some facts, dates, and quotations for prudential motives misled her. On reading a quotation from one of her letters to George, she imagined that George had allowed Roberts to read her letters to him, whereas this single quotation from her own letter actually comes from one of Gissing's letters to Roberts. For months her frantic attempts at refuting Roberts's statements about her relations and domestic arrangements with George involved her in multiple correspondence which only came to an end when her indignation, on the whole legitimate, had spent itself.

Until her death Gabrielle remained unable to forgive and forget. As late as 13 May 1920, for instance, she was still concerned to justify to Clara Collet her domestic arrangements with Gissing at Ciboure in 1902–1903 and thought it worth dealing Roberts a backhanded blow in passing. Years somehow smoothed down her difficulties. Contrary to her gloomy misgivings, none of her relatives, though they had always suspected something "irregular" in her relationship with Gissing, ever ostracized her, and she lost no friend worthy of the name either in England or in France. The delicate manner in which Louis Cazamian dealt with Gissing and Gabrielle in his famous history of English literature, his ignoring Roberts's book as well, show that intelligent, cultured, broad-minded people sided with her even though some of them may have been prepared to acknowledge the interest of Roberts's controversial exercise in biography.[60]

V

From the present-day standpoint, *The Private Life of Henry Maitland* offers a number of more or less apparent characteristics. All the persons mentioned in it, including the author, having died, it is no longer an awkward narrative for anyone, but it continues to irritate scholars who, comparatively unfamiliar with Gissing's life, use it, if at all, with a diffidence prompted by the unreliability of some of its details and by its author's occasional obtrusiveness. Indeed, the book has of late rarely been quoted by responsible scholars because more authoritative works have appeared, based on a wealth of material which was not available to Roberts. However the book retains much of its interest; it remains the admittedly biassed yet stimulating testimony of a man who for years knew Gissing and followed his career as few people did. Now, since Roberts published this biography of his friend in novel form only because of circumstances and since he removed the veil of pseudonymity in the second edition for those persons who had died after 1912, it is reasonable to presume that, if he were still alive, the notion of publishing a new edition with all the veils removed and the exact quotations restored would not displease him. Such an edition would be all the easier to prepare as the material which Roberts used has, with a very few exceptions, found its way into libraries where it can be consulted. The corrections or protests of dramatis personae such as Henry Hick or Gabrielle Fleury would also help to make the book more accurate than Roberts could ever hope to make it.

In this manner, *The Private Life of Henry Maitland,* retitled *The Private Life of George Gissing,* would be given a new lease of life—possibly a longer one than the first—and a posthumous reconciliation could be attempted between men and women who, being all friends of the novelist, should never have lapsed into a controversy which, all too easily understandable in 1912, now bears the mark of human vanity writ large.

10

Waifs of Memory:
Arthur Symons's Confessions

Alan Johnson

Arthur Symons's autobiographical writing provides a useful instance of the genre in the early twentieth century because he produced what amounts to a theory of autobiography as well as autobiography itself. The theory is mainly the product of his brilliant years in the 1890s when he edited the *Savoy* (1896), published *The Symbolist Movement in Literature* (1899), and wrote scores of reviews, introductions, and essays, as well as fiction and verse. Symons's theory of autobiography calls for what he came to think of as a Symbolist record of moments of fleeting experience in vivid, concrete imagery and for the self-contented tone he found in the *Memoirs* of Casanova. Symons turned to the writing of reminiscences in the long years following 1908–10, when he was afflicted with temporary insanity which left him somewhat unstable until his death at seventy-nine in 1945.

Some instances of Symons's autobiographical writing are included in Karl Beckson's *Memoirs of Arthur Symons* (1977), but much of the book's material is, as Symons intended half of his own never-published *Memoirs* to be, a record of his observation of other people. Prior to his attempts to publish his *Memoirs* in 1932–33,[1] he worked for about sixteen years on a project he called his "Confessions."[2] This was never published in its entirety, but Symons published eight or more pieces of it from 1914 to 1930, and a number of manuscript fragments in the Arthur Symons Collection in the Princeton University Library clearly were parts of the project at one time or another. Students of Symons's work have noted the project but apparently have not pieced it together. Professor Beckson, for example, mentions that "in the early 1920s, Symons was writing what he called *Confessions*" and that his published account of his temporary insanity, *Confessions: A Study in Pathology* (1930), "may have grown out of [his] earlier intentions."[3] Indeed it did, appearing in part first in the American periodical, *Two Worlds Quarterly*, 2:123–34, in 1926. The "Confessions" project as a whole constitutes Symons's sustained attempt at autobiography.

The 1930 *Confessions* and the rest of Symons's confessional writing present vivid images of his past experience, as his theory demands, but the tone of this writing is often far from self-contented. One source of Symons's discontent is, as one might expect from his hedonistic theory, a sense of the transience of experience, but this is apparent only in the 1930 *Confessions*. The usual source of the autobiographer's discontent in the various "Confessions" is a sense of wounded vanity. Symons seems to have adopted as a measure of his own achievement the anticonventional, aesthetic personality he had described in many of the subjects of his literary essays. His "Confessions" are riddled with querulous insistence upon his own genius and integrity: he presents himself as a wanderer and immoralist—a Gérard de Nerval, a Verlaine, and a Baudelaire, for example. In this context, the images which crystallize Symons's past experience seem doubly to be, as he calls one of them, "waif[s] of memory."[4] They are living relicts of the dead past, but also, Symons implies, their value is unrecognized by the living present.

Symons's querulousness, along with his Symbolist method and fitful process of publication, makes the "Confessions" material very erratic. Fascinating vignettes give intriguing views of Symons and his era, but the diatribes interrupt the vignettes and may repel many readers. The whole is delightful and excruciating—a fragmentary combination, as it were, of the best anecdotal style of Yeats's *Autobiographies* and the most blatant apologetics of Wilde's *De Profundis*. Like Yeats, who felt that his temperate, intellectually solid attempt to foster Irish national spirit through literature and theater had been defeated by the propaganda of Young Ireland, and like Wilde, Symons seems to have written with a sense of having been displaced. The contrasting poles of contentment and a sense of failure which may be implicit in the works of Yeats and Wilde are explicit in Symons's theory and manifest in his "Confessions."

II

Symons's theory of autobiography, and specifically of "confessional" writing, is apparent in certain of his prose comments on Augustine, Casanova, and Verlaine. These comments show his preference for Casanova's tone and for the imagistic method of Symbolism. In Symons's Introduction to Augustine's *Confessions* in 1897,[5] he defines the Casanovan tone to the tones of Augustine, Rousseau, and Cellini. Augustine's is the tone of penitential recollection of a rejected life; Rousseau's is defensive self-justification; and Cellini's is egoistic self-proclamation. Casanova's tone is contented recollection of a life of pleasure (pp. 1–3). Although Symons does not rank one of these tones clearly above the others in the Introduction, he suggests his preference by an appealing description of Casanova who recollected his experiences "in order that he might be amused . . . and then because he thought the record would do him credit. . . . Always passionate after sensations, and for their own sake, the writing of autobiography was the last, almost active sensation that was left to him, and he accepted it energetically" (p. 3).

Symons's admiration for the Casanovan tone becomes unmistakable in several subsequent essays. In "Casanova at Dux" in the *North American Review* 175 (Sept. 1902), he not only describes his own successful search for some long-missing chapters of Casanova's *Memoirs* but also ranks the *Memoirs* as "one of the greatest autobiographies" and characterizes Casanova as "that rarest kind of autobiographer, one who did not live to write, but wrote because he had lived, and when he could live no longer" (pp. 320–21). Casanova "turns to look back over his past life, and to live it over again in memory, as he writes down the narrative of what had interested him most in it" (p. 346). The description of Casanova as the "rarest kind of autobiographer" is echoed word-for-word in Symons's "Casanova and Venice" in 1918[6] and is expanded in "Confessions and Comments" in *Dramatis Personae* in 1923. There Symons pronounces the *Memoirs* to be "one of the most wonderful autobiographies in the world" and describes Casanova as a writer "who, always passionate after sensations, confesses, in his confessions, the most shameless things that have ever been written: one to whom . . . nothing in the world was indifferent."[7] Despite this sustained admiration for Casanova's self-contented retrospection, however, Symons's own "Confessions" will suggest that he frequently followed the model of Rousseau, whose *Confessions* Symons describes in the Introduction to Augustine and again twenty-five years later in an essay on Proust as a "manifestation of that nervous, defiant consciousness of other people which haunted [Rousseau] all his life . . . the protesting self-consciousness which . . . drove him, in spite of himself, to set about explaining himself to other people, to the world in general."[8]

Symons's preference for the imagistic method in confessional writing is manifest in the Introduction to Augustine and in a brief note on Verlaine's *Confessions of a Poet* (1894) in *Colour Studies in Paris* (London, 1918). In the introduction Symons notes that Augustine's view of "all life only in its relation to the divine . . . brings with it a very impressive kind of symbolism into its record of actual facts" (*Figures of Several Centuries*, pp. 4–5). Augustine renounces purely worldly "'images of earth, and water, and air'" (p. 7), but his "sense of the divine in life, and specially of the miracles which alone count in the soul's summing-up of itself," leads him to focus upon pregnant, momentary details such as a girl's voice calling out the now-famous words *"tolle lege"* and a beggar's joyful voice in Milan. "[I]t is by these apparently trifling, . . . all-significant moments that his narrative moves," Symons concludes, "with a more reticent and effective symbolism than any other narrative known to me" (p. 8). Similarly, Symons describes Paul Verlaine's purely secular account of his youth and marriage in *Confessions of a Poet* as "autobiographical notes" that "tell . . . by means of a series of little facts, little impressions . . . the story of 'une vie beaucoup en nuances'" (*Colour Studies in Paris*, p. 187).

Symons's enthusiasm for the symbolic method in autobiography recalls, of course, his influential formulation of Symbolist theory in the 1890s, particularly in "The Decadent Movement in Literature" in *Harper's New Monthly Magazine* in 1893 and in the essays collected in *The Symbolist Movement in Literature*. As Frank Kermode and others have noted,[9] these essays, written under the influence of Walter Pater as well as the French Symbolists, show that Symons adopted Pater's conception of the self as a mortal agent of sensation in a world of material flux and that for Symons the writer's use of symbols is an attempt to capture fleeting moments of time and to pierce through temporal appearances to some permanent reality or meaning. In "The Decadent Movement," where Symons distinguishes and praises both Impressionists and Symbolists, he praises, for example, the Paterian "desperate endeavor" of the Goncourts "to flash the impression of the moment, to preserve the very heat and motion of life" in images and vignettes (p. 861) along with the attempt of Symbolists such as Maeterlinck to "flash upon you" what Symons enigmatically calls "the finer sense of things unseen, the deeper meaning of things evident" (p. 859). In the later *Symbolist Movement* Symons devotes his attention to the enigma of Symbolism as "a form of expression . . . for an unseen reality apprehended by the consciousness."[10] He quotes Carlyle on the Infinite and Plotinus on substance and soul to explain the "unseen reality" (pp. 2, 95–96) but admits the "final uncertainty" of his metaphysical speculations and thus leaves the reader with Symbolism as an "endeavor to disengage the ultimate essence, the soul, of whatever exists and can be realised by the consciousness" (p. 5).[11] The symbolic "all-significant moments" praised in Symons's Introduction to Augustine are, in the terms of *The Symbolist Movement,* attempts to capture this "ultimate essence" from particular experiences and to effect an "escape" from the "great suspense in which we live. . . . [P]rophets . . . artists . . . lovers . . . have really . . . been fleeing from the certainty of one thought: that we have, all of us, only our one day; and from the dread of that other thought: that the day, however used, must after all be wasted" (pp. 94–95).

III

The scope of the various "Confessions" in which Symons put his theory to the test of practice may be determined from several letters and from uses of the word *confession* in the titles and texts of some of his prose. His earliest reference to his writing of "Confessions" seems to occur in a letter of 7 March 1914, in which he wrote to the American lawyer and patron, John Quinn, that he was trying to publish a description of a dancer he had admired in the 1890s. He calls the piece "a kind of confession."[12] Again on 22 April 1914, in another letter to Quinn, Symons used the term *confession* to describe "Notes in the Sensations of a Lady of the Ballet," which may have been the piece referred to in the earlier letter and was, as he told Quinn, coming out in the April 1914 *International* (Quinn, Box 38). "Notes" chronicles its narrator's friendship with an Alhambra dancer as she pursues a liaison with a certain "Mr. Black." The typescript of this, which is in Princeton's Arthur Symons Collection (Box 13), is dated in Symons's hand "1892–1893," and the totally coherent, vivid style of the piece suggests that the date refers to the time of its composition. Probably when Symons first thought of publishing "Confessions"—presumably about 1914—he began with adaptable material ready at hand.

Another early reference to the writing of "Confessions" is Symons's proposal to Frank Crowninshield, the editor of *Vanity Fair*, in a letter of 18 May 1918 that Symons send notes about some of his "Adventures—some of the nature of Confessions" (Princeton, Box 24). This was an odd proposal because *Vanity Fair* had already published his "Confessions: A Few Thoughts, Portraits and Memories" in its Volume 6 (March 1916), pp. 39 and 130, and a number of other reminiscences which do not use the term *confession* but might be regarded as such.[13] The "Confessions" of March 1916 is a miscellany of recollections of J. K. Huysmans and of

Dieppe, self-characterization, and obituary comments prompted by the recent deaths of Remy de Gourmont and Stuart Merrill.

Apparently the plan for a broadly reminiscential book to be called *Confessions* took shape in Symons's mind by 1920, for on 19 March 1921 he wrote to Selwyn Image: "I spent May and June in Paris, where I began to write my *Confessions*," and he goes on to ask exactly where "the famous Crown tavern" was before its demolition (Princeton, Box 24).[14] Two essays contain an echo of Image's reply to Symons's question about the Crown. On 26 March 1921, Image wrote that "the dear old Crown . . . was . . . north of the Alhambra stage-door" (Beckson, *Memoirs*, p. 125). Symons locates it "between the stage-doors of the Empire and the Alhambra" in "The Hobby Horse," *Vanity Fair* 17 (Feb. 1922): 54, and in "Bohemian Chelsea," *The Double Dealer* 5 (Nov. 1923): 196–98.[15] The first piece sketches a brief history of the *Hobby Horse* journal in the 1880s and 1890s, and the second recollects Symons's acquaintance in and around Chelsea with Charles Conder, Oscar Wilde, and a certain Jenny. To Ernest Rhys, Symons wrote on 15 April 1924 from his home in Kent in the same vein as he had to Image: "I have been here for two months, mostly continuing my Confessions (in MS!)" (Princeton, Box 34). He wrote to Image again for information on 26 December 1924, this time asking for details about Herbert P. Horne for use in "my Confessions" (Princeton, Box 34). This seems to have led to a scathing sketch of Horne, "A Study in Morbidity: Herbert Horne," which was not published until it appeared in Professor Beckson's *Memoirs*.[16]

Symons's single most revealing letter about the "Confessions" project is one he wrote to John Quinn on 12 June 1923:

> For years I have been writing my *Confessions* besides those that have been printed; and I have finished the dramatic and tragic account of my misadventures in Italy at the end of 1908. I have continued this with a minute relation of my awful sufferings in that nightmare of a place in London where I was kept for a year and a half (Quinn, Box 38).

Symons goes on to ask whether he may "bring in" Quinn, who had visited and helped Symons during his recuperation (Lhombreaud, p. 267). Since Quinn first appears in the 1930 *Confessions: A Study in Pathology* (New York: Fountain Press) near the end (p. 69), Symons must have nearly completed the manuscript by the date of the letter. As noted earlier, the account of Symons's "misadventures in Italy" appeared first in *Two Worlds Quarterly* in 1926. It appeared as part of a series which was announced at the end of the journal's first volume (1925–26) as "the

Confessions of Arthur Symons, which will be completed in the four numbers of the second year" (p. 565). There followed "The Confessions of Arthur Symons: Part One" (2: 24–34), "Confessions of Arthur Symons: Part Two: A Study in Lunatic Asylums" (2: 123–34), and "More Confessions" (2: 201–3). "Part One" has been republished in Beckson's *Memoirs*, pp. 70–74, as "[Bohemian Years in London]." It is a potpourri of recollection of a "light love" named Kate, the autobiographical origins of certain of Symons's poems, and self-characterization. "Part Two" is the account of Symons's lapse into madness and brief imprisonment in Italy. "More Confessions" contains a recollection of a visit to Count Stanislaus Eric Stenbock, author of *Studies in Death* (1894), but is more a literary estimate than autobiography. The 1930 *Confessions* presents "Part Two" followed by an account of Symons's year or so in English asylums and long appreciations of Quinn and other helpful friends.

In addition to the essays and notes that are associated with Symons's letters about his "Confessions" project, a number of other pieces, mostly in manuscript, can be linked to the project either because they use the term *confession* or because they are parts of larger pieces of works that do so. The only such piece published in Symons's lifetime seems to be "Confessions and Comments" in *Dramatis Personae* (pp. 132–58), which recalls Symons's association with George Moore in the 1890s, comments on his work, and digresses to other figures such as Zola, Verlaine, and Yeats. Among the manuscript material, two pieces have been published in Beckson's *Memoirs*. The first is a twelve-page typescript beginning, "It was through" (Princeton, Box 1), and appears in the *Memoirs*, pp. 109–14, with excisions. Its content is admirably described by Professor Beckson's title, "[Music Halls and Ballet Girls]." In the typescript Symons refers to what he is writing as "My Confessions" (p. 4). The second piece appears in the *Memoirs*, pp. 75–76, as "[An Actress in Whitechapel]" and is part of a sixteen-page typescript titled "Sensations" in the Princeton Symons Collection (Box 16).[17] The first four pages of this typescript became the *Vanity Fair* "Confessions" of March 1916. The remainder of the piece comments on Balzac and Theodore de Banville and recalls the Tortoni at Paris and four English girls—a dancer, a model, and two actresses, one of them being Rachel Kahn, who becomes Professor Beckson's "Actress in Whitechapel."[18] Symons may well have abandoned his plan to publish a single, all-encompassing book of "Confessions" because of its unwieldiness. There is little doubt, however, of the project's broad extent, of the identity of some of its specific contents, and of its importance to Symons in the 1914–1930 period.

IV

Do Symons's diverse, fragmented "Confessions" fulfill the tenets of his theory of confessional writing? If so, the "Confessions" capture moments of past experience in vivid images and present them in the Casanovan tone—the relaxed tone of "that rarest kind of autobiographer . . . who . . . wrote because he had lived" and for the pleasure of looking over "his past life, . . . liv[ing] it over again in memory." Symons's confessional pieces usually do present vivid images of past experience— Cassy, for example, the seventeen-year-old "Lady of the Ballet" tapp[ing] her umbrella on the ground furiously" in vexation at having been refused permission to leave the Alhambra early in order to join an admirer ("Notes," p. 116); Huysmans in the 1916 *Vanity Fair* "Confessions" "lean[ing] back on the sofa, rolling a cigarette between his thin, expressive fingers, looking at no one, and at nothing" (p. 39); Rachel Kahn "blush[ing] crimson under her paint" as her dressing-room conversation with Symons is interrupted by the violent entrance of her drunken mother (*Memoirs,* p. 76); and the various doors, walls, corridors, and stairways which characterize Symons's incarcerations in the 1930 *Confessions*. The tone of his diverse confessional writings, however, varies greatly from paragraph to paragraph and from piece to piece, ranging between serene Casanovan contentment and the sort of querulous self-justification he attributes to Rousseau in the Introduction to Augustine's *Confessions*: "the protesting self-consciousness which . . . drove him, in spite of himself, to set about explaining himself to other people, and to the world in general."

Because of the diverse, fragmentary, and ultimately nebulous quality of the "Confessions" project as a whole, the range of Symons's tone may be most effectively grasped in a few exemplary pieces. Some pieces such as "Notes in the Sensations of a Lady of the Ballet" and "Bohemian Chelsea" are purely Casanovan or nearly so. In "Notes," unlike most of the confessional pieces, the narrator purports to write as the events he describes are occurring. His tone is wistful regarding the lady of the ballet, Cassy, who remains his friend but Mr. Black's companion; but the narrator is amused at his own quandary and is even self-critical. After the failure of an attempted rendezvous with Cassy, for example, he describes himself walking from the Alhambra to the Embankment and looking into the Thames, "seeing no charm in it, . . . my frail hopes so rudely dashed to the ground. . . . [T]he disappointment has upset me. . . . How absurd, how childish!" (p. 119). And, at the end of the piece, after a lapse and a renewal of his relationship with Cassy, he reflects, "It is March 1893; and now, am I to fall back into the sorceries of Cassy once more, I wonder?" (p. 120).

"Bohemian Chelsea" is written as a reminiscence, rather than observation, about events twenty and even thirty years previous to the time of narration. The tone contains no self-amusement and certainly no self-criticism but also none of the grating passages of self-characterization that mark Symons's Rousseauistic pieces. The tone is one of the self-importance of the enviable person who has been to exotic places, met exotic people, and done exotic things in an exotic past time. "I must confess," the narrator begins, "that I am much less acquainted with modern Bohemian Chelsea than with the actual Bohemia," for he has been to the actual Bohemia (to Casanova's Dux) "twice." He can, and does, speculate on how it would have seemed to Shakespeare and can recall that, "the genius of Wagner having been revealed to me in Bayreuth, the sensation I had in Prague caused by a sunset like a fiery orange, breaking through barred clouds, was the equivalent of the vision of the gate of the Venusberg" (p. 196). The tone of Symons's recollection of London's Bohemia is conveyed by a similar fabric of personal and place names, allusions to art and literature, and vivid visual imagery. Three hundred words or so on a "Fancy Dress Ball the Conders gave . . . in 1904," for example, mention "Augustus John . . . dressed like a *débardeur* of Gavarni"; Charles Conder, "'ce déraciné, toujours amoureux, bohême',," wearing "the costume of a dandy of 1830, that of Balzac's Eugene de Rastignac," with a color scheme that reminded Symons of "one of Whistler's nocturnes"; and four other elaborately described personages of the era. If the tone of "Bohemian Chelsea" is in fact not quite the same as Casanova's in his *Memoirs*, the chief difference is not the presence of proper names or vivid images in Symons's text but its lack of action. The young Casanova about whom the older Casanova writes is always up and doing—travelling, making love, hoaxing someone, or escaping from prison, for example. Symons's narrator has simply been in certain places, seen certain people, and read a multitude of books.

When an unmistakably Rousseauistic tone enters Symons's work, it often results from an interruption of the flow of recollection by a declarative sentence, or even several paragraphs, of self-characterization. The result is an odd mixture of tones in the essay as a whole. An instance of such an essay is the 1916 "Confessions: A Few Thoughts, Portraits and Memories." The piece begins with an apparently objective estimate of Remy de Gourmont and an equally objective description of J. K. Huysmans, but, between this and an objective final paragraph on the poet, Stuart Merrill, the piece abruptly becomes a declaration and demonstration that Symons himself has been a solitary, cruel sensationalist. The preparation for this shift is Symons's perception of De Gourmont as a person of "intellectual curiosity . . . versatility . . . [and] sensitiveness"

whose novels "are studies in . . . fevers of the flesh," and especially
Symons's perception of Huysmans, who is recalled sitting aloofly "at the
house of the bizarre Madame X," as a cutting, contemptuous critic of
"human imbecility." Upon that characterization Symons follows with the
comment, "Always, if I can conceive myself under this image, I have lived
as a solitary in the midst of the world," and he claims for himself a "spirit
of revenge and revolt; . . . an innate sense of cruelty"—for example, "to
many women" (p. 39)—and an allegiance to Pater's "wise precept" of
"burn[ing] always with this hard gem-like flame" (p. 130).

To illustrate his practice of Pater's precept, Symons narrates a vivid,
brief, and abortive encounter with a woman at night on the beach at
Dieppe, and, as if to establish his cruelty, he recalls having someone
pointed out to him in Italy who supposedly possessed the evil eye. Symons
comments, "[A]nd some have supposed that I have a touch of the
Jettatore"—that is, of the evil eye (p. 130). The essay strays from the evil
eye to "Symbolism" in general and symbolism in a public funeral mass
Symons observed in Rome, but he returns to the Paterian theme by
comparing the opportunities for sensation in Rome, Paris, and London
and declaring, "I claim only an equal liberty for rendering every mood of
. . . the beauty and the strangeness and curiosity of the visible world"
(p. 130).[19] In the somewhat wandering central section of the essay, then,
autobiography has become a self-defensive argument.

The same mixture of reminiscence and self-defensive argument is
strikingly present in the *Two Worlds* "Confessions . . .: Part One," which
appears as "[Bohemian Years in London]" in Beckson's *Memoirs,* but
Symons's best-known and, by far, longest autobiographical work, the
1930 *Confessions,* also has a mixed tone. This *Confessions* is unique among
the various other confessional pieces because it comments on his childhood feelings of mortality and sexual guilt, and because one element of the
book's tone seems to reveal the persistence of these feelings in Symons at
the time he wrote it. The 1930 *Confessions* also shows the same frankness,
self-criticism, self-amusement, and intense self-promotion evident in the
shorter pieces. The frankness, criticism, and amusement may be called
Casanovan, but the term must be limited simply to frankness with regard
to much of *Confessions'* eighty-eight pages and twenty-three thousand
words. Not even the "rarest kind of autobiographer" could be expected to
describe his mental collapse and confinement solely "for the pleasure of
writing" if *pleasure* means "merriment." Casanova himself describes his
incarceration by the Venetian Inquisition in "A Venetian Prison" and
"Escape from the Leads" with some bitterness against the injustice and
discomforts he suffered. He is also, however, factual. In the 1930 *Confessions* Symons's tone is produced mainly by the interplay of factuality and

three other elements: self-characterizing declarations, allusions to his literary predecessors and especially to the mental collapse of Gérard de Nerval (1808–1855), and recurrent prison imagery reminiscent of the dark terrors and cruelties in Gothic fiction.

While Symons's self-characterizing declarations always produce a Rousseauistic effect, the effects of the allusions to Gérard and the effects of the prison imagery depend upon their contexts. Through allusions to Gérard at the beginning of the 1930 *Confessions*, Symons seems to claim a stature for himself equal to Gérard's as a tormented but visionary lunatic. By the end, however, Symons's Casanovan amusement at, and criticism of, the literary products of his madness turn the analogy into an objective measure of his inferiority to Gérard. Conversely, early in *Confessions* Symons seems to be an objective reporter when he says that certain buildings in Italy seemed like frightening prisons to him, as he was collapsing into madness. When he uses exaggerated prison imagery to denounce the conditions of his arrest and confinements, however, he as narrator seems under the grip of the same fears still.

The result of the interplay between factuality and other tonal elements is a narrative that opens with Rousseauistic self-characterization and becomes relatively Casanovan regarding Symons's collapse into madness, then intensely Rousseauistic with regard to his arrest in Italy, then Casanovan, even amused, regarding a series of pleasant confinements there and in England, again intensely denunciatory regarding his final place of confinement, in London, and finally, regarding his survival while in this asylum, amused and yet also assertive of the unusual, nervous, even cruel strength of character he feels enabled him to survive—the same sort of character he asserts in outspoken passages of the shorter confessional pieces. The whole tonal effect suggests that Symons's *Confessions: A Study in Pathology* is to some extent a pathological performance. Two passages may serve to exemplify his method and the particular Casanovan and Rousseauistic tones which, in their mixture, create the tonal effect of the 1930 *Confessions* as a whole: the self-characterization with which Symons begins and, second, his account, after denouncing the prisonlike conditions of the asylum in London, of "how [he] contrived . . . to exist" (p. 43) there until his release. The tone in the first passage is Rousseauistic and in the second, mixed.

The Rousseauistic self-characterization with which Symons begins *Confessions* is effected chiefly by references to Gérard, but also by a reference to Paul Verlaine. Symons's first allusion to Gérard is undoubtedly the book's subtitle, *A Study in Pathology*, which in 1930 replaced the forthright and unflattering "A Study in Lunatic Asylums" used in the *Two Worlds* version in 1926. The allusion to Gérard becomes evident when

Symons notes much later in the text of *Confessions* that he has Arvède Barine's *Nevrosés* (1898) before him as he writes. Barine's book consists of four essays, including one entitled "La Folie" on Gérard, which Symons had used as the chief source of facts for his own essay on Gérard, which appeared in the *Fortnightly Review* in 1898 and then in *The Symbolist Movement in Literature*.[20] When Symons mentions *Nevrosés* in the text of *Confessions*, he comments that Barine's essays are "studies in Pathology" (p. 50). The subtitle, then, suggests that Symons saw himself as analogous to Gérard.

Symons makes the analogy explicit in the second paragraph of his text. Having noted the difficulty of explaining the origin of one's own madness, he comments that "many writers have faced this dilemma" (p. 1), and he gives a two-page extract from his 1898 essay on Gérard,[21] although, like most subsequent, similar extracts, it is not enclosed in quotation marks or accompanied by any acknowledgment of the borrowing. The extract describes Gérard as a writer who has experienced what he called a "'descent into [the] Hell'" of madness and concludes that "madness in him had lit, as if by lightning, the hidden links of distant and diverging things" (pp. 2–3). The implication is, of course, that Symons, too, has risen to genius through madness. The comparison is picked up a few pages later as Symons narrates his departure from England for Italy and implies that, once there, he would "dr[i]nk of the cup of dreams . . . Gérard de Nerval drank" (p. 10),[22] and the comparison is recalled again as Symons relates that in Ferrara, just before he wandered from the city and broke down completely, he may have, "with Gérard de Nerval," indulged in insane fantasies (pp. 16–17).

After casting himself in the mold of Gérard in the second paragraph of *Confessions*, Symons expands the self-characterization with an extract from his *Symbolist Movement* essay on Verlaine. This extract describes Verlaine as having had an intense sensitivity to "beauty" and a childlike capacity for varied, vehement moods and as having been an alien from "society" (*Confessions*, pp. 3–5)[23] The excerpt concludes with the generalization, applicable to Symons as well as to Verlaine, that although the "direct antagonism" between the "artist" and society may be avoided by compromise, "there are certain natures to which compromise is impossible." Verlaine is one (p. 5), and, after several paragraphs on Symons's childhood and on Venice, he notes that he, too, has "never understood what a compromise means" and is "generally supposed to be heartless, passionless and indifferent" (p. 9). The reference to Verlaine does not appear in the 1926 version of the narrative and may have been added in the 1930 version because, unlike the earlier one, the 1930 *Confessions* goes on to narrate Symons's confinement in England and to assert that the sternness of his character enabled him to survive.

Despite the seemingly undiluted vanity of Symons's opening comparisons of himself to Gérard and Verlaine, his subsequent account of "how [he] contrived . . . to exist" in the London asylum is a combination of factuality and even self-deprecatory amusement regarding his madness, and self-promoting praise of his initiative and tenacity. Early in this section, for example, he explains that he survived by curiosity about a fellow inmate and by writing. Symons paints an amusing picture of the inmate, a Greek scholar who leapt in the air, thumped his feet in what he claimed was "the rhythm of the angels," and mocked Symons as "The Sensitive Plant" (pp. 44–45). Of his writing done in the asylum, Symons says some was "contemptible" and "quite impossible" (pp. 46, 47). At the end of this self-deprecating estimate, though, he concludes, "Yet, had I not been certain of my own self, . . . I might have withered away," and the sentiment expands into a two-hundred-word celebration of his "strength of will . . . nervous strength . . . almost inflexible belief in [him]self," fidelity to truth, cruel temperament, ungratefulness, and character as "an aristocrat of Letters" (pp. 47–48).

Although the 1930 *Confessions* advances from an initial Rousseauistic self-promotion to a concluding Casanovan factuality and self-judgment, the general tone of the book is Rousseauistic. The work is colored by the intensity of Symons's insistence that if, after all, he has not been a lunatic genius as Gérard was, he has the uncompromising, even cruel strength of nerves and will of a Verlaine. In the 1930 *Confessions*, as in the shorter confessional pieces of the preceding fifteen years, vivid images preserve the past, but Casanovan acceptance and pleasure are tainted and disturbed by a "protesting self-consciousness" such as Symons attributed to Rousseau.

V

To a biographer of Symons, the Rousseauistic petulance that disrupts his Casanovan and Symbolist intent must recall the familiar figure of Symons as an anachronistic Aesthete haunting the Café Royal in London in the years between the two world wars. His principal biographer, Roger Lhombreaud, comments about the Symons of that period, "There must certainly have been something pathetic about him . . . as he tried to grasp anew the atmosphere of former days, days abolished by the cynicism and commercialism of the decades before and after the 1914 war."[24] His mental collapse, of course, made him especially pitiable and, in retrospect, makes him especially poignant. He was, however, responding to a dilemma which seems to have confronted many autobiographers at the end of the nineteenth and the beginning of the twentieth centuries with special force. In the essay, "Time and Autobiography," Burton Pike argues that modern autobiography has been shaped by the secular orientation of the Renaissance, by the "Newtonian idea of time as a succession of equal, mechanical, discrete units," and by a "post-Renaissance emphasis on the primacy and uniqueness of the individual." Because of these three factors, Pike says, "personal death" comes to mean "permanent loss of identity" and becomes a "much more emphatic event than it was in God-oriented times." "Writers," he continues, "who are especially obsessed with the linear brevity of their own lives turn to autobiography as a means of . . . affirming their identity."[25] For Rousseau, for example, "troubled by the . . . ticking of the clock to which his individuality is chained," autobiography becomes a "compulsive necessity" (p. 329). In the nineteenth century, according to Pike, the notion of "History" could provide a "context within which the individual, secular life would retain significance," but "as the twentieth century began, belief in History as the sustaining external principle collapsed"—for example, in the work of Picasso, T. E. Hulme, and Gertrude Stein (pp. 321, 332).

Simultaneous with the collapse of "History" was a radical questioning of the notion of a consistent, unitary self. In *Design and Truth in Autobiography*, Roy Pascal shows the questioning beginning early in the nineteenth century. While Goethe, Rousseau, and Wordsworth, he says, assumed a self and a destiny, "in Stendhal we already see . . . 'What am I?' instead of 'What I am!'"[26] If it is a characteristic of autobiography as a genre to describe the evolution of an inner self, Pascal declares, modern autobiography fails through "self-distrust" which he attributes to "a malaise . . . due to the nature of modern living" (pp. 160–61). From an Existential or perhaps Deconstructionist viewpoint which postdates Pascal's generally Goethean outlook, W. C. Spengemann argues that "ideological upheavals of the nineteenth century" which he does not specify[27] led to a notion of the self as what Wallace Stevens called a "'supreme fiction'" (p. 169)—a poetic creation "continually reshaped by [one's own] efforts to explain, discover, or express it" (p. 167). The genre of autobiography, then, seems to have been doubly in a state of transition at the turn of the twentieth century, confronted on one side by the unmitigated mortality of Newtonian time and on another by the dissolution of the self.

Symons's response to the dual dilemma of maintaining an identity in the face of Newtonian time and the disappearance of personal teleology was, as we have seen, to conceive of identity as the Paterian "hard, gemlike flame" of response to incoming stimuli in the flux of material experience. Words written on a page, symbolic images, become the proof and definition of this identity, and through them one triumphs over Newtonian time even though he may not be able to pierce through temporal appearances to some Carlylean or Plotinian Infinite. However, the Paterian concept of identity poses the challenge of intensity and discrimination. "How," Pater asks in his famous Conclusion, "may we see . . . all that is to be seen . . . by the finest senses? How shall we . . . be present always at the focus where the greatest number of vital forces unite in their purest energy?"[28] The Rousseauistic strain in Symons's autobiography suggests that he was haunted by this challenge and his sense of having failed to meet it. His sense of failure is not simply a personal aberration but a legacy of what he called the Decadent Movement in Literature or what is loosely called Aestheticism.

11

Richard Le Gallienne and the Romanticism of the 1890s

Wendell Harris

We were the last romantics—chose for theme
Traditional sanctity and loveliness;
Whatever's written in what poets name
The book of the people; whatever most can bless
The mind of man or elevate a rhyme;
But all is changed, that high horse riderless,
Though mounted in that saddle Homer rode
Where the swan drifts upon a darkening flood.
—From W. B. Yeats, "Coole Park and Ballylee, 1931"

All heroes, and all lovers, that came to die
Make pity's eyes with grief immortal shine;
Yea! still my cheeks are wet
For little Juliet,
And many a broken-hearted lover's tale,
Told by the nightingale.
Nor have I shame to strive the ancient way,
With rhyme that runs to meet its sister rhyme,
One in some metre that hath learned from time
The heart's own chime.
These ways are not more old
Than the unmeditated modern lay
And all those little heresies of song
Already old when Homer still was young.
—From Richard Le Gallienne, "The Eternal Way"

Yeats's five words, "We were the last romantics," have proved influential in literary history. The idea of a kind of terminal romanticism seemed to help explain a decade in which high aspiration, paradoxical wit, and new attitudes toward the social fabric coalesced with melancholy and despair. Shelley's iconoclasm, Keats's devotion to beauty, and Byron's contempt for the ordinary virtues could be seen as forces transmitted somehow down through the century until finally smashed on the rocks of empiricism, industrialism, and philistinism, triumphant. The early deaths of the romantic poets, through drowning, disease, and martyrdom in a revolutionary cause, offered both dramatic analogues and equally dramatic contrasts to Dowson and Lionel Johnson's fatal love of drink, Beardsley's tuberculosis, and Crackanthorpe's suicide.

The famous lines of "Coole Park and Ballylee" were in a sense explicated by Yeats's autobiographies which helped transmute a generation of writers once regarded simply as outrageous and immoral into that tragic generation in which, Yeats writes, "so many of the greatest talents were to live such passionate lives and die such tragic deaths." Or again, "I had now met all those who were to make the 'nineties of the last century tragic in the history of literature," and yet again, the "Rhymers had begun to break up in tragedy, though we did not know that until the play had finished." [1]

Though at the end of the century the term "romanticism" carried as always many meanings, a central sense was the pursuit of something better or rarer than the earth can provide. However, such a pursuit may present itself quite variously: tragically, comically, absurdly, admirably. Perhaps the 1890s were little more romantic than any other decade, but they were and have continued to be thought so, and if we wish to correct a bit for the luridness and perversity still all too automatically associated with the *fin de siècle,* a look at a figure of the 1890s who found the pursuit of the ideal less tinctured with tragedy is useful. Let us then put the 1890s of Richard Le Gallienne alongside the decade Yeats has created for us.

At first sight we may seem simply to have further vindicated Yeats's melancholy assessment. Though Le Gallienne lived on for years into the twentieth century, long after the worldview and aesthetic goals of the decade had ceased to be intelligible to the majority of readers, he continued to write poetry and prose indistinguishable from that which had delighted a coterie the members of which were dead or dispersed. Scarcely a reviewer of Le Gallienne's early poems failed to speculate with confidence on his promise, few reviewers of his middle poetry failed to comment on the slowness of his literary development, and practically no one bothered to notice his later volumes. Sad enough perhaps, but Le Gallienne's own brand of romanticism engendered an enduring delight in poetry and life despite the brevity of his success. To the end he relished the attitude toward experience expressed in "all those little heresies of song / Already old when Homer was still young."

"Richard Le Gallienne was the first real poet I had ever laid eyes upon in the flesh and it seemed to my rapt senses that this frock-coated young god, with the classic profile and the dark curls curving from the impeccable silk 'tile' that surmounted them as curve the acanthus leaves of a Corinthian capital, could be none other than Anacreon's self in modern shape."[2] Such passages as this in which Oliver Herford is recalling his impression of "the most popular literary idol of the hour" serve as reminders of the position Le Gallienne occupied in literary London in the early 1890s. Nor was it only through his appearance that Le Gallienne laid claim on both sides of the Atlantic to being a poet and man of letters: the Literary Editor of the *Philadelphia Press* described Le Gallienne as "A Poet who can write prose of rare distinction, an epigrammist who can flash wit and wisdom in a bewildering profusion of pregnant phrases, a psychologist who can present objectively his keen, penetrating analysis of human motives and character, a painter who can project his portraits in relief against a happy background of hazy chiaroscuro."[3] Maurice Baring recalls in *The Puppet Show of Memory* that of the poems in the two collections published by the Rhymers' Club, Le Gallienne's "What of the Darkness?" attracted most attention and, according to one critic, "wiped out Tennyson's lyrics."[4] There is a ludicrousness not only in the exaggeration of such descriptions, but in the pose which encouraged them; at the same time there is an attractiveness in the choice of a pose in which grace, chivalry, and cheerful acceptance of the good things of the world displace melancholy, weariness, and perverse paradox.

Le Gallienne's life and literary career has been unstintingly chronicled in Whittington-Egan and Smerdon's *The Quest of the Golden Boy*.[5] He was born on 20 January 1866, the eldest child in the family of John Gallienne, the pious and respected manager of a Liverpool brewery. After a few years in a dame school Richard was enrolled in Liverpool College in 1875, by which time he was already developing vague literary ambitions. When he left the college in 1881 at the age of fifteen, he was apprenticed to a firm of chartered accountants, but soon affecting flowing locks, an Inverness Cape, and the "Le" preceding his name, he devoted his admiration to Oscar Wilde and his energies to poetry. His first volume of poetry, *My Ladies' Sonnets,* was produced by a friendly printer in 1887, though his emancipation from accounting had to wait until 1889, the year in which his second book, *Volumes in Folio,* had the fortune to be the first of the many volumes of poetry to flow from the Bodley Head Press. The appearance of a book-length study of George Meredith in 1890 helped establish his critical credentials.

With his appointment in 1891 as the reviewer and author of the "Logroller" column for the *Star*, Le Gallienne's career as a writer seemed promisingly launched. He married his sweetheart, Mildred Lee, set up a household in London, and participated in the Rhymers' Club. The year 1892 saw the appearance of *English Poems,* a volume which received a number of unfavorable reviews, including one by G. B. Shaw, but Le Gallienne's reputation, aided by several widely publicized literary controversies and some success as a lecturer, was growing. His influence was also growing, for he had become reader for the Bodley Head.

And then in May 1894, Mildred died, leaving one child, Hesper, and a shattered idyll. After a dark and bitter period, his marriage to Julie Norregard and the publication of the first English edition of *The Quest of the Golden Girl*, both occurring on 12 February 1897, seemed to herald a bright new era. But the marriage was under a strain almost from the beginning, a situation which the mounting debts incurred by Le Gallienne's irresponsible handling of money inevitably made worse. His second daughter, Eva, one day to become famous as an actress, was born in 1899.

His financial state drove him to try his fortunes in the United States as lecturer and journalist several times during the next few years, and to leave England permanently in the fall of 1903 after a final separation from Julie, who officially divorced him in 1911. Though the American climate greatly helped the asthmatic condition from which he suffered all his life, the American literary economy was less kind. For years he was harried by debts, though after his marriage to Irma Hinton Perry in 1911, he seems to have achieved not only domestic stability but a precarious financial solvency. For fifteen years he lived in Connecticut and then in Woodstock, New York, writing novels, poetry, essays, and ephemeral pieces for newspapers and magazines, his best-known work from this time being *The Romantic '90s*, published in 1925.

In 1927, Le Gallienne moved to France, where he was able to live parts of each year in Paris and Menton, supporting himself largely by a column, "From a Paris Garret," written for the *New York Sun*. The last of his some fifty books, *From a Paris Scrapbook,* was published in 1938. After the fall of France in 1940, the Le Galliennes were allowed to make their way to Monte Carlo where they lived a hand-to-mouth existence, which Le Gallienne refused to improve at the price of collaborating with the Nazis. They returned at the end of the war to Menton, where he died on 15 September 1947, at the age of eighty-one. Having maintained his faith in the golden girl, and the golden moments of his life, to the end, he has his own claim to be the last romantic.

One comes away from reading Le Gallienne's biography with an overwhelming impression of a long struggle, first for fame and success as a writer and later simply for a livelihood. Le Gallienne was ranked for ten years among the acknowledged minor writers of whom everyone continually expects something better, and endured forty-seven years among those of whom less is expected and who are less remembered. But this impression deserves the sort of qualification produced by reading the brief summary of his life with which H. M. Hyde prefaces the 1951 reissue of *The Romantic '90s*. "Richard Le Gallienne," writes Hyde, "was to the 'nineties what Rupert Brooke was to the succeeding generation of poetry readers. The only difference was that he did not die young, but emigrated to America at the height of his success and lived on to a charming and dignified old age in France."[6] Hyde's account drastically reshapes his life as one suspects Le Gallienne wished it to be recalled, but also, one would like to believe, as Le Gallienne, with his incorrigibly idealistic nature, actually looked back on it in his later years.

Certainly Le Gallienne's 1926 account of the yellow decade, which for him had been golden, is fretted with no hint of bitterness or regret. *The Romantic '90s* is indeed a curious book, devoted much more to Le Gallienne's delight in meeting with the greatest writers of an earlier generation than to his experience with the members of his own well-published coterie. The dominant note of the volume is indeed summed up in the lines from Browning which serve as an epigraph:

> Ah! did you once see Shelley plain,
>   And did he stop and speak to you,
> And did you speak to him again?
>   How strange it seems and new!

Le Gallienne's delight in literature as a treasure horde of precious volumes may have left little room for the development of his own personality as a writer, but it gave perspective on his own generation. He could delight in the spectacle without taking personalities or movements too seriously. He thus recalls the literary events of the nineties as being like "booths at a fair, each with its vociferous 'barker'"—Henley, Yeats, Shaw, Whistler—"inviting us in to the only show on earth."[7] The fair is delightful to attend, but more importantly it is the threshold of the future:

> *Fin de siècle* was the label, with something of a stigma, which was used to cover them all, but, as one looks back, it is plain that here was not so much the ending of a century as the beginning of a new one. Those last ten years of the nineteenth century properly belong to the twentieth

century, and, far from being "decadent," except in certain limited manifestations, they were years of an immense and multifarious renaissance. All our present conditions, socially and artistically, our vaunted new "freedoms" of every kind—including "free verse"—not only began then, but found a more vital and authoritative expression than they have found since because of the larger, more significant personalities engaged in bringing them about.[8]

That movement forward is in fact what Le Gallienne found finally most romantic about the 1890s: "I have called the '90's 'romantic,' not merely because it was romantic to have lived in them, or because they included so many romantic figures, but because their representative writers and artists emphasized the modern determination to escape from the deadening thralldom of materialism and outworn conventions...."[9]

The current of optimism and relish for life with which Le Gallienne always spoke forbade toying with scandal or secret sins either in his own poetry or his later reminiscences. The three little poems whose amorousness caused him to print them "for private circulation only" celebrate the attractiveness of the body as straightforwardly as would a Renaissance courtier. No one reading his comments on Hubert Crackanthorpe or James Welch could find the least hint of the links between Le Gallienne's own sister, later Mrs. James Welch, and Crackanthorpe's suicide. Partly of course this is the conscientious discretion of a brother and friend, but partly it is a reflection of his own sense that personal scandals and foibles were one thing and literature another. Again for him Wilde is a memorable figure because of the qualities of his mind and personality, not the fascinations of scandal or Wilde's potential as a tragic figure.

Hyde's introduction to *The Romantic '90s* usefully emphasizes Le Gallienne's importance for the decade. In his dual role as reader for the Bodley Head and reviewer for the *Star* (a situation nicely symbolized by the two hats he wears in Beerbohm's well-known caricature), he was powerful for several years in London's literary world. As reader for the Bodley Head he accepted and championed the work of Francis Thompson, John Davidson, W. B. Yeats, and Lionel Johnson, as well as that of lesser but historically significant figures like "George Egerton."

As the "logroller" for the *Star,* his praise was unstinting for those he felt deserved it, and he was very often right about who did deserve it. One of the more interesting literary skirmishes of the period was launched by a contributor to the *Westminster Gazette* signing himself the "Philistine," who, in the midst of attacking "sex-mania" in contemporary literature, took Le Gallienne to task for lack of discrimination in his praises of contemporary poets.[10] The "Philistine" especially objected to Le Gallienne's discovery in 1894 of seven new major poets: William Watson, John Davidson, Norman Gale, Arthur Symons, Francis Thompson, W. B.

Yeats, and Rudyard Kipling. Looking back, however, and allowing Le Gallienne some latitude in the use of the phrase "major poet," the seven are not a bad choice upon which to have placed one's bets. Moreover, Le Gallienne's book on Meredith appeared when Meredith's novels were still not widely appreciated and his poetry ignored; his book on Kipling is on the whole a just and balanced evaluation of Kipling's work to that time, and the literary judgments reprinted in *Retrospective Reviews* have been little invalidated by the passage of years. Though never a scholar, Le Gallienne was a wide and discriminating reader. He obviously not only enjoyed playing a part in the literary scene, but understood and rather accurately judged it.

Unfortunately his discrimination and taste too often retired when he sat down to work at his own poetry and imaginative prose. He once described Arthur Symons as "a critic who fondly dreams he is a poet"[11]; the judgment is one he might well have made of himself. The intriguing question about Le Gallienne's career is of course why he never fulfilled his promise as a poet. The authors of *The Quest of the Golden Boy* indicate that their biography is an attempt to answer that question, but in this case biographical detail seems merely to explain personal and financial problems, not literary weakness. Le Gallienne himself seems to have felt, at least at times, that it was the pressure of having to write so much intended merely to earn money that kept him from producing first-rate work. A glance at both the volume and diversity of his published work shows how prodigally he squandered his creative energies. Poems, short stories, novels, essays, reviews, and editing tasks follow one another without pattern, the product of a seemingly directionless pen. Much of this is obviously the result of a publisher's commission rather than the writer's inspiration. But, though Le Gallienne's talents were almost certainly blunted by the necessity of earning his living by hackwork, the hackwork would hardly have been necessary had Le Gallienne's career fulfilled its early promise.

Nor is it enough to say, as does Ellen Moers in a brief review of *The Quest of the Golden Boy*,[12] that Le Gallienne simply had insufficient talent as a writer; the really interesting question is the nature of the specific deficiency in Le Gallienne's equipment as a poet which kept him from ever attaining the success he wished, while allowing him to appear to good judges to be always on the verge of breaking through his limitations. Beside that question lies of course a complementary one—what was the nature of the decade in which Le Gallienne's star could glitter so brightly?

The answer to both is found in the way Le Gallienne's dreamy and bookish romanticism and an idealizing romantic current, which runs through the whole period alongside the more advertised romantic melancholy so intertwined with decadence, reinforced one another. The tired label "decadence" has after all been used to subsume a range of attitudes toward life and literature which are related to each other as much by having had a simultaneous prominence as in any more vital manner. Le Gallienne himself used the term in a variety of ways, capitalizing on its popular interpretation as a perverse hankering after strange sins in the poem "A Decadent to His Soul," while formally defining it more limitedly as "any point of view, seriously taken, which ignores the complete view,"[13] and, when he came to write *The Romantic '90s*, pretty much dismissing the word as meaningless. The qualities which were cited at the time as evidence of "decadent" tendencies were many and diverse—a strong concern for style and form, a revolt against conventional standards, a philosophy of either hedonism or pessimism, a realistic exploration of the unsavory aspects of life, a brooding melancholy—all were "decadent." Le Gallienne's work was a part of the strong current of sentimentally idealistic romanticism of the 1890s, the literary current which he himself saw most clearly when looking back. The last sentence of his significantly titled *The Romantic '90s* describes the "motive philosophy" of the 1890s as "the will to romance." Though the "Ballade of the Poet and the Moon"[14] is one of Le Gallienne's later poems, it represents his unchanging poetic philosophy:

> The day has gone of lovely things,
>   According to the modern bard;
> Of dreariness and dross he sings,
>   And hymns the homely and the hard,
>   The sweat-shop and the engine yard;
> Of these he makes his doleful tune,
>   And plenteous slang doth interlard—
> I still prefer to sing the moon.

A strong love of the romantic poets characterized many of the members of Le Gallienne's coterie, he himself owing an especial debt to Keats. Thus the best passages of "Paolo and Francesca" have something of the music of "The Eve of St. Agnes," his response to older literature as presented in his poems on the love of books expresses the rapture of one who stands silent on a peak, and we are not surprised to come upon a reference to Keats as "He who nearest stood / To Beauty's throne." The result of this admiration for the romantics was the romantically idealized way of looking at the world and the protests against life's failure to measure up to the ideal which make up so much of the literature of the 1890s. That which differentiates Le Gallienne from many of those around him is that he seems to have determined not to lament man's exile from paradise, but to create his own paradise, to live the idyll. For this reason it is wide of the mark to describe Le Gallienne merely as a *poseur*—he was indeed playing a role, but his object was more to live up to the ideal he had chosen than to deceive others. This is expressed in his personal life, for instance, in his constant choice of picturesque residences which were beyond his means: he refused to believe that habitations clearly intended to harbor a poet should not be available to him.

Le Gallienne's way of continuing to find truth and beauty amid an ugly and fallen world was to mix all experience with a romantic distillation from his wide but romantically oriented reading. Thus in "A Bookman's Complaint to His Lady" (included in *Volumes in Folio*, a collection of poems almost entirely devoted to the enchantments of books) we find literature and love related in a way which sums up the perspective from which Le Gallienne regarded both:

> Ah! would that I could make her see
> What is so clear to thee and me,
> How much our happy love-life owes
> To those poor honest folios.
> She little dreams that hidden there
> I found a glass that mirrored her,
> A magic glass which showed her me
> As my own soul's ideal *She*,
> Long ere we met and wedded eyes
> Or made a soft exchange of sighs. [15]

Here we find one explanation of the dismissal of Le Gallienne's poetry today and of his success among a consciously romanticizing readership. It is hard to define the "tension" that we sometimes say we feel in good poetry, but it would seem to include the sense that the poet's mind is actively working, reducing to order, or showing the signfiicance of the hard and unyielding material of human experience. We do not, I think, feel that very often in Le Gallienne's poetry, for his mind is rarely engaged in coming to terms with experience, but rather on the adjustment of experience to an ideal. In this regard there is significance in Yeats's remark that he himself was the only poet among the Rhymers much interested in ideas. After the long series of religious, economic, and aesthetic battles which made up the history of the greater portion of the nineteenth century, many of the younger poets of the 1890s seem to have been without the intellectual energy necessary to achieve an ordering point of view which would give due weight to the claims of both the real and the ideal.

I think such an interpretation serviceable in explaining even the technical weaknesses of Le Gallienne's poetry: he failed to recognize that beauty in verse is the result of more than the rhymed expression of a beautiful or romantic subject, that the beauty is partially produced by the verbal magic which forces words and phrases to take on richer and more complex meanings than in their ordinary use. Again, Le Gallienne's bookishness led him to choose words for their secondary, literary resonances without visualizing the actual objects to which they refer. Thus:

> Rocked ever on thy bosom's fall and rise
> I drink the deep joy of a timeless bliss.[16]

Taken literally the lines are grotesque, but Le Gallienne seems to have had his eye so firmly fixed on their figurative meaning that the literal image did not disturb him—which is another way of saying that his tendency to take the meaning of words and phrases in their ideal, figurative, "poetic" sense betrayed him at times into ludicrous errors of taste. He seems to have been unable to sense how bizarre it is, for another instance, to describe "The floating call of the cuckoo" as "Soft little globes of bosom-shaped sound."[17]

A similar failure of intellectual toughness mars Le Gallienne's essays. Just when he has captured the reader's interest by an apt phrase or unusual turn of thought, he relaxes to pursue a chance conceit, transplant a stylistic turn from a favorite author, or drown thought in sentiment. For instance, despite rather pronounced echoes of Charles Lamb, *A Christmas Meditation* begins well, lighting up some of the less-acknowledged ingredients of the Christmas season, and keeping the sentimental within bounds:

> Unless we are still numbered among those happy people for whom Christmas-trees are laden and lit, this annual prematurity of Christmas cannot but make us a little meditative amid our mirth, and if, while Santa Claus is dispensing his glittering treasures, our thoughts grow a little wistful, they will not necessarily be mournful thoughts, or on that account less seasonable in character; for Christmas is essentially a retrospective feast, and we may, with fitness, with indeed a proper piety of unforgetfulness, bring even our sad memories, as it were to cheer themselves, within the glow of its festivity. Ghosts have always been invited to Christmas parties, and whether they are seen or not, they always come; nor is any form of story so popular by the Christmas fire as the ghost-story—which, when one thinks of it, is rather odd, considering the mirthful character of the time. Yet, after all, what are our memories but ghost-stories? Ah! the beautiful ghosts that come to the Christmas fire!
>
> Christmas too is pre-eminently the Feast of the Absent, the Festival of the Far-Away, for the most prosperous ingathering of beloved faces about the Christmas fire can but include a small number of those we would fain have there; and have you ever realized that the absent are ghosts?[18]

Less than half-way through, however, the thought begins to wander uncertainly, and the essay ends in sentimental conventionalities. The same unevenness is present in the fiction; the charming and overwritten, the clever and the unintentionally ludicrous are inextricably mingled throughout his most successful romance, *The Quest of the Golden Girl*.

Although Le Gallienne was professional enough as a critic and advisor to other writers, there is indeed always something of the dilettante about his own poetry and prose. The majority of the members of the Rhymers' Club and the majority of the contributions to the *Yellow Book* and the *Savoy* were more attentive to the nuances of language, more careful to achieve consistency of style. Thoroughly in love with literature and what he conceived as the literary style, he seems not to have approached his own writing with any intensity of purpose. Perhaps the process of grappling with the technical problems of presenting a darker realism, or a more pervasive melancholy, or a more curious artificiality of vision caused other of the second-rank writers of the time—Crackanthorpe, Lionel Johnson, Symons, Beerbohm—to concentrate and refine their control. But on the other hand Le Gallienne's adolescent freshness of spirit saved him from taking the times or his contemporaries too dramatically. The brooding, at times almost incantatory, prose of Yeats's autobiographies which makes each rereading a return to a remembered pleasure, requires dilution with Le Gallienne's evocation of the delights of being a part of the London literary world of the 1890s.

And a delightful world it was for many a young man or woman, a point more often made by earlier chroniclers of the period than remembered by present readers. Holbrook Jackson, who was sixteen at the beginning of the decade, argued in what is still the best study of the decade "For myself . . . the awakening of the Nineties does not appear to be the realisation of a possibility. Life aroused curiosity. People became enthusiastic about the way it should be used." Osburt Burdett emphasizes the youthful energy of "the Beardsley period": "They were all young men, and the mood, the attitude of mind, that they represented is the mood of excess natural to youthful imagination, especially in an age where everything is made to the measure of a crowd." Again, Bernard Muddiman tells us "It was an attractive period full of the glamour of youth before it went down fighting for Art with a capital *A*, before age had chilled its blood or dulled its vision. And there came, no doubt, an immense vitality for them all, a stimulating energy to each one, from this meeting together in London." [19] Interestingly, as the diaries, letters, and essays of the time manifest, however much the young writers and artists of the 1890s strove to free themselves from social conventions and inhibitions, they looked to the writers of the first four-fifths of the century—Shelley, Keats, Tennyson, Browning, Arnold, Ruskin—with an appreciation of which Le Gallienne's nostalgia was only a heightened version.

Visions of the ideal and beautiful as they ought to be haunt many of the young writers of any decade. In the 1890s the *zeitgeist* (one may as well call a shared mood that results from the combination of an incalculable number of events and influences "the spirit of the time") paradoxically led many of the new writers of the decade to lavish their energy on an atmosphere of sentimental regret or harsh realism. Best seen in the short stories of Harland and Dowson, this mood hangs over the *Yellow Book* especially. But the slogan "art for art's sake" was partly a cry for the right to continue to imagine, create, and contemplate the beautiful amidst an increasingly ugly and disillusioned world, to

> Sing the song of Hope Eternal
> In the face of Facts Infernal.[20]

Le Gallienne's expression of this romantic idealism celebrates the beautiful and idyllic rather than lamenting their passing. "The Eternal Way," part of which I have used as an epigraph, stands as a kind of envoi to *The Junk-Man and Other Poems* of 1920. One suspects that Le Gallienne knew that as poetry it was not as good as it ought to be, but that as a philosophy—a philosophy he was far from alone in espousing in the 1890s—it had served him well enough. It offers an alternative vision to

> Cast a cold eye
> On life, on death,
> Horseman, pass by!

Even in his old age Le Gallienne would have preferred to have his name remembered in association with something a good deal jollier than "The Eternal Way." Perhaps with this little lyric:

> From tavern to tavern
>   Youth passes along
> With an armful of girl
>   And a heart full of song.
>
> From flower to flower
>   The butterfly sips
> O passionate limbs
>   And importunate lips!
>
> From candle to candle
>   The moth loves to fly,
> O sweet, sweet, to burn!
>   And still sweeter to die![21]

12

Bennett's Entertainments

Charles Burkhart

I n Arnold Bennett's huge canon there are plays and poems,
detective stories and movie scenarios, a bit of everything; and
there are one or two great austere novels like *The Old Wives' Tale* and
Riceyman Steps. It seems he would try his capable hand at anything, and his
fecundity, which could run thin, is the opposite of our generation's
literature of silence, whose priest is Beckett, whose sparsities are loaded
with ore. Bennett could write two novels, poles apart in intention and
tone, at the same time: during the composition of *The Old Wives' Tale* he
produced his comic novel *Buried Alive*, and *Clayhanger* was written simultaneously with another entertainment, *The Card.*

"Entertainment" is one of the terms he never used, I believe, for
novels like *Buried Alive* and *The Card,* which form a distinct genre among
his works. Instead he called such novels "fantasias," beginning with the
first of them, *The Grand Babylon Hotel* of 1902, when in a letter to his
agent, J. B. Pinker, he wrote of *The Grand Babylon Hotel* as "one of the first
stories which the author composed especially for serial publication, and
which he has classified as 'fantasias' to distinguish them equally from his
realistic novels and from his satiric novels." [1] "About thirty years ago," he
wrote in his journal, "I was taken to the Savoy Hotel for tea, came out,
went home, and wrote *The Grand Babylon Hotel* in three weeks of evening

work. *The Grand Babylon Hotel* was a mere lark."[2] The subtitle of *The Strange Vanguard*[3] was *A Fantasia*. *A Great Man* was described in a letter to Wells, like *The Grand Babylon Hotel,* as a "lark,"[4] and bore the subtitle *A Frolic*. The eight novels which I am calling "entertainments" Bennett called "humorous" or "light,"[5] but would go so far as to deprecate them as "unserious" or *"un-*literature."[6] In her splendid biography of Bennett, Margaret Drabble distinguishes, as Bennett did, between the "serious" books and the entertainments, and likes to call the latter "extravaganzas."[7] William Lyon Phelps had a sharp phrase for *Hugo* and other early fictions of its type: "light hammock and steamer books."[8] Whatever the name one decides on, whether entertainment, lark, extravaganza, or fantasia, I would include these eight works: *The Grand Babylon Hotel* (1902); *A Great Man* (1904); *Hugo* (1906); *Buried Alive* (1908); *The Card* (1911); *The Regent* (1913); *Mr. Prohack* (1922); and *The Strange Vanguard* (1927).

This list is probably arbitrary, yet certain guidelines have prevailed. I have ruled out short stories because there are so few good ones; and also plays, because, in my opinion, there are no good ones at all, not even *Milestones,* Bennett's great success of 1911, which ran for several years, and which is still revived. I have ruled out whodunits like *Teresa of Watling Street* and the more glib of the potboilers like *The Gates of Wrath.* But I have included two works from the 1920s (*Mr. Prohack* and *The Strange Vanguard*), even though the quality of Bennett's output deteriorated in his later career, in order to round out the picture, to trace this persistent strain to the end, and to substantiate the psychological study they offer of Bennett as man and artist.

None of the eight is, in any case, without merits of its own, even the last two just mentioned. The eight are certainly superior to some of the "serious" novels, novels Bennett believed in, like *The Pretty Lady,* the life of a French prostitute in the West End, of which Walter Allen has written that it is "nothing else but a triumphant exercise in vulgarity . . . Bennett at his least attractive and most flashy . . ."[9] But they also have definite aspects in common.

First of all, these novels are intended to be funny. Generally they succeed. *The Card* is probably the most amusing of all; Bennett included it among his four best novels, and here for once he was an excellent judge of his own work. Even *The Strange Vanguard* has moments of inspired nonsense. There is of course comedy in the grand ironies of *The Old Wives' Tale* or the bitter grotesqueries of *Riceyman Steps,* but it is not the kind of comedy at which one laughs.

The plots of the entertainments are both sensational and highly episodic, just the opposite of the long grave accumulations of event in *The Old Wives' Tale.* Antinaturalistic, they begin with a wild surmise—an extravagant donnée, such as Mr. Theodore Racksole's sudden purchase of the Grand Babylon Hotel, or Hugo's deciding to build the world's best department store, or the great artist Priam Farll assuming the identity of his dead valet—and from there they leap forward in a skittish, disconnected manner. It is quite impossible to keep the plot of *Hugo* straight; it is all revenge, robberies, and false funerals. The plots at their best are serenely nonsensical and abrupt; at their worst, silly, insipid, and contrived. There is always an aura of unreality. What helps to peg them down, among the three traditional staples of the novel, love and money and class, is money. They all concern money most of the time. In these wild tales the hero is basically an adventurer, which does not mean that he is not, and in fact seems to imply that he is, a millionaire. James Hall has a good name for the type: "the commercial picaresque hero"; and he also speaks of the "millionaire's quest" as an archetypal pattern in these and other Bennett novels.[10] All the heroes have a droll sense of fun and a very secure sense of their own identity, neither of which Edwin Clayhanger, for an example from the serious novels, possesses. As for love and class, love is Noël Cowardish and romantic; class is either forgotten or caricatured. All the architecture of fiction is, so to speak, exposed, in the interest of parody, to the extent that one wonders if the term "novel" is adequate, let alone useful, to describe these goings-on. However, one remembers that George Moore, after decades of cogitation, could come up with a definition of the novel no more exact than "an extended prose fiction"—which covers, if not very comfortably, Bennett's entertainments. And it should be added that the novels are not altogether light. There are serious ideas embedded, most notably, perhaps, in *Buried Alive,* which is Bennett's most careful study of the nature of the artist, just as *A Great Man* is his most comic investigation of the subject.

Bennett always had a penchant for odd names, like "Mr. Shushions" in *Clayhanger,* for example. But the gulf fixed between the entertainments and his other novels can be very well indicated by some of the characters in *Mr. Prohack,* the next to the last of the eight: Mr. Asprey Chown, Mr. "Ozzie" Morfey, Mr. Crewd (a detective), and Mr. Softly Bishop (who is not ecclesiastical). We are a long way from realism.

Although they have these features in common, the eight entertainments have their differences from one another as well as from Bennett's other work. How unlike *The Grand Babylon Hotel* is Bennett's last serious effort, *Imperial Palace,* which is a much-labored monument to his fascination with the complexity of modern institutions like hotels and department stores and theaters. *The Grand Babylon Hotel* was the most successful of his early novels before *The Old Wives' Tale;* it had a "sensational success."[11] When the American millionaire, Mr. Theodore Racksole, buys the Grand Babylon because the chef refuses to serve his daughter Nella with the beefsteak and bottle of Bass she wants for her dinner, a series of impetuous and improbable events is inaugurated which ends with the death of the villainous Jules, the head waiter, and the marriage of the spirited Nella to Prince Eugen of Posen, wherever that is. At the same time the story is airy and highspirited, it also shows Bennett's inveterate command of social and economic data.

The Grand Babylon Hotel is cheerfully without a theme; the subsequent entertainment, A Great Man, had a more serious concern than Bennett at first quite realized. He called it "purely humorous," and remarked, "Personally I don't see how anyone can read the book without laughing."[12] It would be hard to. The hero, Henry Shakspere Knight, is ludicrously without literary talent, but ends up phenomenally successful as novelist and playwright; he is rich, marries the perfect woman, fathers twins. Margaret Drabble says of Shakspere Knight (which is his name as novelist laureate), "The charm of the hero is that, unlike Bennett, he is a complete innocent, not financially (for he is shrewd, quite the card in his dealings) but artistically, and has no notion that his clearly dreadful novels are not the height of literary talent."[13] Henry has a cousin Tom who is just as raffish as he is stuffily respectable, and who is as genuinely gifted as Henry is amateur. But nothing ruffles Henry's complacency, not when Tom is made a Chevalier of the Legion of Honor nor when his wife Geraldine lets slip, "Well, of course . . . everybody knows that Tom is a genius."[14] The very vivid character of the amoral Tom makes one wonder if Shaw had read this clever and lively novel before he wrote The Doctor's Dilemma, which was produced two years later, in 1906, and is also a study of the artistic temperament.

In that year Bennett wrote Hugo, surely the most fantastic of all his tales. Hugo is the creator of a paragon of department stores, somewhat resembling Harrod's, which he names after himself and governs with a suave, benevolent despotism. The murder mystery of the plot is impossibly complex; but the details of the way the store is run are, as is typical with Bennett, intriguing, the comic spirit is never long absent, and, for Bennett, the story is surprisingly sexy. "This dim book," is what Dudley Barker, one of Bennett's best critics, has called it,[15] but it is better than that. It is too odd to be dim, though it is true that there isn't an idea in it—only careful research, surrealistically conveyed.

Buried Alive (1908) returns to ideas. It is the story of a great painter with the fine name of Priam Farll who, shy by nature, abandons the public world and assumes the identity of his valet, Henry Leek (another good name), who has died—and who is buried in his place in Westminster

Abbey. He then marries a comfortable lady named Alice and leads a placid hidden life with her in Putney until the paintings she has been selling through the local tobacconist for five guineas are discovered and identified by a shrewd dealer, and a lawsuit which rocks England ensues. His true identity revealed, Priam escapes England with Alice to avoid furor and fame, and presumably lives happily ever after, painting Impressionist masterpieces which his wife regards with tolerance and some pity. It is a thoughtful piece; James Hepburn calls it "perhaps the best of Bennett's comic novels."[16] Margaret Drabble calls it "a highly successful book about art and the artist. It deploys the stock notions of what artists ought to be like and what they are really like with a good deal of skill."[17] Bennett himself seems consistently to have admired *Buried Alive* and recommended it to correspondents, as in a letter to William Dean Howells in which he admitted that he had written "unserious books" to make money, but added, "I consider *Buried Alive*, though as you say a farce, as a quite serious 'criticism of life', and I mean to continue at intervals in this vein."[18] A stage version of *Buried Alive* called *The Great Adventure* was produced in 1913 and was, next to *Milestones*, his chief hit on the stage.[19]

But *The Card*, published in 1911, has always been the most popular of the entertainments. It was first made into a film in 1922, and again, most successfully, with Alec Guinness as the card, Denry, in 1952. "One can't always be producing big books," wrote Bennett to his agent,[20] but *The Card* turned out bigger than he had expected: it was produced as a straight play, as a musical comedy, translated into many languages (including Arabic), always in print.[21] I believe that there are two clear reasons for this. In a letter to the Duchess of Sutherland, the original of the Countess of Chell in the novel, Bennett said, ". . . the whole book is written in a fiercely sarcastic vein. . . . "[22] The satire is brilliant indeed, of life in the Potteries; of Denry the Card, most humorous of entrepreneurs; of business and politics and marriage and snobbery and human nature itself. The second reason is the setting. Like any author Bennett wrote best out of his deepest self, and the Potteries of his totally observant childhood and youth had ineffaceably conditioned him. *The Card* is one of those rare comedies that lift one's spirits.

It had the sort of acclaim that demands a sequel, and Bennett produced it in *The Regent* (whose subtitle was *A Five Towns Story of Adventure in London*) in 1913. It is the further adventures of "Denry" (Edward Henry) Machin, now Alderman Machin, the hero of *The Card*. Its title comes from the theater Denry the Audacious builds just off Piccadilly Circus. Another financial coup, more satire: this time of theatrical types, especially those to be found in the more ethereal reaches of verse theatre, and of their shallowness and affectation. There is an aging star named Rose Euclid, a scenery designer named Saracen-Givington, a matinee idol, no longer young, named Sir John Pilgrim, an author/actor named Seven Sachs, a militant suffragette named Isabel Joy, and a photographer named Rentoul Smiles. Denry survives them all, even the beautiful Elsie April, secretary of the Azure Society which "leads the New Thought movement in England," and remains faithful to skeptical Burslem values and to his wife Nellie, who is another Alice of *Buried Alive*. After both financial and artistic success with the Regent ("You've saved the intellectual theatah for London, my boy!"), Denry goes home: "I've done with London. The Five Towns are good enough for me":[23] a conclusion which conveys the coziness of the story. *The Regent* is inferior to *The Card* in just the ways most sequels are inferior.

The last two entertainments reveal the fatigue and failure of Bennett's creativity in the latter part of his life. Where they should be imaginative, they are contrived; where energetic, belabored; where comic, flippant or slick. *Mr. Prohack* of 1922 begins well with sharp dialogue and the promising situation of a staid but smart civil servant inheriting a fortune. He has a fey wife and a "modern" son and daughter, in whom the youth of the 1920s are figured. None of the domestic trials, flirtations, large parties, and altercations, seem to go anywhere, and take too long to do so. Despite the fact that Charles Laughton had a great success in the play based on this novel in 1927, despite its having been made into a popular radio serial in Britain, despite Walter Allen's opinion that *Mr. Prohack* is "one of his most successful light novels," I am more inclined to agree with Dudley Barker, who writes, "It is a novel that starts almost as well as, say, *Buried Alive*, but wanders off into incredibilities, and ends by being merely boring. After a few deep breaths, the impulse dies."[24]

Barker is equally negative about the last of the entertainments, *The Strange Vanguard* of 1927. He calls it "the blot among his last series of novels," and summarizes the "ridiculous" tale of a millionaire "immersed in a ridiculous plot to buy a firm of dressmakers to whom his wife is refusing to pay a bill; precisely the sort of subject that brought out Bennett's worst writing qualities, particularly his facetiousness."[25] Walter Allen calls it "unreadable,"[26] and Reginald Pound says that it is "yet one more 'fantasia,' attempting to blend cosmopolitanism in Italy with Five Towns character and producing an unsatisfying and somewhat insipid result."[27] The plot is feeble and the characters are too rich or homey or pert or debonair, like second-rate Noël Coward. Perhaps the uncertainties, overreaching, attenuation, and unfunniness of the following passage may stand for all that could be said against *The Strange Vanguard*; it is the paragraph which ends chapter 10, called "The Snore":

Suddenly came a new sound through the open window of a cabin. Mr. Sutherland's cabin. A steady, not unmusical snore. Mr. Sutherland's snore. Mr. Sutherland, like many persons considering themselves to be the martyrized victims of insomnia, had been mistaken as to his entire wakefulness. There was something at once grotesque, comic and formidable about the noise of that snore from the nose of Harriet's admirer. Harriet tried to master her sensations, failed, screamed, and finally yielded herself, not without hysteria, to something which she had thought would be laughter but which seemed, even to her own ears, most curiously to resemble sobbing.[28]

The pep and aplomb of the earlier entertainments are gone; it is sad to see such empty verbalizing. The skill of an entirely professional man of letters of course remained, but the springs of joyful creativity, nowhere more evident than in his entertainments, had run dry. Bennett was no longer capable of the early jeux d'esprit like *Hugo* and *The Card*, and his later career, even though it had its solid achievements, is sadder for their loss.

Bennett's professionalism, sometimes rather maliciously equated with journalism, remains remarkable. What is most interesting about the entertainments, however, is not their skill or lack of it but what they tell us about Bennett himself and about his creativity, energy, and art. Some have their own value; *A Great Man, Buried Alive,* and *The Card* are compellingly humorous or thoughtful, and we might well read them even if *Anna* or *Old Wives'* or *Riceyman* did not loom in the background. Yet all of them are minor works, and as such are more transparent and accessible than the well-wrought and deliberate artistries of the best of the Potteries stories.

Bennett gave of himself more obviously than he knew in the entertainments. They were so rapidly written, even by his own standards, that there was not much time for disguises. He bragged about his speed: *The Grand Babylon Hotel* was written in "three weeks of evening work," as we know, and *A Great Man* was: "One writing. No draft. Practically no erasures, and about two months' work at most."[29] Though *Hugo* took "over three months,"[30] *Buried Alive* and *The Card* and *The Regent* were all finished in two months apiece.[31] The last two entertainments were slower, *The Strange Vanguard* requiring as much as five months.[32] Yet to add it up, these eight novels took less than two years, a more-than-Balzacian outpouring; and of course Bennett was writing reams of essays, criticism, scenarios, other novels, at the same time. While the composition of *Clayhanger* drove him "nearly . . . mad,"[33] his lighter works were agreeable diversions.

Thus in the entertainments Bennett did not have time to distance or transform himself, had he wished to. While he was writing *A Great Man* he recorded in his journals, very acutely:

It seems amusing enough, and very good in places. But if I treated this as a draft, and really thought out types and made the book fuller, I could make it much better. However, I have a mania for producing a lot just now. And further, this sort of book, though I can do it, is scarcely my natural *genre*. I do not take quite the same terrific interest in it as I take in a serious book, nor do I get quite the same satisfaction out of a passage which I know to be well done. And often I have the greatest difficulty in starting my day's work. I am all right when I have started. But the starting is *penible*.[34]

It was a question of tapping his fantasies, and then of giving them rein. V. S. Pritchett praises Bennett as "the connoisseur of the normal, the ordinary, and the banal,"[35] just the opposite of his role in the entertainments.

Realism was what Bennett believed in, but what a constraint it was: "the damnedest nerve-shattering experience."[36] It was a choke, a halter, and for his creativity's health he had to break loose at times and let the Dionysian in him run rampant, to compensate for those shattered nerves. How frequently he resorted to fantasy we have already seen, how he shook off *The Old Wives' Tale* and plunged into *Buried Alive,* or leapt from *Clayhanger* into *The Card.* Almost all critics and biographers of Bennett stress the autobiographical nature of his novels, but all novels derive at greater or less remove from the lives of their makers; what is different in Bennett is that in an unusual way, fantasies operate as direct expressions of wish fulfillment. They are basic Bennett. Although Mr. Prohack, like Bennett, takes dancing lessons and has insomniac nights, although yachts, witty young women, and luxurious hotels appear in Bennett's fantasy heroes' lives as in his own, the difference is the sea change they have undergone. It is all much nicer in novels. Fame, for which Bennett struggled so hard, is the easiest of acquisitions to his foolish hero Henry Shakspere Knight; prudence, care with cash, financial commonsense are all obliterated in the charming figure of Charlie Prohack. Success comes very easily to the heroes of *A Great Man, Buried Alive,* and *The Card,* in comparison with Bennett's own struggles. Drabble says, "The Card himself is clearly a fictitious character, a kind of dream hero, who says all the things one would like to have said oneself, a master of *l'esprit de l'escalier.*"[37] For "one" read Bennett, who never overcame his stammer. Alice Clarrice in *Buried Alive* is, like Nellie in *The Card* or Maidie in *The Strange Vanguard,* the dream wife—easy, adoring, housewifely, unproblematical. Gambling, French "cocottes," yachts: Bennett knew them in his life, but prudently; in his fiction they are transfigured into easy, harmless, and somehow inexpensive diversions. The entertainments are play, though the figure of the overachiever Bennett as *homo ludens* seems incongruous. He escaped in the fantasies to perform, as Walter Wright says, "his impulsive acts in a never-never world which has, to be sure, a coherence and logic of its own, but was created deliberately to be unlike anything actual."[38]

Whether one calls them escape, relief, purgative, self-parody, whether in them he was Denry, Shakspere Knight and his cynical cousin Tom, or the grand manipulator like Mr. Racksole or Hugo or Mr. Sutherland, the entertainments kept Bennett afloat in his real and imaginary yachts. As fantasy literature the entertainments have their own place; as guides to Bennett's greater work and to Bennett himself, if only by force of contrast, they are a sure sign and direction.

13

Publishable and Worth It

Forster's Hitherto Unpublished Fiction

Frederick P. W. McDowell

rctic Summer and Other Fiction, a volume in the monumental Abinger Edition of E. M. Forster, is unusually interesting for students of modern literature and for Forster scholars.[1] In this volume the editors (Oliver Stallybrass and, after his death, Elizabeth Heine) have reprinted works that Forster either abandoned or never submitted for publication; even those that seem to be complete units were probably not finished to his full satisfaction. Except for eight short fragments at the end of the volume, the reprinted items are more than fragments and possess, some of them, considerable literary value, in addition to being sources of record for what they tell us about Forster himself and for the light that they shed on his other works. The stories—"Ralph and Tony," "The Tomb of Pletone," "Unfinished Short Story," and perhaps "Little Imber"—are equal in merit to those gathered in *The Life to Come and Other Short Stories,* and "Ralph and Tony," I think, ranks among Forster's best works in the short story. *Arctic Summer* is, from some points of view, a finished work, and regarded in that light, it takes a modest place with the other Forster novels. *Nottingham Lace* is an apprentice work; it does not rank so highly as most of the other titles gathered here, but does have considerable interest as Forster's first attempt to dramatize an alienated, isolated protagonist who has some of his own characteristics. If Forster could have rounded off the protagonist's conflicts with his immediate family, the first section of *Nottingham Lace* might have been publishable. Forster might also have placed the other works with a modicum of revision, except for "Little Imber," with its explicit homosexual elements, and the fragments.

Though most of the works are so nearly finished, they nevertheless reveal that Forster had some difficulty in establishing his narrative line in them; he tended to be indecisive as to the direction that a narrative, so far articulated, would take in its further development. He seems, in short, to have been at the mercy of the "story" element in fiction, for which he was to register a lack of enthusiasm in *Aspects of the Novel*. All of these works show some failure in the implementation of an initial vision, in inventiveness, but the failures are much less crucial than Forster thought, with the result that most of these works are more complete than he gave them credit for being. In perusing them, we recognize that Forster experienced difficulty in extending beyond the envisaging of an arresting initial situation. But these initial sequences have the unity, the intensity, and the complexity that characterize excellent short fictions, and are best considered in this light. Such an approach would be able to disregard the attempts, mostly abortive, at a full amplification of the initial *donnée* and to accept the *donnée* itself as Forster had so far articulated it. In *Nottingham Lace* Edgar Carruthers' persecution by his family and relatives and his expansive relationship with Sidney Trent form such an aesthetic unit, if we disregard the attempts made to extend the narrative in the Edgar–Miss Logan, the Jack Manchett–Piggy Trent, and the Edgar–Jack Manchett sequences. It is legitimate, I think, to regard *Arctic Summer* as relatively complete in the "Main Version" with the fateful termination of the relationship between the brothers, Clesant and Lance March (Lance commits suicide after Clesant curses him for his sexual transgressions). Alternatively, we could regard the Italian chapters of the Main Version (the first five), which Forster revised for a reading at the Aldeburgh Festival of 1951, as comprising a viable aesthetic unit with Venetia Borlase's headlong disruption of the developing friendship between her husband Martin Whitby and Clesant Marsh.

I

In *Nottingham Lace* (1889–1902) Forster felt that he was functioning technically as a novelist but that he was too uninvolved in his creation: "The apparatus was working, not inaccurately, but feebly and dreamily, because I wasn't sure it was there."[2] The fragment is eminently readable, however, and reveals how adept Forster was from the first as a novelist of manners. He began like Jane Austen but was later to incorporate a visionary element into his fiction, deriving from the romantic poets, Meredith, Hardy, and Emily Brontë. As a novelist of manners he had a sure instinct for the niceties of class distinctions, for social snobbery, and for the exaggerated deference extended by polite society to the claims of decorum and propriety. As the work opens, Mrs. Manchett decides that curtains of Nottingham lace prove unmistakably that the Trents, moving in across the way, are impossibly vulgar and that she cannot afford, therefore, to know them. She reckons without the knowledge that Sidney Trent is to be a schoolmaster for her sons and that complete aloofness is consequently impossible; she reckons without the unthinking actions of her husband, who brings Sidney Trent back with him after meeting him at a cricket match; she reckons without Edgar Carruthers' naiveté and lack of sophistication (he finds it impossible to resist the advances of Trent and he tells Trent that Mrs. Manchett will call on his mother); and she reckons without a knowledge of the aggressiveness, the impatience, the vigor, and the iconoclasm of Sidney Trent himself. She is mortified at his offering to carry some of her groceries without his having been introduced to her; and she is humiliated at having to receive him when her husband brings him home. With Mrs. Manchett appearances rather than sterling virtues count; with Austen-like expertise, Forster emphasizes how shallow are her distinctions: "Mrs. Manchett sat down and talked till tea-time. Beginning with the lady opposite, like all great talkers she gradually reached the universal—the mass of people who were 'not quite.' These fell into three classes: those who had called on her, those who had not, and those whom she did not mean to call on. The third class was the most exhilarating, and on it she declaimed till tea came" (p. 2).

Psychologically, Forster's main preoccupation in this tale is with the analysis of Edgar Carruthers' mind and personality. He suffers from a painful isolation, much like the isolation that Rickie Elliot (*The Longest Journey*) and Forster himelf had to undergo as dayboys before coming to Cambridge. Edgar is the sensitive adolescent who lives in his imagination and for whom the arts are crucial in a society which champions distinction in athletics for its youth and the making of money for those who have completed their stay in a public school. Poetry, art, music, and intellectual discourse to the extent that they are available make his life tolerable in his philistine surroundings. The opportunity to talk about the arts and ideas lures him to Trent, at first with the encouragement of his uncle and then in opposition to him.

The antagonism of Manchett, an aggressive philistine, toward Edgar develops into actions of cruelty and sadism. After having promoted a relationship between Edgar and Trent with the hope of developing his nephew physically, he becomes lukewarm when he finds that Trent is the son of a draper, and he finally forbids Edgar any further association with Trent. Mr. Manchett takes this stand as a result of Edgar's defiance. Manchett has become prosperous and no longer wants Edgar's father, an archeologist in India, to pay for his son's lodging. But Edgar, wishing to retain this vestige of independence from his relatives, stands up to his uncle and refuses to give his consent to the new financial arrangement. Infuriated at this opposition to his wishes, Manchett boxes his nephew sharply on the ears; Edgar then breaks down with pain and humiliation. Manchett cannot endure tears in a man and forbids his unmanly nephew to see the manly Trent. The spectacle of a well-intentioned young man being broken by the cruelty of a near relative is, in fact, more painful than anything else in Forster with the exception of the persecutions of Aziz in *A Passage to India* and the deaths in the late stories, "The Life to Come" and "The Other Boat."

The hapless Edgar fares no better at the hands of his absent father, after Edgar, with Trent's assistance, sends a cable to him in India describing the situation at the Manchetts and asking help. Far from helping or even trying to understand his son, the elder Carruthers cannot resist the appeal to his cupidity and accepts Manchett's offer of free lodging for Edgar. His callousness to his son anticipates Mr. Elliot's dehumanized treatment of his son, Rickie, in *The Longest Journey*, while Manchett and Carruthers between them anticipate the impersonal and peremptory quality toward their inferiors exhibited by the Pembrokes of *Journey*, the Wilcoxes of *Howards End*, and the Anglo-Indians of *A Passage to India*. Forster knew well apparently, from experience or from inference, even before the appearance of Samuel Butler's *The Way of All Flesh*, the discordancies, the masked sadism, and the violence, latent and overt, that often underlay the ostensibly harmonious life of the family in the Victorian Age. As a result of Edgar's having challenged the authority of uncle and father, he finds himself alone in a hostile world, a weak individual unable to cope with the brutality and the cruelty of the people in his family and compelled to forego a helpful relationship with his friend Trent.

In the portrait of Edgar Carruthers are overtones of Forster himself: Edgar's decency, his hesitancies, his aesthetic temperament, his lack of personal force, his deference, his nervous constitution, his sensitivity, his ranging intellectual interests, his strong intuitive perceptions, and his valuing of personal relationships are, in large degree, Forster's own attributes. Edgar also anticipates the characters in the fiction who most resemble Forster: Philip Herriton in *Where Angels Fear to Tread*, Rickie Elliot in *The Longest Journey*, and, to some extent, Margaret Schlegel of *Howards End*.

In Nottingham Lace Sidney Trent becomes a touchstone for value and the moral guardian of the protagonist; he instructs a weaker and less experienced person in the ways of the world and in the possibilities for the spiritual life. With something of the brashness and crudity of Gino Carella in *Where Angels Fear to Tread,* but something also of his genuineness, he has, moreover, some of the insight and the sympathetic awareness of Caroline Abbott of *Angels,* Stewart Ansell of *The Longest Journey,* and Margaret Schlegel of *Howards End.* He differs from them, however, in his unabashed assertion of his vulgarity, the iconoclastic dimensions of which he cherishes, in particular as it upsets the decorum of Mrs. Manchett and her associates. In a sense he uses bourgeois aggressiveness in himself to combat bourgeois complacency and conformity in others, qualities endemic in the Sawston adults governing the worlds of family, school, and business, people who do not understand the intellectual and see in him only a threat to the placid prosperity that they could otherwise, without calling it into question, enjoy. At the time of his first visit to the Manchetts, Trent is determined not to be more vulgar than he can help, though he realizes that it is an uphill contest for him to control some of his basic instincts:

> He was perfectly aware that he was "vulgar," "ill-bred," "a rough diamond," "one of nature's gentlemen"—the various phrases had been applied to him by acquaintances of various malignity—but he did not see why or how he should alter. When occasion demanded however he could suppress the more offensive manifestations, such as lounging, laughing a certain laugh, making jokes of a certain calibre, bantering his hostess and being over-assiduous in his attempts to make her guests eat. He had to keep his hand on the reins, but it was possible (p. 17).

In his humble origins he most completely resembles Stewart Ansell, among the guardian figures in Forster, but he is less refined and controlled and more petulant. Ansell has gained the acceptance by his peers at Cambridge, the kind of acceptance that Trent cannot hope for in narrow-minded Sawston but that he longs for with his whole being.

Nottingham Lace is praiseworthy for its portrait of the unsettled young man, presentation of the sadistic philistine in Mr. Manchett, sketch of the absurd Mrs. Manchett, and acid insight into family relationships. Crudely envisioned and lacking in imaginative range, at many points it suggests the stylistic mastery and the psychological insight present in Forster's later works.

II

Superficially it might seem perplexing that the virtually completed "Ralph and Tony" (dating from 1903–1904) should have remained obscure for so long and that Forster apparently never mentioned it or made any efforts to publish it. But considering the autobiographical aspects of the story (Ralph Holme and his mother closely resemble Forster and his mother) and the personal longings that Ralph explicitly and implicitly expresses in it, the reader can better appreciate why Forster did not make the story public. It would have been too close to a confession for a reticent individual like Forster to have made, and the homosexual aspects of the story could have been embarrasing to him. Whether his mother could have tolerated in print the thinly disguised portraits of herself and her son is questionable. Whatever the cause, we have been deprived of a complex, moving, and accomplished work of narrative art.

The tale explores a personal relationship that is, from the first, marked by extremity and violence. Tony is a London medical student whose spiritual home is the mountains and whose inner being is marked by the freedom and the explosiveness of untamed nature: "He was in fact a pure pagan, all the more complete for being unconscious, living the glorious unquestioning life of the body, with instinct as a soul" (p. 89). He is vacationing with his sister Margaret in the Tyrol when an unprepossessing Englishman, Ralph Holme, and his mother intrude upon his privacy and, without realizing quite that they are doing so, upon his sense of personal sanctity. Tony feels physical revulsion in the presence of one whom he deems "affected, decadent, morbid, neurotic" and whom he calls "an affectionate worm" (p. 69). Tony's antipathy increases in proportion to Ralph's growing devotion to him. Ralph perhaps innocently touches some strand in Tony that the latter would wish to deny; Ralph reaches through, as it were, to some central core of his being that causes him to acknowledge guilt. Tony's fierce expressions of loathing toward Ralph comprise an expression by his conscious mind of unconscious impulses that he is reluctant to face—undoubtedly, homosexual feeling. How else account for the violence that follows Ralph's prostration before Tony when Ralph pleads with Tony to love him? Cruelty, violence, and sadism are likely to be concomitants of the awakening of unexpected passion that society proscribes. On an expedition into the mountains to walk to the summit of Giau mountain, Tony derives sadistic pleasure from telling Ralph all his defects and then lying to him to prevent him from going further up the mountain with him and Margaret. Brother and sister on the way down experience a transcendent expansion of their souls as a result of a thunderstorm overtaking them, "Tony singing or rather howling, mad with bodily excitement and the joy of life" (pp. 73–74). Such uninhibited emotion would have been impossible to express in Ralph's presence. Brother and sister come upon him kneeling, seemingly in prayer to the mountains; but this quasi-intellectualizing of strong emotion excites Tony's scorn and active contempt.

Before his involvement with Ralph, Tony had appeared to be a primitive sensibility in close rapport with nature. We view him at the time mostly through the eyes of the admiring Margaret, who sees him always against the mountains, as "a radiant demigod who had seen into heaven," as lovable, tall, strong, "a beautiful half-wild animal," only content on the heights, where he finds satisfaction in being with the chamois hunters, "living among clouds and glaciers, faring roughly among rough men" (pp. 69–70). As we first see him, he is a personification of Nature and her energies, and he possesses, therefore, the large contours and the suggestive proportions of an archetypal or mythic presence. Though Margaret feels strong sympathy with her brother, she also begins to feel that his behavior, especially toward Ralph, is extreme—overly militant and overly aggressive. Ralph has disturbed Tony's equilibrium forever, and Tony struggles against this, to him, sinister influence. Tony represents, in essence, innocence that is corrupted by experience, although the agent of that corruption is a man of sincerity and integrity.

The tale comes to climax after the scene when Tony is brutal to Ralph, continually kicking him in anger at the suggestion that Tony should love him. Ralph's profession of love had been the result of his intense quest, as he explains to Margaret, to find some sort of standard. Though it would be easier not to involve himself in the search for Justice, he feels he must not give over his endeavor. Margaret recognizes also that Ralph needs love and, specifically, needs to be loved by those whom he loves. After an outburst from Tony, Margaret thinks of herself as a possible recipient of Ralph's love; at another point she has a vision of a relationship that might become transcendent between the two men if Tony would allow himself to respond. Ralph is attracted to Margaret as well as to Tony, and he proposes to Tony that he marry Margaret so that the three might live together. After Tony's violent rejection of him, Ralph feels that he must prove himself to himself; otherwise, he cannot survive with his self-image so torn asunder. Early in the story he had said that he had "never been to the top of anything" in his life (p. 68); he fails to reach the top of the Giau mountain on the walk with Tony and Margaret. He must now climb to the top of the mountain that he calls Justice in order to prove that he can achieve something tangible and at the same time attain some transcendent state which will give him peace and insight: a sense of serenity and a feeling of identity with the cosmic processes.

Ralph gets higher into the mountains than he has ever been before. He would persist in his dangerous climb on an untenable path, perhaps courting the death that might give at last some coherence to his fragmented life. Against Ralph's will, Tony intervenes, knocks him senseless, and carries him to safety, but is himself physically overcome by his exertions. It develops that Tony has a weak heart—has in fact always had one without knowing it. This defect of body will not only prevent him from pursuing an active life again in the mountains but keep him from even being in their presence because of the adverse effects of altitude upon the heart. Tony is humiliated that he, who has always been as a god, is in fact mortal and can suffer from disease, like Ralph or any other human being. If he is diseased in body, might he not also be diseased in spirit?

Nevertheless, Tony also undergoes an enlargement of spirit at the same time that, in another direction, his spirit contracts. In a dream that descends on him in his sickbed, he sees humanity climbing a great mountain, and only surviving through the forces of love and mutual understanding. This dream impels him to act. Though he is weary and can only act with great effort, he summons Ralph in order to suggest a reconciliation. He now sees Ralph in altered perspective and can now appreciate that he has been "so heroic under the extreme misery, so utterly true in word and spirit." Victory or defeat? Whose victory or defeat? Tony at least learns that he cannot live forever at the extremities of emotion and that personal relationships must supplement the impersonal joy deriving from nature. But the progress is costly because the hero and the god are reduced to the human and the encompassable. Ralph will undoubtedly experience renewal, but is this a renewal at the expense of his friend upon whose vitality he may, vampirelike, have been feeding? Will Tony's passion and the violence induced by passion be effectively subdued? Can homosexual love find more than a covert expression in a *ménage à trois*?

The story is fascinating to consider in light of all the speculative issues that it raises but leaves suspended. It is also prototypic, in that it adumbrates the relationships between men that are so much a part of the Forsterian universe: Philip Herriton and Gino Carella, Rickie Elliot and Stephen Wonham, Rickie and Stewart Ansell, Maurice and Clive Durham (and Alec Scudder), Aziz and Fielding, are those that most readily come to mind. The clarity of line and structure in the tale, despite its complexities, its masterful relating of the psychic conflicts of the characters to external Nature, and its symbolic extensions, insinuations, and ramifications all contribute to its force and persuasiveness and make of "Ralph and Tony" an exciting addition to the Forster canon.

Three other stories are relatively complete as they are printed here for the first time. "The Tomb of Pletone" reveals Forster's fascination with the Mediterranean civilizations, and it belongs with sketches in *Abinger Harvest* such as "Cnidus," "Cardan," and "Gemisthus Pletho." "The Tomb of Pletone" is, in effect, an expansion of the last paragraph of "Gemisthus Pletho" and recounts the circumstances whereby Sismondo Malatesta was able to bring Pletho's tomb back to Rimini from Mount Taygetus near Sparta. An Italian banker and a one-time classics scholar, Astorre also intends to bring his friend of long ago, Jacobo Vernagallo, to Italy. Malatesta just manages to get the tomb on board ship before the Turks overrun the area. Astorre is not so fortunate. He is a man of good intentions that are undercut by lack of personal force though, paradoxically, during a crisis he had saved the ship, forcibly taking the place of an incompetent helmsman. Astorre is killed by accident, or perhaps by Malatesta's design, as he helps carry the tomb down a flight of stairs. In this story Forster captures the individualism and the largeness of outlook, the violence and the love of learning, the cruelty and the capacity for passionate friendship, the worship of the life-energies and the contempt for the individual life, characteristic of the Italian Renaissance. As a story based in history, it is, I think, more successful than "The Torque," which is reprinted in *The Life to Come and Other Stories* because the characters are not so limited, defined, and distorted by their primal sexual natures.

"Unfinished Short Story" is perhaps as finished as it needs to be, considering that the central situation in the tale concerns the fragmented and apparently meaningless existence of Gregory Dale, an English official stationed at a ministry in Egypt. His existence is one of quiet desperation. In the first part, he is at odds with his wife and an aristocratic patron, Lady Concannon, and disillusioned with his life in Cairo. In the second, he tries to escape tedium by recourse to a lively prostitute in Alexandria, a Mademoiselle Marcelle: he forces himself to act as the world does but derives little pleasure from his escapade. In the third, he is lifted out, but only temporarily, from his barren routine by a flight in an airplane over Alexandria and Akoubir, a flight which Forster describes with much gusto and vividness. The parts of the story are apparently unconnected, but they have a deeper unity as they comment upon the futility of Dale's entire existence. Forster is expert at eliciting the psychic ramifications of his materials: the drabness of the Alexandria red light district and the acuteness of his sensations as he flies over the city dramatize Dale's life of dullness as it is punctuated by occasional thrills.

"Little Imber" contains an appealing element of whimsical fantasy, though the depiction of the sexual encounter lacks subtlety and emotional depth. In spite of his homosexuality, in *Where Angels Fear to Tread, The Longest Journey,* and *Maurice* Forster regarded paternity as representing a crucial fulfillment for the individual, his sympathetic characters in these books desiring for themselves the only certain immortality, perpetuity through their progeny. Forster was intrigued with the notion of personal continuance being made possible through one's descendants. The difficulties, needless to say, for a homosexual to overcome in achieving paternity are formidable. "Little Imber" solves the problem through the means of wish-fulfilling fantasy. At a time in the future when males are scarce, two venturesome men (one elderly and the other a youth, Little Imber by name), who are hired by the state to impregnate women, discover that life may be generated by the contact of one male with another. So the problem of continuing the race is solved, and the desire of the male to attain immortality without resorting to intercourse with women is satisfied. And sensual pleasure is not ruled out. The line of the story is a bit simplistic perhaps, yet an energy and geniality of presentation prove effective within the tale's rather narrow dimensions.

III

Arctic Summer is the most considerable of these reprinted works and, even in its unfinished state, may come to rank high among Forster's works. Forster seems to have thought well of it, since he made a final revision of the first five chapters for the Aldeburgh Festival of 1951. In his "Note on *Arctic Summer*" written at that time, he indicated that his purpose in writing the novel had been to contrast two essentially admirable types and to show their interactions upon each other. He had wanted to present "the antithesis between the civilized man, who hopes for an Arctic Summer, and the heroic man who rides into the sea" (p. 162). In this note he expressed regret that he could not envision the requisite large event toward which his whole narrative might move.

Though we cannot deny Forster's statement that the work is unfinished, there is nevertheless a cohesiveness in the first five chapters which gives that section of the narrative a unity that we associate, customarily, with the short story. That section of the work is enclosed by Clesant March's heroic rescue of Martin Whitby from the wheels of a moving train in Basle station at the beginning and Martin's impulsive action in chapter 5 to save himself in a fire at a cinema in Milan, deserting his chauffeur, his companion, in so doing. Between the episodes occurs the most intensely rendered event, the humiliation of March by Venetia Borlase Whitby, Martin's overly confident and assertive wife. Looking at the work as a whole, we can discern a greater unity and a more coherent development than Forster may have thought were there. Granted that the work is unfinished, there might have been no necessity to go further with it than the last incident presented in it, that of Lance's suicide, brought on by the violence of his brother Clesant's condemnation of him for sexual transgression.

Since the work is entitled *Arctic Summer* and since Martin Whitby is the man who wishes for such a season of continual light, a new era "in which there will be time to get something really great done," we can regard him as the principal character. He is the main focus of interest in the first five chapters, the point of view character at least. Subsequently, the heroic challenger to the civilized life, a warrior or warrior in the making, Lieutenant March, becomes the focus of Forster's attention, and the point of view is either March's or that of an omniscient narrator.[3] Martin Whitby is a conscientious civil servant at the Treasury and has a marked sense of responsibility, of integrity, of self-identity. He anticipates the Fielding of *A Passage to India,* and like that Bloomsbury-oriented individual, he possesses "good will plus culture and intelligence." He also evinces the sensitivity of Fielding in social relationships. In contrast with Martin, his wife Venetia lacks tact and social imagination, though she has her husband's integrity and honesty. She is the Adela Quested to his Fielding. Martin's thoughts about himself as he leaves Tramonta Castle best sum up him and his type: "He felt so happy as he came down the stairs and so efficient. He knew himself to be clever and kind and moral and energetic, and to be surrounded by friends who were like him. He knew this— without self-consciousness and without conceit: the truth—for it was one—lay in his soul like a star" (p. 147). He has gained much from the sensitivity and the restraint embodied in his mother, who had developed these qualities from the Quaker heritage at its best. The inner light, which the Quakers cultivated rather than the light of the physical sun, caused Martin paradoxically to value more highly than he would otherwise that same sun—or the sensuous aspects of experience: for him, finally, "the physical joined with the spiritual into one glory" (p. 130). Like the Margaret Schlegel of *Howards End,* he has been able to "connect" the various facets of his experience into a meaningful synthesis. Though he became a skeptic and denied even the undogmatic Quaker faith, it was a skepticism more in name than in fact, for "though he doubted a purpose behind the Universe, he never ceased to act as if there was a purpose" (p. 131).

Though as a youth he was overwhelmed by beauty and "the wonder of life," he had also developed an acute sense of moral discrimination, and came to see that the cultivation of "romance and adventure" is unsound as an organizing principle for one's life. Yet Beauty did not vanish for him: "it transferred itself from monkey tricks to his work, and dwelt in the masses of the hills" (p. 131). It also evolved into a sense of Form; and it is in

Italy that he is conscious of this transmuting of aesthetic impressions into some organizing entity. In Italy romance and sentiment merge into an austere beauty with some implicit social and philosophical dimensions, which are there precisely because they have not been too directly sought: "She [Italy], like himself, had abandoned sentiment; she existed apart from associations by the virtues of mass and line: her austere beauty was an image of the millenium towards which all good citizens are cooperating" (p. 129). The ideas of Roger Fry animate these speculations of Martin, as Elizabeth Heine in her informed Editor's Introduction rightly observes (pp. xviii–xix). Italy, for Martin, nourishes the idea of an abstract and vitalizing "Significant Form," and her greatest art to him points to a significance that is other than representational. Though Martin's matured philosophy gives him stability, he is sometimes self-conscious and feels that what he does, although it matters, attracts too little notice. At this point he says he would be a pessimist but for his belief in Form, which hints at civilization as it will be rather than as it now is. Venetia shares the progressivism of her husband, but everything about her is more arid. She feels, for example, that Martin may be too visionary for his own good and that his propensity toward the subjective may be making him restless.

Martin truly loves his wife, and is only intermittently aware of her limitations. Venetia and her sister Dorothea wish to "tidy" the world, to reconstruct it according to rational principles; and for such people, "romance, whether in action or in thought, is a relic of the age of untidiness" (p. 131). Her sincerity and the strength of her beliefs, her clear if simplified vision, attracted him at a time when he was undergoing his crisis of loss of faith. Liking for her led to genuine passion, which, with the great ardors passed, led to a companionship marked by a new tenderness. So by the time he has come out to Italy, "Martin's inner life was complete," and he can think of Venetia with benignity, gratitude, and affection. Although she can reassure him that his "cowardice" at the cinema was a slowness of the will rather than a fixed attribute, he is also uncomfortable with her somewhat easy rationalization of his state. He reluctantly concludes that there are subtleties toward which she seems to be insensitive: "There were tangles in life unguessed by her tidy mind. There was—how should one express it?—Tramonta" (p. 160).

Martin Whitby's experience at Tramonta, the events that lead up to it, and the crucial event subsequent to it when Venetia mishandles young March, represent the chief challenge to Martin at this time. His own life, he sees, may be less complete than he had thought: for better or worse, he realizes that there are values other than those bounded by his liberalism, values other than Venetia's solid conceptions of human beings and society, values too, in a masterwork of graphic art, that range beyond the formal properties that organize it. The agent of Martin's enlargement is the Lieutenant March who had saved his life at Basle Station; later Martin senses in March a decisiveness that might allow him—Martin—to "tighten up the will." Everything conspires to make Martin's journey to Tramonta Castle with Venetia and her mother memorable. At the Castle, Martin undergoes an experience which reorients him and loosens his hitherto solid grasp on life. As we have just seen, Martin had assimilated the doctrines of Roger Fry by denigrating the contents of works of art and by placing, instead, an emphasis upon their formal properties. As soon as Martin enters the Castle unmediated emotion—or Romance—comes flooding back, though Form still stands firm in the foreground. Martin describes the powerful if somewhat awkward frescos in terms of their subject matter, a departure from his usual criticisms of art according to the principles of Fry: "very moving: warriors about to fight for their country and faith" (p. 148). One face in the frescos arrests him with its uncanny resemblance to young March; one of the latter's ancestors, it turns out, had served an Italian noblemen three hundred years ago at the battle of Lepanto. Now Martin understands why March had wished to come here: to renew his own identity by establishing an identity with an heroic ancestor. A strong but perplexing emotion overcomes Martin when he thinks of the picture and of his rescuer: a power behind both, a power that had saved him "to which he could give no name" (p. 149). With his rational faculties he feels ignorance and shame when he later recalls his emotion; but it had been all-powerful at the time. It also persists to color permanently his impressions of Tramonta and to exert a subversive influence upon him, although with his intelligence he discerns something alien and snobbish about Tramonta and the feudal values for which it stands.

The remainder of his time in Italy becomes for him spurious and shallow, now that "Romance," which had "blessed" him at Tramonta Castle, no longer pervades his perceptions. As with other expressions of the rational mind, the doctrine of Significant Form, despite the genuine authority that it exerts, had also for Forster its inherent limitations. P. N. Furbank is perceptive in viewing the novel as turning, in a sense, "on Martin's unlearning of Fry's doctrines."[4]

The most powerful scene in *Arctic Summer* occurs when the high-minded and somewhat officious Venetia decides, on the spur of the moment, to take the youthful March in hand and to lecture him about the unimportance of family and ancestry. Martin discerns that she is invading the private life of the young man which he jealously guards from intrusion by outsiders; March can hardly contain his disgust as Venetia persists in her inquiries. Martin understands that March's visiting Tramonta Castle is a personal ritual for him, since he had already declined to accompany them in the Whitby motor car. Venetia tactlessly asks him whether his portrait (reflected in the soldier's face in the fresco) is at Tramonta or whether it is not; she does not realize that plain questions are sometimes destructive. There may be no plain answer to such a question. Although Venetia is well-meaning and has Martin's love, she is limited in her insight into human nature beause she tends to interpret all phenomena in terms of her own clear-cut values; she is deficient in humor, human warmth, and sympathy. Applied with rigidity, her supposedly liberal values become illiberal. Her meddlesomeness effectually brings an end, for a considerable time, to the budding friendship between the two men. The suggestion also obtrudes that Venetia is possessive of Martin and therefore jealous of a possible rival; she acts in part to ward off the maturing of the friendship involving her husband and his rescuer. March is unable to see, however, that Venetia's actions were as painful to Martin as they were to him. He is able to appreciate Martin's letter of apology as sincere, in spite of some reservations that he and his brother Lance have about its tone.

Clesant March's uncle, Arthur Vullamy, a Tory in his attitudes and an advocate for the established privileges of the upper middle class, appears in the novel after Clesant returns to England and confirms him in his negative reactions toward Martin. As the spokesman for the chivalric idealism that he encourages in the March family, he is forthright, and to some extent Forster would share his feudalistic views; but Forster, it seems, is more on the side of Martin, the spokesman for Bloomsbury, whom Vullamy condemns for his tolerance, his noncombativeness, and his analytic mind.[5] Martin, Vullamy says, is "quietly" against morality, religion, the throne, and all else for which the established classes stand; his aim is "to modify, till everything's slack and lukewarm" (p. 171). Martin represents in large part Forster himself in his most usual guise, and Forster could be considered one of "these crawling non-conformist intellectuals" whom Vullamy condemns Martin for being. From one point of view, Martin could be thought of as one of Dante's dwellers in Limbo, being neither for God nor against; from another point of view, he could be regarded as a truly enlightened man and the finest examplar of the humanistic tradition as opposed to the chivalric. If the dialectic of the work would indicate that Forster has some reservations about Martin, Martin's attitudes are nonetheless largely his own. Martin's values, Forster seems to imply, ought to be tempered by influences more forthright and direct, by influences that are ineffable and transcendent in kind, influences which he might have assimilated quickly from fuller contact with his opposite, Clesant March.

March has saved Martin's life and is capable of extraordinary self-possession and courage in a crisis, in contrast to Martin's slowness of will in an emergency. He affirms his values with passion and is willing to sacrifice himself regardless of the consequences. As Forster said in a letter to Forrest Reid quoted in the Editor's Introduction, "From boyhood he asked for straight issues—to lay down his life for God or King or Woman—and has to learn that in this latter day straight issues are not provided" (p. xxi). In the concluding chapters of the novel, which are laid in England, Clesant learns this lesson painfully. His brother Lance, who in part subscribes to Clesant's romantic values, fails to live up to the ideals envisioned for him by Clesant. At Cambridge, Lance has not been able to resist sexual passion; he has seen fit, as Clesant says, to "take to filth and go with women" (p. 191). As a result, Clesant curses his brother in front of Martin and Vullamy. The curse is so much in excess of its cause that we can perhaps ascribe it to unconscious—but all-possessive—homosexual emotion (the only forceful personal emotions in the tale emanate from the close relationship between the brothers). There is, moreover, a homoerotic element in the more unrestrained forms of hero-worship; and it is as a model for his own potential as hero that Clesant regards his brother. The desecration of that ideal by Lance's actions is too much for Clesant to endure without a violent reaction.

Clesant's violence disturbs both Martin and Vullamy, Martin especially, who reflects that Clesant has shown "the violence of inexperience, the cruelty of one who has never been tempted himself" (p. 192). He has been too extreme, and Lance kills himself as a result of his brother's violent expression of disillusionment. Can heroism, by its very nature, exist in moderation, as in Clesant March? Forster almost implies that it cannot and that its demands upon others may be too exalted for ordinary mortals to encompass. If the absoluteness of the young warrior's values can in one sense serve as a source of renewal for the overly intellectual Martin, they can also be destructive when self-control, self-restraint, and reasonableness are lacking.

What was Forster to do with his romantic hero? The future for a man of Clesant's sort had become increasingly problematic, given the refractory circumstances of the modern age; and after Gallipoli in 1915, with the symbolic death of Rupert Brooke, the chivalric hero had become an anachronism, at best a denizen of a mythic realm unobtainable by other mere soldiers. The processes of history overtook Forster, the creative artist, in his writing of this book. Or what is just as likely, Forster had completed it in the only way possible with Lance's suicide, an event which forms an appropriate symbolic commentary upon the idealism of both Clesant and Lance, possibly even upon Martin's quite different aspirations. Might not Forster, almost in spite of himself, have found the only event toward which this novel might move? Is there any role possible in the modern age except a destructive or a self-destructive one for a man of

Clesant March's single-minded idealism? Or can the more rationally defined aspirations of the humanistic Martin Whitby achieve a truly satisfying expression in the contemporary wasteland? The realities of the Great War, in any case, negated the possibility of the heroic. The age of chivalry was not only dead but it was impossible to resurrect it in any form at all. So there was nothing for Forster's chivalric figure to do. The future of the "decent" intellectual of Bloomsbury, the other chief type in the novel, seemed almost as uncertain, although that type proved to have considerable lasting power in university, literary, and artistic circles and in public life. Forster in his "Note" says that his two male characters might both have ended in defeat, but that he was not interested in tracing the series of events leading to such a dénouement. The novel reveals the supersession of the heroic type, so that any connection between a man of that kind and another would no longer be possible. The work as it now stands reveals the impossibility of the kind of connection that Forster had originally envisioned, and to that extent Forster went as far as he could with his novel. The effect of Forster's story is nostalgic; implicit in it is regret for the passing of a kind of individual whose strength of commitment might have done something to revitalize and reintegrate a fractured society.

The "Radipole Version" is, I think, inferior to the "Main Version" of *Arctic Summer*, but does illustrate the troubles that Forster had writing it. If he could not move forward, he might go back and begin again. In the "Radipole Version" the domestication of the action in the public school environment only serves to diminish both of the chief characters and exposes Clesant to the danger of becoming unconvincing by being too overtly assimilated into a specific social scene, a danger that Forster mentions in his Note, possibly with the benefit of hindsight.

In her Editor's Introduction, Elizabeth Heine provides the intellectual and biographical background against which the work should be viewed. The Tripoli Fragment of the novel demonstrates that, at some point, Lieutenant March was to test himself on the field of battle, involving himself on the side of Tripoli in the 1911 dispute between Tripoli and Italy. Here would be a crusade made to order for Forster's latter-day medieval hero. Rupert Brooke, Forster's friend, was formative upon both male characters, as Elizabeth Heine has indicated. His influence appears in Martin's intellectual interests (Martin's socialism and his views concerning state support for the arts), and it also appears in Clesant's militant idealism and again in his puritanical views. Elizabeth Heine also demonstrates the crucial role of Conrad's *Lord Jim* in the conceptions behind the novel: Jim's quixotic knight-errantry is present in Clesant, and his paralysis of will in an emergency appears in Martin.

It is greatly satisfying to have these previously unpublished works available in an edition so impeccably and comprehensively edited. They have not only the interest that attaches to anything written by a first-rate writer, but they are sometimes first-rate—or close to first-rate—themselves. Critics certainly cannot afford to neglect "Ralph and Tony" and *Arctic Summer* in any complete discussion of Forster and his career. The density, the complexities, and the ambiguities, characteristic of Forster the writer and thinker at his best, are sufficiently present in these works to establish their authenticity and stature.

Notes to the Chapters

Preface

1. Walter Pater, *The Renaissance* (Chicago: Academy Press, 1977), p. xxiii.
2. Helmut E. Gerber, "The Nineties: Beginning, End, or Transition?" in *Edwardians and Late Victorians,* ed. Richard Ellmann (New York: Columbia University Press, 1960), p. 77. I am also indebted for my remarks to Gerber's lecture, "English Literature (1880–1920): A Speculative Overview," recently published in *English Literature in Transition,* special ser. no. 3 (1985), pp. 14–29.
3. *The Poems of Gerard Manley Hopkins,* ed. W. H. Gardner and N. H. MacKenzie, 4th ed. (London: Oxford University Press, 1970), p. 66.

1. Some Aspects of Aestheticism

1. See, for example, Elsie B. Adams, *Bernard Shaw and the Aesthetes* (Columbus: Ohio State University Press, 1971); Amy Cruse, *The Victorians and Their Reading* (Boston: Houghton Mifflin, 1962); Marotino D'Amico, "Oscar Wilde between 'Socialism' and 'Aestheticism'," *English Miscellany* 18 (1967):111–39; Lorentz J. H. Eckhoff, *The Aesthetic Movement in English Literature* (Oslo: Oslo University Press, 1959); Hoxie N. Fairchild, *Gods of a Changing Poetry,* vol. 5 of *Religious Trends in English Poetry* (New York: Columbia University Press, 1962); Albert J. Farmer, *Le Movement esthetique et décadent en Angleterre (1873–1900)* (Paris: H. Champion, 1931); William Gaunt, *The Aesthetic Adventure,* rev. ed. (London: Jonathan Cape, 1975); Albert Guerard, *Art for Art's Sake* (Boston: Lothrop, Lee, and Shepard, 1936); R. V. Johnson, *Aestheticism* (London: Methuen, 1969), and "Pater and the Victorian Anti-Romantics," *Essays in Criticism* 4 (1954):42–57; Morse Peckham, "Aestheticism to Modernism: Fulfillment or Revolution," *Mundus Artium* 1 (1967):36–55; Louise Rosenblatt, *L'idée de l'art pour l'art dans la littérature anglaise pendant la période victorienne* (Paris: H. Champion, 1931); Irving Singer, "The Aesthetics of 'Art for Art's Sake'," *Journal of Aesthetics and Art Criticism* 12 (March 1954):343–59; John Wilcox, "The Beginnings of l'art pour l'art," *Journal of Aesthetics and Art Criticism* 11 (June 1953):360–77.

2. "Truth in Labelling: Pre-Raphaelitism, Aestheticism, Decadence, Fin-de-Siecle," *English Literature in Transition* 17 (1974):201–22.

3. Elizabeth Aslin, *The Aesthetic Movement: Prelude to Art Nouveau* (London: Elek, 1969).

4. Robin Spencer, *The Aesthetic Movement: Theory and Practice* (London: Studio Vista, 1972).

5. A staff seminar paper given by A. G. Lehmann at the University of Reading in May 1956.

6. Ibid., p. 6.

7. Ibid., p. 7.

8. Ibid.

9. Ibid.

10. *The Works of Max Beerbohm,* 5th ed. (London: John Lane, 1923), p. 46.

11. *Time Was* (London: Hamish Hamilton, 1931), p. 36.

12. *The Dictionary of National Biography* peddles the story about Knight censoring himself, but the latest scholarship is dubious. For Knight's views, see *An Analytical Enquiry into the Principles of Taste* (London, 1805), pp. 70–72, 181, and especially 102 and 151. For recent views about the suppression of *An Account,* see *The Arrogant Connoisseur: Richard Payne Knight 1751–1824,* ed. Michael Clarke and Nicholas Penny (Manchester: Manchester University Press, 1982).

13. *Quarterly Review* 98 (1856): 433 and *passim.*

14. "*Punch* and the Syncretics: An Early Victorian Prelude to the Aesthetic Movement," *Studies in English Literature* 15 (1975): 627–40.

15. Horne's essay appeared as a preliminary to his tragedy *Gregory VII* (1840).

16. *Poems of William Edmonstoune Aytoun* (London: Milford, 1921), p.499.

17. Ibid., p. 311.

18. Ibid., p. 330.

19. Ibid., p. 333.

20. Charles Kingsley, *Two Years Ago* (London: Macmillan,1881), 1:57.

21. Ibid., 1:247.

22. Ibid., 1:250–51.

23. Ibid., 1:255.

24. Ibid., 1:257.

25. Ibid., 1:260.

26. Ibid., 2:281–82.

27. Ibid., 1:247.

28. A useful book which summarises the history of Guilds and Sisterhoods in the Anglican Church is Arthur W. Crickmay, *A Layman's Thoughts on Some Questions of the Day* (London: Mowbray, 1896).

29. See Sason Chitty, *The Beast and the Monk* (London: Hodder and Stoughton,1974).

30. *The Poems of Charles Kingsley,* with an introduction by Ernest Rhys (London: Dent, 1927), p. 32.

31. *The Saturday Review,* October 10, 1863, p. 488.

32. Ibid., p. 489.

33. Ibid.

34. *The Saturday Review,* 31 January 1863, p. 138.

35. *Punch,* 26 December 1874, p. 270.

36. *Punch's Almanac for 1875,* 17 December 1874, unpaginated.

37. *Punch,* 2 May 1874, p. 189.

38. Charles L. Eastlake, *Hints on Household Taste in Furniture, Upholstery and Other Details,* 4th ed. (London: Longmans, Green, 1878), pp. 135–36. Sir Nikolaus Pevsner discusses Eastlake's *Household Taste* and R. W. Edis's *Decoration and Furniture of Town Houses* in *Studies in Art, Architecture and Design: Victorian and After* (Princeton: Princeton University Press,1968).

39. *Punch,* 17 March 1860, p. 107.

40. *Punch,* 5 February 1876, p. 33.

41. Ibid.

42. Ibid.

43. *Punch,* 7 September 1878, pp. 98–100; 14 September 1878, pp. 110–112; 21 September 1878, pp. 122–24; 28 September 1878, pp. 134–35; 5 October 1878, pp. 144–45; 12 October 1878, pp. 159–60; 19 October 1878, pp. 178–79; 26 October 1878, pp. 183–89.

44. *Punch,* 17 July 1860, p. 9.

45. "The Grasshopper," Lord Chamberlain's Papers, British Library Add. MSS. 52722, pp. 78–79.

46. Ibid., p. 117.

47. *Fun,* 11 December 1878, p. 235.

48. "The Colonel," Lord Chamberlain's Papers, British Library Add. MSS. 52722.

49. Ibid.

50. *Punch,* 12 May 1877, p. 216.

51. Reprinted from *The World.*

52. *The Monks of Thelema,* Library Edition (London: Chatto and Windus, 1887), pp. 313–14.

53. *Punch,* 31 July 1875, p. 24; 25 September 1875, p. 124.

54. Rhoda and Agnes Garrett, *Suggestions for House Decorations* (1877; reprint, New York: Garland Press, 1978), p. 69.

55. Eastlake, p. 119.

56. W. J. Loftie, *A Plea for Art in the House with Special Reference to the Economy of Collecting Works of Art* (London: Macmillan, 1876), p. 68.

57. *Art in the House* (Boston: L. Prang, 1879), pp. 216–17.

58. Ibid., p. 226.

59. Ibid., p. 207.

60. Ibid., p. 259.

61. Falke, p. 314.

62. Ibid., p. 315.

63. See, for example, Aslin, pp. 160 ff.

64. Falke, p. 319.

65. Mary Eliza Haweis, *Beautiful Houses,* 2d ed. (London: S. Low, Marston, Searle, & Rivington, 1882), pp. 3–5.

66. Ibid., p. 6.

67. Ibid., p. 91.

68. Ibid., p. 106.

69. Lady Archibald Campbell, *Rainbow-Music or the Philosophy of Colour Grouping* (London: Bernard Quaritch, 1886), pp. 6, 14. See also John Stokes, *Resistible Theatres* (London: Elek, 1972), pp. 58–60.

70. Ibid., pp. 16–18.

71. Ibid., p. 29.

72. *The Art of the House* (London: G. Bell, 1897), p. 9.

73. *Punch,* 24 February 1877, p. 84; *Fun,* 23 February 1881, p. 74.

74. *Punch,* 24 February 1877, p. 84.

75. *The Tragic Muse* (London: Macmillan, 1891), p. 31.

76. W. H. Mallock, *The New Republic,* a new edition (London: Chatto and Windus, 1879), p. 262.

77. W. Besant and J. Rice, *The Monks of Thelema,* (London: Chatto and Windus, 1887), pp. 36, 37, 286.

78. Ibid., pp. 288–89.

79. Ibid., p. 126.

80. Ibid., p. 22.

81. *The Diary of W. M. Rossetti 1870–1873,* ed. Odette Bornand (Oxford: Clarendon, 1977), furnishes a useful context.

82. Robert Buchanan, *The Martyrdom of Madeline* (London, n.d.), p. 171.

83. W. H. Lecky, *History of European Morals from Augustus to Charlemagne* (London: Longmans, Green, 1911), 2:283.

84. *Harper's New Monthly Magazine* 64 (1882): 455.

85. Ibid., p. 619.

86. See Alice Corkran, "The Kyrle Society," *Merrie England,* July 1884, p. 154. "The Kyrle Society," *Oxford and Cambridge Undergraduates Journal,* 3 February 1881, pp. 182–83, praises the Society and calls for volunteers. Other literature on the Society includes *Extracts from Octavia Hill's "Letters to Fellow Workers" 1864–1911,* confided by her niece, Elinor Southwood Ovry (London: Adelphi Book Shop, 1933). J. Rutter, *The Nineteenth Century: A Poem in Twenty-Nine Cantos* (London: Burleigh, 1900), pp. 53–56, outlines the Society's aims in amiable doggerel. The Mitchell Library, Glasgow, has the annual reports of the Glasgow branch for 1886 and 1887; the Bristol Central Library of the Bristol branch from 1908 to 1913. I have not found any manuscript material from the papers of Octavia or Miranda Hill relating directly to the Society's foundation.

87. For Octavia Hill, see Charles E. Maurice, *The Life of Octavia Hill as Told in Her Letters* (London: Macmillan, 1913).

88. *Punch,* 19 February 1881, p. 84.

89. May Morris, *William Morris: Artist, Writer, Socialist* (1936; reprint, New York: Russell & Russell, 1966), 1:199.

90. Ibid., p. 200.

91. "Colour, Space and Music for the People," *Nineteenth Century* 15 (May 1884): 745. Another article by Octavia Hill, "Open Spaces of the Future," also mentions the work of the Society.

92. The annual reports of the Birmingham Society extend from 1882 to 1912. *The Birmingham Kyrle Society and the Birmingham Guild of Handicraft* report for 1890 reprints a speech by Montague Fordham, which actually quotes approvingly "the socialist poet, Morris," p. 7.

93. Letter from Mark P. Rathbone in *Liverpool Daily Post,* 21 December 1921. The Rathbones were a family of Liverpool merchant princes. See also issues for 30 December and 31 December, 1927. Brief references to the Liverpool Society appear also in Ivy A. Ireland, *Margaret Beavan of Liverpool* (Liverpool: Henry Young, 1938), and Margaret B. Simey, *Charitable Effort in Liverpool in the Nineteenth Century* (Liverpool: University Press, 1951). The earliest reference to the Liverpool Society appears in a letter from Mr. (late Sir) Lewis Beard, the Honorary Secretary to the Liverpool Corporation in October 1883. Articles on the Liverpool branch can also be found in *The Liverpool Review,* 4 December 1886, p. 1006; 19 November 1887, p. 110; 15 December 1894, p. 3.

94. Mary (Smith) Berenson [Mary Logan], *Guide to the Italian Pictures at Hampton Court, with Short Studies of the Artists, The Kyrle Pamphlets, No. II* (London: A. D. Innes, 1894), p. [v].

95. L. Ormond, *Costume* 2 (1968), p. 33; and Aslin, pp. 145–59 and *passim*. See also *Costume* 8 (1974), p. 26, for Rossetti's views. The standard work is S. M. Newton, *Health, Art and Reason: Dress Reformers of the 19th Century* (London: John Murray, 1974).

96. *The Woman in White* (London: Chatto and Windus, 1875), p. 21.

97. A. Dunnett, "Breeching the Atlantic," Reading University M. A. thesis, 1977, p. 29.

98. Ibid.

99. The "Souls" appear in numerous autobiograpies, biographies, and memoirs, and in novels such as H. G. Wells, *The New Macchiavelli* (1911), and E. F. Benson, *Dodo* (1893). An account of their origin may be found in A. G. K. Liddell, *Notes from the Life of an Ordinary Mortal* (London: J. Murray, 1911), pp. 212–13. This describes gatherings at Lord Cowper's seat in the early 1880s at Wrest. *The Souls, An Exhibition*, compiled and catalogued by Jane Adby and Charlotte Gere, March 1982, at the Bury Street Gallery, Cork Street, London, may be said to begin a study of their aesthetic milieu. The same authors have recently produced a fuller study, *The Souls* (London: John Murray, 1985). Mark Girouard relates them to nineteenth-century notions of chivalry and gentility in *The Return to Camelot* (New Haven and London: Yale University Press, 1981), pp. 208–13 and 225. For the hints about Balfour's "spankings" see Max Egremont, *Balfour: A Life of Arthur James Balfour* (London: Collins, 1980), p. 63.

2. Collecting the Quarrels: Whistler and *The Gentle Art of Making Enemies*

1. From a Sickert letter to *Art News*, dated 21 April 1910, published in Richard Friedenthal, ed., *Letters of the Great Artists*, 2 vols. (New York: Random House, 1963), p. 189.

2. From the MS European diary of Thomas Sergeant Perry, entry for 15 August 1888, in the Colby College Library.

3. Walter Sickert, *A Free House*, ed. Osbert Sitwell (London: Macmillan, 1947), pp. 51–52.

4. Max Beerbohm, "The Mirror of the Past," ed. Lawrence Danson, *Princeton University Library Chronicle* 43 (Winter 1982): 108–9.

5. Joseph and Elizabeth Pennell, *The Life of James A. McNeill Whistler*, 2 vols. (Philadelphia: J. B. Lippincott,1908), 2:100–13, Ch. 34.This biography has most of the details about the pursuit of Ford not otherwise credited below, and is supplemented here by Octave Maus, "Whistler in Belgium," *The Studio* 32 (1904): 7–23, on the Antwerp trial.

6. Whistler's correspondence with Ford is quoted in the suppressed Ford edition of *The Gentle Art of Making Enemies* (London: Frederick Stokes and Brother, 1890), from the copy in the Pattee Library, the Pennsylvania State University, hereafter described in the text. The Whistler version quoted from is *The Gentle Art of Making Enemies* (London: Heineman, 1892).

7. Maus, "Whistler in Belgium."

8. Whitelaw Reid's role, as well as George Smalley's remark, are from *Royal Cortissoz*, ed., *Life of Whitelaw Reid,* 2 vols. (New York: Charles Scribner's Sons, 1921), pp. 131–32.

9. Ford's edition, pp. 22–23. Other quotations from Ford are from this edition.

10. Frederick Keppel, *One Day with Whistler* (London: F. Keppel, 1904), privately printed pamphlet.

11. George Moore, *Modern Painting* (London: Walter Scott, 1893), pp. 5–6.

12. Max Beerbohm, *Yet Again* (London: Heinemann, 1928), pp. 108, 110.

13. G. K. Chesteron, *Heretics* (London: John Lane, 1909), pp. 239–41.

14. D. B. Wyndham Lewis, "Whistler," *English Wits,* ed. Leonard Russell (London: Hutchinson, 1940), p. 87. Bayliss, a minor artist rather than an influential critic like Taylor or Quilter, succeeded Whistler as president of the Royal Society of British Artists in 1888, when in reaction to Whistler's attempt to reform the staid group and remake it in his own image, he was ousted. His quarrels with all three are highlights of both versions of *The Gentle Art.*

15. George Moore, *Avowals* (London: privately printed, 1936), p. 23.

16. Frank Harris, "Whistler: Artist and Fighter," *Contemporary Portraits* (New York: Kennerley, 1915), pp. 85–86.

3. Schopenhauerian Compassion, Fictional Structure, and the Reader: The Example of Hardy and Conrad

1. Preliminary attempts to compare the two writers have appeared, e.g., Edward Wagenknecht, "'Pessimism' in Hardy and Conrad," *College English* 3 (1942), 546–54. Contrasts have also emerged, e.g., Kellog W. Hunt, "*Lord Jim* and *The Return of the Native*: A Contrast," *English Journal,* 49 (1960), pp. 447–56.

2. See also my "Compassion and Fictional Structure: The Example of Gissing and Bennett," *Studies in the Novel* 15 (1983): 293–313.

3. Structure may refer to a number of features in fiction. As used in this essay the term refers to the architectonic of a work, a design not dependent on plot pattern but comprised of a more pervasive and inherent principle of cohesion or of disintegration. Structure may exhibit external features (often corresponding to plot pattern) and internal features (either supportive or subversive to the external features). In *Jude* the hourglass shape, to be remarked, constitutes an external mode of structure and the spiral shape exemplifies an internal mode of structure. See my "Fictional Structure and Ethics in the Edwardian, Modern and Contemporary Novel," *Philological Quarterly* 62 (1984): 279–303.

4. The problem is manifest in G. W. Sherman's *The Pessimism of Thomas Hardy* (Rutherford, N. J.: Fairleigh Dickinson University Press, 1976) and is redressed in Ian Gregor's "*Jude the Obscure,*" in *Imagined Worlds: Essays in Some English Novels and Novelists in Honor of John Butt,* ed. Maynard Mack and Ian Gregor (London: Methuen, 1968), pp. 237–56; and in J. Hillis Miller's *Thomas Hardy: Distance and Desire* (Cambridge: Harvard University Press, 1970), p. 44.

5. See, e.g., Harvey Curtis Webster, *On a Darkling Plain: The Art and Thought of Thomas Hardy* (Chicago: University of Chicago Press, 1947); J. O. Bailey, "Hardy's Visions of the Self," *Studies in Philology* 56 (1959): 74–101; and

Bailey, "Evolutionary Meliorism in the Poetry of Thomas Hardy," *Studies in Philology* 60 (1963): 569–87.

6. William R. Rutland, *Thomas Hardy: A Study of His Writings and Their Background* (Oxford: Blackwell, 1938).

7. Eden Phillpotts, "Thomas Hardy and Schopenhauer," in *From the Angle of 88* (London: Hutchinson, 1951), pp. 68–76; Evelyn Hardy, *Thomas Hardy: A Critical Biography* (London: Hogarth Press, 1954), pp. 53, 286.

8. For example, Paul Neugebauer, *Schopenhauer in England: Mit Besonderer Berücksichtigung Seines Einfluesses auf die Englische Literatur* (Berlin: Doktordruck-Graphisches Institute Paul Funk, 1932), pp. 33–39.

9. As argued by Friedrich Wild, *Die Englische Literatur der Gegenwart seit 1870: Drama und Roman* (Wiesbaden: Drosburen, 1931), pp. 118–21, 159–68.

10. As remarked by Samuel C. Chew, "Homage to Thomas Hardy," *New Republic* 23 (21 June 1920): 22–26; Webster, pp. 196–98; and Bailey, p. 574.

11. Carl J. Weber, "Hardy's Copy of Schopenhauer," *Colby Library Journal* 4 (1957): 217–24.

12. Edward Wright, "The Novels of Thomas Hardy," *Quarterly Review* 199 (1904): 499–523; Harold Williams, "Thomas Hardy (1840)," in *Two Centuries of the English Novel* (London: Smith, Elder, 1911), pp. 283–303. See also Helen Garwood, *Thomas Hardy: An Illustration of the Philosophy of Schopenhauer* (Philadelphia: Winston, 1911).

13. Barry Schwartz, *"Jude the Obscure* in the Age of Anxiety," *Studies in English Literature* 10 (1970): 793–804.

14. Thomas Hardy, *Jude the Obscure,* ed. C. H. Sisson (Harmondsworth, England: Penguin, 1978), p. 451. Page references to subsequent quotations from this edition appear parenthetically in the text.

15. Arthur Schopenhauer, *The World as Will and Idea,* trans. R. B. Haldane and J. Kemp (London: Kegan Paul, Trench, Trübner, 1891), vol. 2, p. 411.

16. Lawrence Jones, "Thomas Hardy's 'Idiosyncratic Mode of Regard,'" *ELH* 42 (1975): 437.

17. Compare Schopenhauer, vol. 1, pp. 142, 419.

18. Schopenhauer, vol. 1, p. 400.

19. Schopenhauer, vol. 3, pp. 430–31.

20. How the Will turns against itself is, by Schopenhauer's own admission, a difficult and paradoxical concept. It is best explained by George Gissing. "The Hope of Pessimism," in *George Gissing: Essays and Fiction,* ed. Pierre Coustillas (Baltimore: Johns Hopkins University Press, 1970), pp. 76–97. On *Maya* Schopenhauer writes: "Maya is . . . this visible world in which we are, a summoned enchantment, an inconstant appearance without true being, like an optical illusion or a dream, a veil which surrounds human consciousness, something of which it is equally false and true to say that it is and that it is not" (vol. 2, p. 9).

21. As contended by Roy Morrell, *Thomas Hardy: The Will and the Way* (Singapore: University of Malaya Press, 1965).

22. Arnold Bennett, "Tendencies of Modern Literature," *T. P.'s Weekly* 14 (1909): 7–10.

23. As remarked by Jerome Hamilton Buckley, *The Triumph of Time* (Cambridge: Harvard University Press, 1966), p. 63.

24. Herbert Leslie Stewart, "Thomas Hardy as a Teacher of His Age," *North American Review* 208 (1918): 584–96.

25. In a thought-provoking, if sometimes mistaken essay by Morton Dauwen Zabel, "Hardy in Defense of His Art: The Aesthetic Incongruity," *Southern Review* 6 (1940): 125–49.

26. Phillpotts, pp. 74–75.

27. Schopenhauer, vol. 1, pp. 485-90, 530–31.

28. Schopenhauer, vol. 1, pp. 455, 490.

29. Lewis P. Horne, "'The Art of Renunciation' in Hardy's Novels," *Studies in the Novel* 4 (1972): 556–67. See also Norman Holland, *"Jude the Obscure*: Hardy's Symbolic Indictment of Christianity," *Nineteenth-Century Fiction* 9 (1954): 50–60.

30. Schopenhauer, vol. 1, pp. 526–28, endorses the idea of Christian renunciation, which he believes to have been improved upon by Buddhism and, finally, by his own philosophy.

31. Richard Benvenuto unconvincingly argues that Jude's love implies the intrinsic value, overlooked by the narrator, of individual lives: "Modes of Perception: The Will to Live in *Jude the Obscure," Studies in the Novel* 2 (1970): 31–41.

32. Philpotts, p. 69.

33. On the whole critics have disapproved of Hardy's characterization of Father Time. A cautionary note is in order, for possibly the idea of children appearing more aged than those of preceding generations may have had greater currency at the end of the nineteenth century than we now suspect. Theodore Roosevelt's sister, Anna, was thought by her family not only to be competent beyond her years but also to look tired, painfully sad, and years older than she was: David McCullough, *Mornings on Horseback* (New York: Simon & Schuster, 1981), pp. 32–35.

34. Geoffrey Thurley, *The Psychology of Hardy's Novels: The Nervous and the Statuesque* (St. Lucia, Queensland: University of Queensland Press, 1975), pp. 184–85.

35. Ian Gregor, "Hardy's World," *ELH* 38 (1971): 274–93.

36. Miller, p. 208; cf. pp. 259–60.

37. The conflicting points of view are typified by "Architecture and Thomas Hardy," *Architect and Building News* (London) 119 (20 Jan. 1928): 119–21, 139, 147; and William Lyon Phelps, "The Novels of Thomas Hardy," *North American Review* 190 (1909): 502–14.

38. Edmund William Gosse, "Mr. Hardy's New Novel," *Cosmopolis* 1 (1896): 60–69.

39. Florence Emily Hardy, *The Later Years of Thomas Hardy, 1892–1928* (New York: Macmillan, 1930), p. 40.

40. See Fernand Lagarda, "Apropos de la construction de *Jude the Obscure*," *Caliban* 3 (1966): 185–214.

41. See David Lodge, *"Jude the Obscure*: Pessimism and Fictional Form," in *Critical Approaches to the Fiction of Thomas Hardy*, ed. Dale Kramer (London: Macmillan, 1979), pp. 193–201.

42. See Margaret Makar, "Hardy's Poetry of Renunciation," *ELH* 45 (1978): 303–24; and Daniel R. Schwarz, "Beginnings and Endings in Hardy's Major Fiction," in *Critical Approaches*, pp. 17–35.

43. "The typological vision generally accompanies a profound determinism that always threatens to become pessimism": Sherman, p. 230. Cf. Schopenhauer, vol. 3, p. 227.

44. On the allusions to Christ, see Lodge, pp. 193–201.

45. Schopenhauer, vol. 3, p. 267.

46. Miller, p. 39.

47. Daniel R. Schwarz, "The Narrator as Character in Hardy's Major Fiction," *Modern Fiction Studies* 18 (1972): 155–72; and Dale Kramer, *"Jude the Obscure*: Doctrine or Distanced Narrative," in *Thomas Hardy: The Forms of Tragedy* (Detroit: Wayne State University Press, 1975), pp. 136–65. The opposite view, that the narrator insists on his knowledge and on the reader's dependence upon him, is argued by John Sutherland, "A Note on the Teasing Narrator of *Jude the Obscure,"* *English Literature in Transition* 17 (1974): 159–62; Sutherland is right to note the narrator's manner of getting the reader's attention, but the reason for this behavior lies in Hardy's intention to disrupt the reader's usual acceptance of the viewpoint of a third-person narrative voice.

48. See Miller, p. 6.

49. Robert W. Stallman, "Hardy's Hour Glass Novel," *Sewanee Review* 55 (1947): 283–96; reprinted in *The House That James Built and Other Literary Studies* (East Lansing: Michigan State University Press, 1961), pp. 53–63.

50. Where it is remarked as the true symbol of nature: Schopenhauer, vol. 3, p. 267. On another literary experiment in spiral structuring, vis-à-vis a revision of Schopenhauerian aesthetics, see my "Schopenhauer, Maori Symbolism, and Wells's *Brynhild,"* *Studies in the Literary Imagination* 13 (1980): 17–29.

51. Frank R. Giordana, Jr., *"Jude the Obscure* and the *Bildungsroman,"* *Studies in the Novel* 4 (1972): 580–91.

52. E. g., J. Pitt, "Things and Other Things: Letters to Living Authors—VII. Mr. Thomas Hardy," *Good Words* 43 (1902): 647–76; Wilfred S. Durant, "The Disciple of Destiny," *Fortnightly Review* 91 (1909): 1117–24.

53. Usually for inadequate catharsis, e.g., W. M. Payne, "Recent Fiction," *Dial* 20 (1 Feb. 1896): 76–77; Williams, pp. 283–303.

54. D. H. Lawrence, "Hardy's 'Prédilection d'artiste,'" in *Phoenix* (New York: Viking, 1936), pp. 434–40. See also Arthur Mizener, *"Jude the Obscure* as Tragedy," *Southern Review* 6 (1940): 193–213. The opposite position is taken by Zabel, pp. 125–49, and Ted R. Spivey, "Thomas Hardy's Tragic Hero," *Nineteenth-Century Fiction* 9 (1954): 179–91.

55. My distinction between tragedy and pathos is indebted to excellent studies by two of my colleagues: Warwick Wadlington, "Pathos and Dreiser," *Southern Review* 7 (1971): 411–29; and Anthony Channell Hilfer, *The Ethics of Intensity in American Fiction* (Austin: University of Texas Press, 1981). Pathos is the dominant mode of literary naturalism, a problematical term but one which has been applied to Hardy: D. F. Hannigan, "Mr. Thomas Hardy's Latest Novel," *Westminster Review* 142 (1896): 136–39; William Newton,"Chance as Employed by Hardy and the Naturalists," *Philological Quarterly* 30 (1951): 154–75; and Newton, "Hardy and the Naturalists: Their Use of Physiology," *Modern Philology* 49 (1951): 28–41.

56. A sense of tragedy would indeed be evoked if, as David DeLaura has argued, Jude fails because of the gap between his humanitarian ideal and his historical situation: "The Ache of Modernism in Hardy's Later Novels," *ELH* 34 (1967): 380–99 (cf. Miller, p. 213); and it would be evoked as well if, as Bert G. Hornback has argued, Hardy's characters are not determined, but have the power to choose: *The Metaphor of Chance: Vision and Technique in the Works of Thomas Hardy* (Athens: Ohio University Press, 1971).

57. James R. Kincaid, "Hardy's Absences," in *Critical Approaches,* p. 205. Hardy's use of a pseudo-tragic figure who cheats the reader of fulfillment of expectations elicited by the novel is discussed in Robert Evans' "The Other Eustacia," *Novel* 1 (1968): 251–59. And on the frustration of the reader's search for

an authoritative interpretation of the text, see Ramón Saldívar's *"Jude the Obscure*: Reading and the Spirit of the Law," *ELH* 50 (1983): 607–25.

58. Miller formulates Hardy's artistic objective: "The wider, the more detached, the more impersonal, the more disinterested, the more clear and objective a man's view is the closer he will come to seeing the truth of things as they are"; art "holds things at a distance and imitates in another pattern the objective patterns in the outside world which have held his attention through their power to generate an emotional fascination. Such an art is at once a reaction to the external world, and a protection against it. It is a transformation of the reaction into a shape which imitates it at a distance." Two corrections are needed here: one, the external world of phenomena evinces patterns only insofar as conscious minds seek those patterns and in the process posit them, and this is also true of art; second, artistic detachment for Hardy, at least in *Jude,* also requires profound philosophical compassion.

59. Thomas Hardy, *Tess of the D'Urbervilles: A Pure Woman Faithfully Presented* (1891), ed. William E. Buckler (Boston: Houghton-Mifflin, 1960), p. xxii. Pertinent is James Gindon's discussion of Hardy in *Harvest of the Quiet Eye: The Novel of Compassion* (Bloomington: Indiana University Press, 1971), pp. 78–101.

60. Schopenhauer, vol. 1, p. 271. See also Gissing, p. 95.

61. By John A. Palmer, *Joseph Conrad's Fiction: A Study in Literary Growth* (Ithaca: Cornell University Press, 1968).

62. Edward Said, *Joseph Conrad and the Fiction of Autobiography* (Cambridge: Harvard University Press, 1966). See also Ian Watt, *"Heart of Darkness* and Nineteenth-Century Thought," *Partisan Review* 45 (1978): 108–19.

63. John Galsworthy, *Castles in Spain* (New York: Scribner's, 1927), p. 121; Galsworthy, "Reminiscences of Conrad: 1924" in *Two Essays on Conrad* (Freelands: privately printed and Cincinnati: Ebbert and Richardson, 1930), p. 52. See also Bruce Johnson, *Conrad's Models of Mind* (Minneapolis: University of Minnesota Press, 1971), pp. 41–53. Johnson argues that Conrad repudiated Schopenhauer's denial of the ego through selflessness and emphasized art celebrating individual will as the crucial source of value. In "Conrad's 'Pessimisim' Re-Examined" (*Conradiana* 2, no. 3 [1969–70], 25–38) Lee M. Whitehead suggests that critics have overestimated the presence of Schopenhauerian pessimism in Conrad's writings.

64. William W. Bonney, *Thorns and Arabesques: Contexts for Conrad's Fiction* (Baltimore: Johns Hopkins University Press,1980), pp. 3–11.

65. See Lillian Feder, "Marlow's Descent Into Hell," *Nineteenth-Century Fiction* 9 (1955): 280–92; and Robert O. Evans, "Conrad's Underworld," *Modern Fiction Studies* 2 (1956): 56–62.

66. Joseph Conrad, *Heart of Darkness,* ed. Robert Kimbrough (New York: Norton, 1971), pp. 14, 17. Page references to subsequent quotations from this edition appear parenthetically in the text.

67. On the role of the harlequinesque Russian in the novel, see C. F.Burgess, "Conrad's Pesky Russian," *Nineteenth-Century Fiction* 18 (1963): 189–93; John Edward Hardy, "'Heart of Darkness': The Russian in Motley," in *Man in the Modern Novel* (Seattle: University of Washington Press, 1964), pp. 17–33; Mario D'Avanzo, "Conrad's Motley as an Organizing Metaphor in *Heart of Darkness,"* *College Language Association* 9 (1966): 289–91; John W. Canario, "The Harlequin in *Heart of Darkness,"* *Studies in Short Fiction* 4 (1967): 225–33; Jack Helder, "Fool Convention and Conrad's Hollow Harlequin," *Studies in Short Fiction* 12 (1975): 361–68; and Emily K. Yoder, "The Demon Harlequin in Conrad's Hell," *Conradiana* 12 (1980): 88–92.

68. The *danse macabre* figures in Cecil Scrimgeour's "Jimmy Wait and the Dance of Death: Conrad's *Nigger of the Narcissus*," *Critical Quarterly* 7 (1965): 339–52.

69. Alan Warren Friedman errs, I think, in believing that "Marlow seizes grotesquely on the morality of ideas" but is correct in adding that for Marlow ideas "remain . . . problematical, a matter demanding continual struggle, always in motion": "Conrad's Picaresque Narrator: Marlow's Journey from *Youth* to *Chance*," in *Multivalence: The Moral Quality of Form in the Modern Novel* (Baton Rouge: Louisiana State University Press, 1978), pp. 108–40. Others have singled out certain ideas which Marlow is said to endorse, even imperialism (Leo Gurko, *Joseph Conrad: Giant in Exile* [London: Macmillan,1962], pp. 148–53). On other features of Conrad's attitude toward ideas, see Allan O. McIntyre, "Conrad on the Function of the Mind," *Modern Language Quarterly* 25 (1964): 187–97.

70. William Bysshe Stein, "The Lotus Posture and *Heart of Darkness*," *Modern Fiction Studies* 2 (1956–57): 167–70. See also Stein, "Buddhism and 'Heart of Darkness,'" *Western Humanities Review* 11 (1957): 281–85; Stein, "Bodhisattva Scenario," *Orient/West* 9 (1964): 37–46; and H. C. Brashers, "Conrad, Marlow, and Gautama Buddha: On Structure and Theme in *Heart of Darkness*," *Conradiana* 1, no. 3 (1969): 63–72. In *"Heart of Darkness* and the Problem of Emptiness" (*Studies in Short Fiction* 9 [1972]: 387–400) Bruce Johnson explains, "The emptiness, indeed nothingness, so often intimated, continually eludes the Buddha defense, which after all is equipped for nearly the opposite kind of threat." This position supersedes the issue of whether Marlow in some sense discovers a moral universe, e.g., Jerome Thale, "Marlow's Quest," *University of Toronto Quarterly* 24 (1955): 351–58; and Robert F. Haugh, *Joseph Conrad: Discovery in Design* (Norman: University of Oklahoma Press, 1957), pp. 35–40.

71. Arnold Bennett, "The Progress of the Novel," *Realist* 1 (1 April 1929): 3–11. See also note 2. A distinction between simple and complex altruism in *Heart,* albeit with inadequate grounding in the Schopenhauerian context with which the discussion begins, is provided by Lawrence Graver, *Conrad's Short Fiction* (Berkeley: University of California Press, 1969). See also Garry Geddes, "The Structure of Sympathy: Conrad and the Chance That Wasn't," *English Literature in Transition* 12 (1969): 175–88; and Juliet McLauchlan, "The 'Something Human' in *Heart of Darkness*," *Conradiana* 9 (1977): 115–25.

72. See Bruce R. Stark, "Kurtz's Intended: The Heart of *Heart of Darkness*," *Texas Studies in Literature and Language* 16 (1974): 535–55; and James Ellis, "Kurtz's Voice: The Intended as 'The Horror,'" *English Literature in Transition* 19 (1976): 105–10.

73. See Gerald B. Kauvar, "Marlow as Liar," *Studies in Short Fiction* 5 (1968): 290–92. Other features of the lie are discussed by Kenneth A. Bruffee, "The Lesser Nightmare: Marlow's Lie in *Heart of Darkness*," *Modern Language Quarterly* 25 (1964): 322–29; and Ted E. Boyle, "Marlow's 'Life' in 'Heart of Darkness,'" *Studies in Short Fiction* 1 (1964): 159–63.

74. See Robert Kimbrough's annotations: *Heart of Darkness*, pp. 33, 57. That, finally, *Heart* is more concerned with adjustment than with judgment is noted by Sanford Pinsker, *The Language of Joseph Conrad* (Amsterdam: Rodopi, 1978), p. 48. See also John A. McClure, "The Rhetoric of Restraint in *Heart of Darkness*," *Nineteenth-Century Fiction* 32 (1977): 310–26.

75. See Stark, pp. 546–48.

76. This dual position is what Peter J. Glassman slights when he concludes that Marlow and the narrator, recoiling from experience, define themselves by an

aversion to life: "The Horror: *Heart of Darkness,*" in *Language and Being: Joseph Conrad and the Language of Personality* (New York: Columbia University Press, 1976), pp. 198–249. On the other hand, involvement does not necessarily imply Conrad's disapproval of Marlow's response, as argued by Eliose Knapp Hay, *The Political Novels of Joseph Conrad: A Critical Study* (Chicago: University of Chicago Press, 1963).

77.   On Kurtz and Marlow as artists, see Elsa Nettels, "'Heart of Darkness' and the Creative Process," *Conradiana* 5, no. 2 (1973): 66–73.

78.   On the correspondence between this passage and Conrad's method, see Stewart C. Wilcox, "Conrad's 'Complicated Presentations' of Symbolic Imagery in *Heart of Darkness,*" *Philological Quarterly* 39 (1960): 1–17. On Marlow's trouble with language, see Bruce Johnson, "Names, Naming, and the 'Inscrutable' in Conrad's *Heart of Darkness,*" *Texas Studies in Literature and Language* 12 (1971): 675–88; and on Marlow's use of language as both an abstraction and as a tool of vision, see Jerry Wasserman, "Narrative Presence: The Illusion of Language in *Heart of Darkness,*" *Studies in the Novel* 6 (1974): 327–38; and Jeremy Hawthorn, *Joseph Conrad: Language and Fictional Self-Consciousness* (Lincoln: University of Nebraska Press, 1979), pp. 7–36.

79.   Roger Ramsey, "The Available and the Unavailable 'I' in Conrad and James," *English Literature in Transition* 14 (1971): 137–45; Elsa Nettels, "James and Conrad on the Art of Fiction," *Texas Studies in Literature and Language* 14 (1972): 524–43; and Ian Watt, "Marlow, Henry James, and 'Heart of Darkness,'" *Nineteenth-Century Fiction* 33 (1978): 159–74. On the void at the center see Albert Spaulding Cook, "Plot as Discovery: Conrad, Dostoevski, and Faulkner," in *The Meaning of Fiction* (Detroit: Wayne State University Press, 1960), pp. 202–41.

80.   The topography of the telling, oscillating between a collective "we" and an isolated "I," is discussed in L. J. Morrissey's "The Tellers in *Heart of Darkness:* Conrad's Chinese Boxes," *Conradiana* 13 (1981): 141–48. On Conrad's notion of art as a means of bringing things together and of keeping them at a distance, see J. Hillis Miller, "Joseph Conrad," in *Poets of Reality: Six Twentieth-Century Writers* (Cambridge: Harvard University Press, 1965), pp. 13–67.

81.   On Melville and Conrad, see Frank MacShane, "Conrad on Melville," *American Literature* 29 (1958): 463–64; Jesse D. Green, "Diabolism, Pessimism, and Democracy: Notes on Melville and Conrad" *Modern Fiction Studies* 8 (1962): 287–305; and Leon F. Seltzer, "Like Repels Like: The Case of Conrad's Antipathy for Melville," *Conradiana* 1, no. 3 (1969): 101–5.

4. Hardy's Interest in the Law

1.   Richard H. Taylor, ed., *The Personal Notebooks of Thomas Hardy with an Appendix Including the Unpublished Passages in the Original Typescript of "The Life of Thomas Hardy"* (New York: Columbia University Press, 1979), p. 241.

2.   Ibid., p. 230.

3.   Ibid., p. 70.

4.   D. F. Barber, ed., *Concerning Thomas Hardy: A Composite Portrait from Memory* (London: Charles Skilton Ltd., 1968), p. 28.

5.   Ibid.

6.   J. O. Bailey, *The Poetry of Thomas Hardy: A Handbook and Commentary* (Chapel Hill: University of North Carolina Press, 1970), p. 534.

7. Evelyn Hardy, ed., *Thomas Hardy's Notebooks and Some Letters from Julia Augusta Martin* (London: Hogarth Press,1955), pp. 82–83.

8. Ibid., p. 82.

9. Ibid., p. 83.

10. Harold Orel, ed., *Thomas Hardy's Personal Writings, Prefaces, Literary Opinions, Reminiscences* (Lawrence: University of Kansas Press, 1966), p. 229.

11. Bailey, pp. 533–34.

12. Taylor, pp. 124–25.

13. Florence Emily Hardy, *The Life of Thomas Hardy 1840–1928* (1928, 1930; reprint, London: Macmillan and Co., Ltd., 1962), p. 124.

14. G. Stevens Cox believes that the murderer was James Seale, who committed a murder in the little village of Stoke Abbott, near Beaminster, and was hanged as a consequence at Dorchester on 10 August 1858. "The Dreadful Murder at Stoke Abbott and the Public Execution of James Seale," *The Thomas Hardy Yearbook 1970* (No. 1), pp. 85–93.

15. F. E. Hardy, pp. 28–29.

16. Ibid., p. 153.

17. Ibid., p. 162.

18. Ibid., p. 214.

19. Ibid., p. 255.

20. Ibid., pp. 294–295.

21. F. B. Pinion, *A Hardy Companion: A Guide to the Works of Thomas Hardy and Their Background* (London: Macmillan, 1968), p. 293; *The Variorum Edition of the Complete Poems of Thomas Hardy,* ed. James Gibson (New York: Macmillan, 1979), p. 780.

22. F. E. Hardy, p. 317.

23. Taylor, pp. 8–9.

24. F. E. Hardy, pp. 107–8.

25. Taylor, p. 129.

26. F. E. Hardy, p. 392.

27. Ibid., p. 189.

28. Ibid., p. 213.

29. Ibid., p. 454.

30. Ibid., p. 374.

31. Bailey, pp. 419–20.

32. F. E. Hardy, p. 126.

33. Ibid., p. 209.

34. Richard Little Purdy and Michael Millgate, eds., *The Collected Letters of Thomas Hardy,* (Oxford: Clarendon Press, 1980), vol. 2, 1893–1901, pp. 15–16.

35. Ibid., pp. 223, 229.

36. Ibid., p. 272.

37. F. E. Hardy, p. 41.

38. Ibid., p. 240.

39. Ibid., p. 227.

40. Ibid., p. 236.

41. Ibid., p. 395.

42. R. J. White, *Thomas Hardy and History* (London: Macmillan Press Ltd., 1974), p. 6.

43. Lennart A. Bjork, ed., *The Literary Notes of Thomas Hardy* (Goteborg, Sweden: Acta Universitatis Gothoburgensis, 1974), vol. 2, p. 620.

44. Evelyn Hardy and F. B. Pinion, ed., *One Rare Fair Woman: Thomas Hardy's Letters to Florence Henniker 1893–1922* (London: Macmillan, 1972), p. 170.

45. Bjork, vol. 2, p. 620.

46. For a quick and readable review of the ways in which Hardy's understanding of legal niceties pertaining to the profession of an author surpassed that held by many of his contemporaries, see John Gross's *The Rise and Fall of the Man of Letters: Aspects of English Literary Life since 1800* (London: Weidenfeld and Nicolson, 1969) and, of course, Hardy's own correspondence.

47. Purdy and Millgate, vol. 1, p. 290.

48. Ibid., vol. 2, p. 62.

49. F. B. Pinion, p. 496.

50. F. E. Hardy, p. 251.

51. Orel, p. 34.

52. Purdy and Millgate, vol. 2, p. 154.

53. *Dorset County Chronicle,* February 18, 1886, as quoted by Edward C. Sampson, "Thomas Hardy: Justice of the Peace," *Colby Library Quarterly* 13, no. 4 (December 1977): 264.

54. Sampson, p. 270.

55. *Dorset County Chronicle,* September 5,1918, as quoted by Sampson, p. 271.

56. F. E. Hardy, p. 227.

57. Ibid., p. 167.

58. Purdy and Millgate, vol. 2, p. 50.

59. Robert Gittings and Jo Manton, *The Second Mrs. Hardy* (London: Heinemann, 1979), pp. 123–25.

5. The Nature of Things: Hopkins and Scotus

1. Thomas Aquinas, *Summa Theologica* Ia. 85, 1.

2. Thomas Aquinas, *Summa Contra Gentiles* 4. 81.

3. Ibid., 2. 54; 1. 22.

4. Gerard Manley Hopkins, *The Poems of Gerard Manley Hopkins,* ed. W. H. Gardner and N. H. Mackenzie, 4th ed. (London: Oxford University Press, 1967), pp. 211–12; *Liber Usualis with Introduction and Rubrics in English,* ed. Benedictines of Solesmes (Tournai, Belgium: Desclée, 1938), pp. 1855–56.

5. Hopkins, *Poems,* p. 79.

6. James Finn Cotter, *Inscape: The Christology and Poetry of Gerard Manley Hopkins* (Pittsburgh: University of Pittsburgh Press, 1972), p. 126.

7. Gerard Manley Hopkins, *The Sermons and Devotional Writings of Gerard Manley Hopkins,* ed. Christopher Devlin, S.J. (London: Oxford University Press, 1959), p. 151.

8. *Summa Theologica,* Ia. 5. 2.

9. Hopkins, *Poems,* p. 105.

10. John Duns Scotus, *Commentaria Oxoniensia* 4. 45. 3, no.17.

11. John Duns Scotus, *Quodlibitales* 13. 8010.

12. John Duns Scotus, *De Anima* 22. 3.

13. *Commentaria Oxoniensia* 4. 45. 2; and *Quodlibitales* 7, no. 8.

14. John Duns Scotus, *Quaestiones subtilissimae super libros Metaphysicorum* 2. 1, no. 2.
15. *The Poems of Gerard Manley Hopkins,* p. 267.
16. *Commentaria Oxoniensia* 4. 13. 1, no. 8.
17. *Commentaria Oxoniensia* 2. 3. 6, no. 5; *Quaestiones subtilissimae super libros Metaphysicorum* 7. 13, no. 7.

6. A Reconsideration:
Confessions of a Young Man as Farce

1. Several recent studies of *Confessions* analyze its autobiographical characteristics. See Robert Michael Scotto's "Self-Portraits of the Apprentice Artist: Walter Pater's *Marius,* George Moore's *Confessions,* and James Joyce's *A Portrait of the Artist*" (Ph.D. diss., City University of New York, 1970); Betty Lucille Drawbaugh's "The Autobiographical Works of George Moore" (Ph.D. diss., Columbia University, 1972); Brian Greenwood Donovan, "George Moore's Fictive Autobiography" (Ph.D. diss., University of Minnesota, 1974); Michael M. Riley's "Persona and Theme in George Moore's *Confessions of a Young Man,*" *English Literature in Transition* 19 (1979): 87–95; and Jean C. Noël's "George Moore's Pluridimensional Autobiography (Remarks on his *Confessions of a Young Man*)," *Cahiers du Centre D'Etudes Irlandaises* 4 (1970): 49–66.
2. Jacques-Emile Blanche, "Mes Models: George Moore," *Nouvelles Litteraires* 7 (16, 23 June 1928): 6, 6.
3. John A'Dreams, *"Confessions of a Young Man,"* Hawk 1 (10 April 1888): 172.
4. George Moore, *Confessions of a Young Man*, ed. Susan Dick (Montreal and London: McGill-Queen's University Press, 1972), p. 165. All further references to *Confessions* are made from this text and noted parenthetically.
5. Ronald Paulson, *The Fictions of Satire* (Baltimore, MD: Johns Hopkins University Press, 1967), p. 4.
6. Paulson, p. 6.
7. David Worcester, *The Art of Satire,* 2nd ed. (New York: Russell & Russell, 1960), p. 37.
8. Edith Kern, *The Absolute Comic* (New York: Columbia University Press,1980), p. 115.
9. Morton Gurewitch, *Comedy: The Irrational Vision* (Ithaca and London: Cornell University Press, 1975), p. 128.
10. Gurewitch, p. 136.
11. Gurewitch, p. 135.
12. Gurewitch, p. 150.
13. Gurewitch, p. 159.
14. Gurewitch, p. 153.
15. See Noël's "George Moore's Pluridimensional Autobiography (Remarks on his *Confessions of a Young Man*)," *Cahiers du Centre D'Etudes Irlandaises* 4 (1970): 44–66.
16. See Moore's *Literature at Nurse, or Circulating Morals* (London: Vizetelly, 1885), an attack on circulating libraries, particularly Mudie's, for their exercise of censorship. Moore was angered that Mudie refused to stock adequately *A Modern*

Lover and *A Mummer's Wife.* For more details, see Edwin Gilcher's *A Bibliography of George Moore* (DeKalb, IL: Northern Illinois University Press,1970), pp. 15–16.

17. Susan Dick presents a concise background to the Colin Campbell divorce case, a trial held in 1886 which the papers happily exploited, p. 250, n. 12.

18. Nathan A. Scott, Jr., "The Bias of Comedy and the Narrow Escape to Faith," *Comedy: Meaning and Form,* ed. Robert Corrigan (San Francisco: Chandler Publishing Co., 1965), pp. 167–86, explores how the radical nature of comedy helps to assist us in capturing what in human experience is lost to time.

19. Susanne K. Langer, "The Comic Rhythm," *Comedy: Meaning and Form,* ed. Robert Corrigan (San Francisco: Chandler Publishing Co., 1965), pp. 102–25, asserts that the underlying feeling of comedy is a "pure sense of life," that the basic nature of comedy is the bawdy and sensuous.

20. For some reactions to Moore's attacks on Hardy, Conrad, and other writers, see "George Moore Popular Idol at Last: Takes Fling at Everybody," *Boston Herald,* 3 April 1928, p. 28; "Mr. Moore on Hardy," *Manchester Guardian,* 4 April 1928, p. 9; Hadden Knight, "Did Mr. Moore Mean It?" *London Daily Express,* 5 April 1928, p. 8.

7. In Excelsis: Wilde's Epistolary Relationship with Lord Alfred Douglas

1. *The Autobiography of Lord Alfred Douglas* (1929; reprint London: Martin Secker, 1931), p. 114.

2. André Gide, *Oscar Wilde: In Memoriam* (Paris: Mercure de France, 1913), p. 12.

3. Letter of [ca. 16 April 1894], *The Letters of Oscar Wilde,* ed. Rupert Hart-Davis (London: Rupert Hart-Davis, 1962), p. 354. Further references to all letters, including *De Profundis,* are to this edition and will be given parenthetically in the text.

4. In *Intentions,* ed. Robert Ross (1891; reprint, London: Methuen, 1908), pp. 23–24.

5. "The Critic as Artist, Part I," in *Intentions,* p. 150.

6. Quoted in H. Montgomery Hyde, *The Trials of Oscar Wilde* (1948; reprint, New York: Dover 1973), p. 101.

7. Quoted in Hyde, *Trials,* p. 117. Wilde's friend Pierre Louÿs published a sonnet in French based on this letter in *The Spirit Lamp* (4 May 1893), an Oxford undergraduate periodical edited by Douglas.

8. "The Decay of Lying," in *Intentions,* p. 15.

9. Several months later Douglas planned to publish these three letters in an article he had written for the *Mercure de France,* but with the aid of Robert Sherard, Wilde managed to prevent publication. A French translation of this manuscript is at Princeton; an English translation by Stuart Mason is at the William Andrews Clark Memorial Library (UCLA). Douglas claimed to have destroyed the originals, and Hart-Davis prints the English translation by Mason (see Hart-Davis, p. 393 n. 1). Two of the three surviving letters by Douglas to Wilde are at the Clark, one of which was written while Wilde was in Holloway.

10. The manuscript was given to Wilde by prison officials on the day of his release. Wilde gave it to Robert Ross, who had two typed copies made, one of

which he sent to Alfred Douglas, who denied ever receiving it (see his *Autobiography*, p. 135, for his rather implausible explanation). In 1905 Ross published a highly expurgated version under the title *De Profundis* (London: Methuen) which was approximately half the original's length and gave no indication that it was addressed to Douglas. In 1908 Ross included a slightly less expurgated version in the Collected Edition, and in the following year he turned over the manuscript to the British Museum with the proviso that no one see it for fifty years. The second typescript was given by Ross to Vyvyan Holland, Wilde's youngest son; this typescript was used for the text of *De Profundis* published by Holland in 1949. This version, according to Hart-Davis (p. 424 n. 1), contained "several hundred errors," many of which were errors in Ross's typescript. The original manuscript was made available to the public in 1959, and Hart-Davis was the first to make an accurate transcription.

   11. Hyde, *Oscar Wilde: A Biography* (New York: Farrar, Straus and Giroux, 1975), p. 233.
   12. Douglas, *Autobiography*, p. 135.
   13. "The Portrait of Mr. W. H.," *Blackwood's Edinburgh Magazine* 146 (July 1889): 1–21; reprinted in *Lord Arthur Savile's Crime and Other Prose Pieces*, ed. Robert Ross (London: Methuen, 1908), p. 147.

8. Oscar Wilde's *Salome,* the Salome Theme in Late European Art, and a Problem of Method in Cultural History

   1. Carl E. Schorske, *Fin-de-siècle Vienna: Politics and Culture* (New York: Alfred Knopf, 1980), p. xix.
   2. The major studies are by Rafael Cansinos Assens, *Salome en la Literatura* (Madrid: Editorial-America, 1919); Hugo Daffner, *Salome: Ihre Gestalt in Geschichte und Kunst* (Munich: H. Schmidt Verlag, 1912); John S. White, *The Salome Motive* (New York: New York City Opera Co., 1947); and Helen Grace Zagona, *The Legend of Salome and the Principle of Art for Art's Sake* (Paris: Librarie Minard, 1960). Other extensive treatments may be found in such works as Mario Praz's *The Romantic Agony* and Frank Kermode's *Romantic Image*.
   3. Of course probably all works of art are in some sense "irrational," and "irrationality" can be manifest in many ways: it is one of the staple elements of comedy, certainly, but it appears in other guises as well—consider for example, Wylie Sypher's discussion of the tensions in mannerist art in his *Four Stages of Renaissance Style* (Garden City, N.Y.: Doubleday & Co., 1955), pp. 162 ff. The distinctive kind of irrationality to which I refer appears in works of high art with growing frequency in the latter half of the nineteenth century and thereafter and is marked by striking contradictoriness, inconsistency, or disconnectedness—in short, by some distinct "lack of match" between elements in a work which calls attention to itself and contributes in a major way to the effect the work of art creates. Twentieth-century constructions like Meret Oppenheim's fur-lined teacup represent extremes of the kind of irrationality which concerns me here. It is possible, I think, to trace the emergence of this phenomenon in art from a beginning in eighteenth-century Europe: see, for example, George Rosen's

"Forms of Irrationality in the Eighteenth Century" in *Irrationalism in the Eighteenth Century*, Studies in Eighteenth-Century Culture, vol. 2, ed. by Harold E. Pagliaro (Cleveland and London: Case Western Reserve University Press, 1972), 255–88; however, from the late nineteenth century onward it becomes far more common in European art and appears in such diverse movements as dadaism, surrealism, and the theater of the absurd.

4. Translation based on the text in *Oeuvres Complètes*, ed. Henri Mondor and G. Jean-Aubry (Paris: Editions Gallimard, 1961), pp. 47–48, but incorporating a variant provided on p. 1445. Except for Wilde's *Salome*, this and all subsequent translations are mine.

5. My references to Moreau's principles of "the beauty of inertia" and of "necessary richness" are indebted to the discussion of those principles in Ary Renan's *Gustave Moreau 1826–1898* (Paris: *Gazette des Beaux Arts,* 1900), particularly pp. 26, 33, and 36–44.

6. On page 49 of the transcription of Moreau's *Notebook III* in the Moreau Museum, Paris, he described Salome as "that woman who represents the eternal feminine . . . in search of some vague ideal. . . . She is the emblem of sensuality, of unhealthy curiosity, and of that terrible fate reserved for searchers after a nameless ideal."

7. In a manuscript note in the Moreau Museum, reproduced in Julius Kaplan's *Gustave Moreau* (Greenwich, Connecticut: New York Graphic Society, 1974), p. 144, Moreau wrote: "Thus in my Salome I wanted to portray the image of a sibyl and of a sacred enchantress with a special quality. I had in that light conceived her costume, which is like a reliquary."

8. Kaplan, p. 35.

9. Wilde certainly knew des Esseintes' well-known meditations on the Mallarmé and Moreau works in *A Rebours* (Paris: Bibliothèque-Charpentier, 1923), pp. 69–78 and 259–61, though it should be stressed that certain supposed features of Moreau's picture—for example, those conveyed by Huysmans' lines, "Her breasts undulate, and, from the rubbing of her / necklaces which swing about, their nipples grow erect"—bear no obvious relation to Moreau's painting, whatever they may convey about des Esseintes' fevered imagination.

10. Alan Bird, *The Plays of Oscar Wilde* (New York: Barnes and Noble, 1977), p. 74.

11. *The Complete Works of Oscar Wilde,* vol. 10. (New York: Doubleday, Page & Company, 1923), pp. 128–31. Further citations to this edition are indicated by page numbers inserted parenthetically in the text.

12. Keven Sullivan, *Oscar Wilde* (New York: Columbia University Press, 1972), p. 23.

13. Beardsley's illustrations for *Salome,* including those which were suppressed or not included in the first edition, are conveniently reproduced in Aubrey Beardsley, *Zeichnungen* (Berlin: Gerhardt Verlag, 1966), fols. 1–17.

14. Quoted in Stanley Weintraub, *Beardsley: A Biography* (New York: George Braziller, 1967), p. 70.

15. See, for example, Norman Del Mar, *Richard Strauss: A Critical Commentary on His Life and Works* (New York: Macmillan Company, 1962), pp. 238–86.

16. Richard Strauss, *Recollections and Reflections* (New York and London: Boosey and Hawkes, 1953), p. 152.

17. Gary Schmidgall, *Literature as Opera* (New York: Oxford University Press, 1977), p. 281.

18. Useful surveys are provided by Alessandra Comini's *Gustav Klimt* (New York: George Braziller, 1975) and in Carl E. Schorske's *Fin-de-siècle Vienna* (see note 1).

19. See, for example, the "Salome" titled reproduction in *Die Kunst* 25 (1912): 173.

20. Comini, p. 22.

21. Comini, p. 25, provides a photograh of Fanchette Verhunk and invites comparison with the figure of *Judith II*.

22. See, for example, Werner Hofmann's *Gustav Klimt*, trans. Inge Goodwin (Boston: New York Graphic Society, 1971), p. 59. Even the original *Judith II*, now in the Galleria Internazionale d'Arte Moderna in Venice, has on its frame a brass museum plaque which gives the title "Salome" in parentheses.

23. Flaubert's story is almost certainly the source of some of the details Wilde incorporated in his play, including the name *Iokanaan* for John. Heine's *Atta Troll* has sometimes been suggested as a source for Wilde's Salome kissing Iokanaan's head, though this attribution has been questioned by Richard Ellmann in "Overtures to Wilde's *Salome*," *Yearbook of Comparative and General Literature*, vol. 17, 1968, and Ellmann's objections themselves questioned by Philip Cohen in his *The Moral Vision of Oscar Wilde* (1978).

24. Heinrich Heine, *Sämtliche Schriften* (Darmstadt: Wissenschaftliche Buchgesellschaft, 1971), 4:547.

25. See particularly the discussion of the "fatal woman" theme in Mario Praz's *The Romantic Agony* (London: Oxford University Press, 1951), especially chapters 4 and 5; the "dancer" motif is discussed extensively in Frank Kermode's *Romantic Image* (London: Routledge & Kegan Paul Ltd., 1957), chapter 4.

26. One cannot object, certainly, to studies which limit themselves to systematically exposing the confusions surrounding vague categories sometimes widely used in cultural history—I have in mind works like Richard Gilman's recent *Decadence: The Strange Life of an Epithet* (New York: Farrar, Strauss, and Giroux, 1979). But it is even more important, I think, to attempt the more constructive task of identifying well-defined lines of development in the arts which are often masked by the vagueness of terms which have come to be applied to them in slipshod ways. I have tried, for example, to do that while sorting out some of the confusions surrounding that notoriously slippery term *impressionism* in a study titled "Swinburne, Hopkins, and the Roots of Modernism," *University of Hartford Studies in Literature* 11 (1979): 157–72. An excellent recent example of the kind of constructive effort I have in mind is Marshall Brown's "The Logic of Realism: A Hegelian Approach," *PMLA* 96 (1981): 224–41.

9. The Publication of *The Private Life of Henry Maitland*: A Literary Event

1. See Pierre Coustillas, "Thomas Seccombe writes the Gissing entry in the *D.N.B.*," *Gissing Newsletter*, October 1977, pp. 1–18, and January 1978, pp. 18–34.

2. Roberts wrote the following articles and reviews in Gissing's lifetime: "George Gissing," *Novel Review*, May 1892, pp. 97–103; "Mr. Gissing's New

Novel [*The Crown of Life*] and—Mr. Gissing," *Review of the Week*, 4 November 1899, pp. 16–17; and "George Gissing," *Literature*, 20 July 1901, p. 52.

3. "In Memoriam: George Gissing," *Church Times*, 8 January 1904, p. 33. The *Westminster Gazette* ("George Gissing: A High Churchman," 9 January 1904, p. 8) commented on this article, which drew a protest from Roberts in the form of a letter to the editor ("George Gissing," 11 January 1904, p. 12). Another letter, this time to the editor of the *Church Times* ("The Late George Gissing," 15 January 1904, p. 11) was followed by some editorial comment on 29 January 1904, p. 130.

4. Published anonymously in the *Albany Magazine*, Christmas 1904, pp. 24–31. Reprinted in *George Gissing: Critical Essays*, ed. J. P. Michaux (London: Vision, 1981).

5. See especially chapter 1, in which the characteristic Gissing notes abound.

6. Unpublished letter in the Berg Collection of the New York Public Library.

7. "Tritt" was collected in *Midsummer Madness*, one of Roberts's many volumes of short stories (London: Eveleigh Nash, 1909). I am indebted to Professor T. E. M. Boll for drawing my attention to it. For comments on this story, see Pierre Coustillas, "Plitt into Tritt: Gissing's Travelling Companion in a Short Story by Morley Roberts," *Gissing Newsletter*, January 1983, pp. 1–30.

8. See Pierre Coustillas, "The Stormy Publication of Gissing's *Veranilda*," *Bulletin of the New York Public Library*, 72 (November 1968): 588–610.

9. All the letters from Clara Collet to Morley Roberts quoted in this article are in the Berg Collection, New York Public Library. Citations from his replies are from copies in the present writer's collection. The originals of the letters from Gabrielle Fleury to Clara Collet are in the possession of Robert Collet.

10. Letter of 21 December 1904.

11. Letter of 7 February 1905.

12. Letter to Clara Collet of 19 February 1905.

13. Letter of 28 November 1907.

14. Frank Swinnerton, *George Gissing: A Critical Study* (Port Washington, N.Y.: Kennikat Press, 1966), p. [8].

15. See the *Observer*, 10 November 1912, p. 5.

16. 15 November 1912, p. 12.

17. C. Lewis Hind, "Fact in Fiction: The Life of George Gissing as a Novel," *Daily Chronicle*, 30 October 1912, p. 4. See also Hind's *More Authors and I* (London: John Lane, 1922), pp. 129–34.

18. Anon., "The Private Life of Henry Maitland," *Daily Telegraph*, 1 November 1912, p. 4.

19. James Douglas, "George Gissing," *Star*, 2 November 1912, p. 4.

20. James Douglas, "The Grave-worm," *Daily News and Leader*, 5 November 1912, p. 6. See also "A Scholar's Tragedy" in the same number, p. 8. These comments on the book were in turn commented upon at length by F.S.A.L. in "Books and Their Writers," *Yorkshire Observer*, 9 November 1912, p. 12.

21. The following correspondence appeared in the *Daily News and Leader*: "The Biographic Novel," 8 November, p. 8 (W. L. George); 9 November, p. 5 (a friend of Mrs. Gissing); 11 November, p. 8 (May Sinclair and Reginald Turner); "Authors and Their Victims," 12 November, p. 8 (W. J. Locke and M. P. Willcocks); 13 November, p. 8 (R. Ellis Roberts); 14 November, p. 8 (Ena Fitzgerald); "Authors and Their Victims: Mr. Thomas Hardy on the Modern Novel," 15 November, p. 6 (extract from a letter to James Douglas) and "The Biographic Novel" on the same page (A. St. John Adcock); "Authors and Their Victims," 18 November, p. 8 (B. Low).

22. Claudius Clear [W. Robertson Nicoll], "George Gissing," *British Weekly*, 7 November 1912, p. 173. Reprinted in a slightly revised form in Nicoll's *A Bookman's Letters* (London: Hodder & Stoughton, 1913), pp. 288–96.

23. See Gissing's letter of 28 August 1900 to Edward Clodd in *The Letters of George Gissing to Edward Clodd*, ed. Pierre Coustillas (London: Enitharmon Press, 1973), p. 69.

24. C. K. S[horter], "A Literary Letter: Concerning George Gissing," *Sphere*, 16 November 1912, p. 182.

25. Respectively F. G. Bettany, "The World of Books: George Gissing," 3 November 1912, p. 4, and Anon., "Henry Maitland," 13 November 1912, p. 4.

26. "A Literary Letter," *Sphere*, 23 November 1912, p. 210.

27. Anon., "The Candid Friend," *Nation* (London), 16 November 1912, pp. 323–24.

28. R. E. R., "George Gissing," *Pall Mall Gazette*, 27 November 1912, p. 5.

29. T., "George Gissing: The Tragedy of a Moral Weakling," *Christian Commonwealth*, 20 November 1912, p. 127.

30. Anon., "The Private Life of Henry Maitland," *Spectator*, 1 February 1913, p. 199.

31. "The 'Whole Truth' in Biography," *Evening Standard and St. James's Gazette*, 28 November 1912, p. 11.

32. "Fiction," December 1912, p. 162.

33. "The Real Gissing," *Bookman* (London), December 1912, pp. 173–74.

34. "The Truth about Gissing," *Rhythm* (Literary Supplement), December 1912, pp. i–iv. Reprinted in the *New York Times Review of Books*, 13 January 1913, p. 9.

35. Anon., "New Novels: The Private Life of Henry Maitland," *Westminster Gazette*, 23 November 1912, p. 14.

36. "H. G. Wells, Morley Roberts and George Gissing," *T. P.'s Weekly*, 20 December 1912, p. 821. The same journal had previously published an anonymous review of the book, "Fiction That Dons the Attire of Fact," 22 November, p. 675, and this had been followed by "George Gissing" and "T. P.'s Letter-Box," 29 November, pp. 710 and 712; "Mr. Harrison and Mr. Gissing," 6 December, p. 752; "T. P.'s Letter-Box," 13 December, p. 798 (three letters to the editor).

37. For further reviews and comments in the English press see: "Recent Fiction," *Yorkshire Post*, 13 November 1912, p. 5; "Literary, Dramatic and Musical Notes," *Author*, 1 December 1912, pp. 73–74; Mimnermus, "Book Chat," *Literary Guide and Rationalist Review*, 1 December 1912, p. 190; and Thomas Seccombe, "Henry Maitland," *New Witness*, 19 December 1912, pp. 213–14.

38. Frank Swinnerton, *George Gissing: A Critical Study* (London: Martin Secker, 1912), p. 42.

39. Anon., "Body-snatching in Fiction," *Literary Digest*, 21 December 1912, pp. 1180–81.

40. Respectively "Writers and Books," p. 8, and "Truth about Gissing," p. 1.

41. Anon., "Morley Roberts's New Book," 25 January 1913, p. 11; Upton Sinclair, "Is It 'Scandal' to Invade the Private Life of Geniuses?", 15 March 1913, p. 12; and Anon., "George Gissing, Novelist, as Pictured by a Friend," 12 April 1913, p. 8.

42. E[dwin] F[rancis] E[dgett], "George Gissing: A Biography in Masquerade as a Novel," *Boston Evening Transcript*, 1 February 1913, Part 3, p. 4.

43. "New Lights on Gissing," *Bookman*, February 1913, pp. 655–57.

44. P. E. More, "George Gissing," *Nation*, 13 March 1913, pp. 256–57.

45. Anon., "Was George Gissing a Distinguished Failure?", *Current Opinion*, February 1913, pp. 143–44.

46. Anon., "George Gissing," *Independent*, 20 March 1913, p. 655.

47. Anon., "Henry Maitland's Private Life," 17 May 1913, pp. 1136–37.

48. "Genius and Privacy," *Academy*, 29 March 1913, pp. 389–90. The letter from H. G. Wells about this article appeared in the number for 12 April, pp. 478. Echoes of Sinclair's article are to be found in "Literary Notes," *Australasian*, 10 May, p. 1099.

49. [H. H. Champion], "The Private Life of Henry Maitland," *Book Lover* (Melbourne), February 1913, p. 16.

50. The following Australian reviews have been found: "Gissing," *Bulletin*, 30 January 1913, red page; "Review of Books: A Page from Life," *Register*, 1 February 1913, p. 4; "Recent Fiction," *Sydney Morning Herald*, 8 February 1913, p. 4; "New Books," *The Age* (Melbourne), 15 February 1913, p. 4; "A Novelist's Own Tragedy," *Advertiser*, 23 February 1913, p. 6; "The Life of Gissing," *Argus*, 28 February 1913, p. 5; "Literature: Publications," *Queensland*, 8 March 1913, p. 20; "In Bookland," *Brisbane Courier* (Courier Home Circle Supplement), 12 March 1913, p. 6. I am indebted to C. M. Wyatt for most of these Australian references.

51. "A Memorial to George Gissing," *The Times*, 5 March 1913, p. 11, and "A Memorial to George Gissing: Proposal to Found a Scholarship," *Manchester Guardian*, 5 March 1913, p. 7. In the latter newspaper the appeal was accompanied by a leading article on page 6 and an assessment of the novelist's work, entitled "George Gissing," by A. C. Benson, on page 14.

52. Anon., "Project of Dishonour: Protest Against the Gissing Memorial," *Manchester City News*, 8 March 1913, pp. 6–7. The campaign went on in the next three numbers: "Gissing Scholarship: Remarkable Outburst of Opinion," 15 March, p. 5; "George Gissing: The Proposed Scholarship," 22 March, p. 6; "The Gissing Scholarship: Views of the Proposed Memorial," 29 March, p. 3.

53. W.H. Hudson, *Men, Books and Birds* (London: Eveleigh Nash & Grayson, 1925), p. 115.

54. Letter of 9 February 1913 (University of Pennsylvania).

55. Four letters from Hick to Roberts dated 26 July 1912, 3 November 1912, 15 December 1912 and 22 February 1917 are in the Berg Collection.

56. Undated letter, c. 5 November 1912, in the Berg Collection.

57. Letter of 31 October 1912 to Clara Collet.

58. The literary papers of Alice Ward in the Coustillas collection.

59. See her letter (in French) of 1 January 1913 printed in full by Pierre Coustillas, "Une lettre inédite de Gabrielle Fleury à Clara Collet," *Etudes Anglaises*, April–June 1962, pp. 167–71.

60. The copy of Cazamian's book inscribed by the author to "Madame Fleury-Gissing" is in the Coustillas collection.

10. Waifs of Memory:
Arthur Symons's Confessions

1. For the date and contents of Symons' projected *Memoirs*, see *The Memoirs of Arthur Symons*, ed. Karl Beckson (University Park and London: Pennsylvania State University Press, 1977), pp. 2–4; Roger Lhombreaud, *Arthur Symons: A Critical Biography* (Philadelphia: Dufour, 1964), p. 303; and my "Beckson's

Symons," *English Literature in Transition: 1880–1920* 21 (1977): 67–70. I am indebted to Professor Beckson for his informative and gracious correspondence regarding Symons.

2. See, for examples, the untitled, twelve-page typescript beginning, "It was through," p. 4, in the Arthur Symons Collection, Box 1, at Princeton University Library. For permission to use and quote materials in this collection I am indebted to the library. The Literary Estate of Arthur Symons has kindly given me permission to quote from these and Symons's other unpublished writings.

3. Beckson, p. 261, n. 3.

4. "Confessions: A Few Thoughts, Portraits and Memories," *Vanity Fair* 6 (March 1916): 130.

5. London: Walter Scott, 1898. The Introduction is reprinted as "St. Augustine" and dated 1897 in *Figures of Several Centuries* (New York: E.P. Dutton, 1916), pp. 1–12, which is the text quoted below.

6. *Anglo-American Review* 1 (July 18, 1918): 233, reprinted as "The Memoirs of Casanova," *Vanity Fair* 12 (June 1919): 106–12.

7. *Dramatis Personae* (Indianapolis: Bobbs Merrill, 1923), pp. 144–45.

8. *Figures of Several Centuries*, p. 1. Cf. "A Casuist of Souls," *Vanity Fair* 20 (March 1923): 108.

9. Frank Kermode, *Romantic Image* (London: Macmillan,1957), p. 108; also Barbara Charlesworth, *Dark Passages: The Decadent Consciousness in Victorian Literature* (Madison and Milwaukee, 1965), pp. 110, 112; and my "Arthur Symons' 'Novel à la Goncourt'," *Journal of Modern Literature* 9 (1981–82): 56–59.

10. *The Symbolist Movement in Literature,* ed. Richard Ellmann (1899; reprint New York: E. P. Dutton, 1958), p. 1.

11. Kerry Powell's conclusion that in *The Symbolist Movement* Symons uses Symbolism as "a refuge from unpleasant reality in the embrace of sheer illusion" points usefully to Symons' escapist thoughts but neglects his ultimate uncertainty. See Professor Powell's "Arthur Symons, Symbolism, and the Aesthetics of Escape," *Renascence* 29 (1977): 157.

12. Box 38 in the John Quinn Memorial Collection, Manuscripts and Archives Division, the New York Public Library, Astor, Lenox and Tilden Foundations, to which I am indebted for permission to use this and other letters cited below.

13. See, for example, "When Italy Was Pro-German," *Vanity Fair* 5 (July 1915): 35; "Paul Verlaine in London," *Vanity Fair* 6 (June 1916): 61; and "Quiet Days in Dieppe," *Vanity Fair* 9 (December 6, 1917): 9–10, among some twenty-five critical and reminiscential notes Symons published in *Vanity Fair* from his earliest, in 1915, to the date of his letter.

14. In *Parisian Nights* (Westminster: Cyril Beaumont, 1926), Symons refers to the visit to Paris in "Lautrec and the Moulin Rouge" and in "A Voyage of Discovery" (pp. 1 and 31) as the occasion for gathering evidence about Verlaine and Baudelaire. Those essays contain much more evaluation of others than reminiscence about Symons himself, but possibly he regarded them as confessional, along with other apparent products of the visit to Paris—for example, "Parisian Nights and French Music-Halls," *Vanity Fair* 15 (Jan. 1921): 43, 88; "Spiritual Adventures in Paris," *Bookman* (New York) 52 (Feb. 1921): 481–85; and "The History of the Moulin Rouge," *English Review* 34 (Jan. 1922): 5–12.

15. "Bohemian Chelsea" was reprinted in *Mes Souvenirs* (Chapelle-Reanville, Eure: Hours Press [1929]), pp. 21–30.

16. *Memoirs,* ed. Beckson, pp. 125–28. Probably the dinner mentioned on

p. 126, at which Image told Symons about Horne, occurred in 1925 in response to Symons' letter and not, as he says, in 1924. Some phrases describing Horne in "A Study in Morbidity" resemble, and seem to be taken from, the *Vanity Fair* note, "The Hobby Horse."

17. Professor Beckson, p. 258, cites the Princeton typescript, "Impressions: III." "Impressions: I–III" (Box 10) is a short version of the sixteen-page "Sensations."

18. Other notable manuscripts are "Confessions—Dan Leno" (Princeton, Box 6), which is a brief appreciation of that comedian, and "Pages from the Life of Muriel Broadbent" (Princeton, Box 14), an introduction to three stories, two of them previously published, based upon the life of Muriel, who had been Symons' friend and Horne's mistress. Still other manuscripts incorporate all or parts of the ones already mentioned. The sixteen-page "Sensations" is duplicated not only by "Impressions: Parts I–III" (Box 10) but also by three other manuscripts: its pp. 7–16, but without the Rachel Kahn anecdote, make up the untitled, eight-page typescript (carbon) which begins, "I never felt myself at home," in the folder, Unidentified MSS (2), in Box 1; a typescript of pp. 14–16 of the sixteen-page "Sensations" relating to Sylvia Goffe is appended to the typescript in Box 13, "November 16, 1917," which recalls Augustus John and parallels "Augustus John" in Box 11; and pp. 5–7 on the Tortoni appears in "The Boulevards," pp. 1–4, in Box 3. A second typescript titled "Sensations" (Box 16) of twenty pages is the source of the *Two Worlds* "Confessions . . .: Part One" but also includes a final, unpublished section about a vacation-time mistress, Giulia Curanico (pp. 14–20). The untitled typescript beginning, "To take one instance out of many," in the Unidentified MSS (2) folder in Box 1 is a carbon copy of this "Sensations," pp. 2–8 and 11–13; and "Giulia Curanico" in Box 7 is a revised carbon copy of the twenty-page "Sensations," pp. 14–19.

19. For Symons's first use of this sentence, see his Preface to *Silhouettes,* rev. ed. (1896), reprinted in Karl Beckson, ed., *Aesthetes and Decadents of the 1890s* (New York: Random House, 1966), p. 161.

20. For the debt to Barine, see *Fortnightly Review* 63 (new series, January 1898): 81 n. 1.

21. Cf. *The Symbolist Movement in Literature,* pp. 6, 9–10, 14–16, and 19.

22. Cf. *The Symbolist Movement in Literature,* p. 11.

23. Cf. *The Symbolist Movement in Literature,* pp. 43–45.

24. Lhombreaud, p. 299.

25. Burton Pike, "Time and Autobiography," *Comparative Literature* 28 (1976): 328.

26. Roy Pascal, *Design and Truth in Autobiography* (Cambridge: Harvard University Press, 1960), p. 249.

27. W. C. Spengemann, *Forms of Autobiography* (New Haven and London: Yale University Press, 1980), p. xv.

28. Walter Pater, *The Renaissance,* Modern Library ed. (New York: Random House, n.d.), p. 197.

11. Richard Le Gallienne and the Romanticism of the 1890s

1. *The Autobiography of William Butler Yeats* (New York: Macmillan, 1953), pp. 104, 180.

2. Herford, "Introduction," *A Jongleur Strayed* (Garden City: Doubleday, Page, 1922), p. xv. See also J. Lewis May's account of his first meeting with Le Gallienne in *The Path through the Wood* (New York: Lincoln Macveagh, Dial Press; Toronto: Longmans, Green,1931), pp. 160–63.

3. Quoted in "Richard Le Gallienne and a New Rhetoric," *Cosmopolitan* 25 (August, 1898): 458.

4. Baring, *The Puppet Show of Memory* (London: William Heinemann, 1922), p. 150.

5. Whittington-Egan and Smerdon, *The Quest of the Golden Boy* (London: Unicorn Press, 1960; Barre, Mass.: Barre Publishing Company, 1962).

6. Hyde, "Introduction," *The Romantic '90s* (London: Putnam, 1951), p. xxii.

7. *The Romantic '90s* (1926; reprint, London: Putnam, 1951), p. 19.

8. Ibid., p. 78.

9. Ibid., p. 157.

10. See J. A. S[terry?], *The New Fiction: A Protest against Sex-Mania* (London: Westminster Gazette, 1895) which reprints the controversy.

11. *Attitudes and Avowals* (New York and London: John Lane, 1910), p. 310.

12. Moers, "Literary Economics in the 1890's: Golden Boys for Sale," *Victorian Studies* (December 1963): 185–91.

13. *Retrospective Reviews* (London: John Lane, 1896), 1: 25.

14. *The Junk-Man and Other Poems* (Garden City: Doubleday, Page, 1920), p. 27.

15. *Volumes in Folio* (London: E. Mathews, 1889), pp. 32–33.

16. "A Dream Wife," *My Ladies' Sonnets*, p. 31.

17. "An Impression," *Robert Louis Stevenson: An Elegy and Other Poems* (Boston: Copeland and Day; London: John Lane, 1895), p. 47.

18. *Vanishing Roads* (New York: G. P. Putnam's Sons, 1915), pp. 244–45.

19. Jackson, *The Eighteen Nineties* (New York: Knopf, n.d.), p. 14; Burdett, *The Beardsley Period* (London: John Lane, 1925), pp. 11–12; Muddiman, *The Men of Nineties* (London: Henry Danielson, 1920), p. 7.

20. "A Song of Singers," *The Lonely Dancer* (London: John Lane; New York: John Lane Company; Toronto: Bell and Cockburn, 1914), p. 184.

21. "Snatch," *Robert Louis Stevenson*, p. 23.

12. Bennett's Entertainments

1. Letter to J. B. Pinker, 6 September 1911; *Letters of Arnold Bennett*, ed. James Hepburn (London: Oxford University Press, 1966), 1: 162.

2. 25 September 1929; quoted in Reginald Pound, *Arnold Bennett* (London: William Heinemann, 1952), p. 335.

3. I will use the English titles of Bennett's books where they differ from the American. In America *The Strange Vanguard* was called *The Vanguard*, *The Card* was called *Denry the Audacious*, and *The Regent* was called *The Old Adam*.

4. Letter to H. G. Wells, 25 May 1905; *Letters*, 2: 189.

5. "It [*The Card*] is purely humorous and light, but it is true to life"; letter to J. B. Pinker, 13 January 1909; *Letters*, 1: 119.

6. "*Un*-literature" is his term for *Hugo* in a letter to Violet Hunt of 21 June 1906; *Letters*, 2: 205.

7. Margaret Drabble, *Arnold Bennett* (New York: Alfred A. Knopf, 1974), p. 351 and elsewhere.

8. As quoted in J. B. Simons, *Arnold Bennett and His Novels* (Folcroft, PA: Folcroft Press, 1936; repr. 1969), p. 231.

9. Walter Allen, *Arnold Bennett* (London: Home & Van Thal, 1948), p. 91.

10. James Hall, *Arnold Bennett: Primitivism and Taste* (Seattle: University of Washington Press, 1959), pp. 17–22, 11–15.

11. Introduction, *Letters*, 1: 21.

12. Letters to J. B. Pinker, 22 November 1903, postmarked 14 March 1904; *Letters*, 1: 41, 45.

13. Drabble, p. 115.

14. *A Great Man* (1904; repr. London: Methuen,1925), p. 240.

15. Dudley Barker, *Writer by Trade: A View of Arnold Bennett* (London: George Allen & Unwin, 1966), p. 116.

16. *Letters*, 1: 101 n.; James Hepburn, *The Art of Arnold Bennett* (Bloomington: Indiana University Press, 1963), p. 200.

17. Drabble, p. 160.

18. Letter to William Dean Howells, 1 March 1911; *Letters*, 2: 274.

19. Drabble, p. 180; Barker, p. 147.

20. Letter to J. B. Pinker, 9 February 1910; *Letters*, 1: 132.

21. Drabble, p. 158.

22. Letter to the Duchess of Sutherland, 23 June 1911; *Letters*, 2: 285.

23. *The Regent* (1913; repr. London: Methuen, 1965), p. 253.

24. *Letters*, 1: 367 n.; Drabble, p. 351; Allen, p. 91; Barker, p. 205.

25. Barker, p. 228.

26. Allen, p. 99.

27. Pound, p. 331.

28. *The Strange Vanguard* (1927; London: Cassell, 1928), pp. 68–69.

29. Letter to H. G. Wells, 25 May 1905; *Letters*, 2: 189.

30. Letter to J. B. Pinker, 27 April 1904; *Letters*, 1: 50.

31. *Arnold Bennett: The Journals*, ed. Frank Swinnerton (Hammondsworth: Penguin, 1971), pp. 232, 235 (2 January 1908; 29 February 1908); pp. 252, 257 (8 January 1909; 2 March 1909). *Letters*, 2: 103 n.

32. *Journals*, p. 514 (8 July 1926).

33. Hepburn, p. 185.

34. *Journals*, p. 90 (28 February 1904).

35. V. S. Pritchett, *The Living Novel* (New York: Reynal & Hitchcock, 1947), p. 132.

36. In a letter to George Sturt quoted by Hepburn, p. 185, his "serious" work is so described.

37. Drabble, p. 159.

38. Walter Wright, *Arnold Bennett: Romantic Realist* (Lincoln: University of Nebraska Press, 1971), pp. 142–43.

13. Publishable and Worth It: Forster's Hitherto Unpublished Fiction

1. E. M. Forster, *Arctic Summer and Other Fiction*, ed. Elizabeth Heine (London: Edward Arnold; New York: Holmes and Meier, 1980). Unless otherwise stated, all quotations are from this text.

2. Ibid., "Editor's Introduction," p. ix.

3. Forster does not use March's given name, Clesant, until chapter 4 of the main version of the novel. Generally, I will refer to him as March when I discuss the events of the first five chapters and will use Clesant when I discuss the events in chapter 6 and following.

4. P. N. Furbank, *E. M. Forster: A Life,* 2 vols. (London: Secker & Warburg, 1977), 1:207.

5. I disagree with Barbara Rosecrance in *Forster's Narrative Vision* (Ithaca and London: Cornell University Press,1982, pp. 174–77) that Vullamy is Forster's spokesman in the novel. Vullamy represents views toward which Forster is partly sympathetic, but he represents only one aspect of a situation which has notable elements of complexity and ambiguity. Vullamy's formulation of the good as enclosed in military prowess and inherited tradition and of evil as residing in the forces of intellect which challenge these entities is not necessarily Forster's, though in some sense Forster does identify with heroism and tradition in the person of Clesant March in the novel. Certainly Martin's perception at the time of Lance's crisis that Vullamy is unkind and does not love his nephews but rather is only proud of them would indicate less than Forster's full endorsement of Vullamy. Kindness is, of course, one of Forster's cherished humanistic values. Neither can I agree with Rosecrance that Forster in this novel repudiates Martin Whitby's civilized ideas and values. Rather, they are admirable as far as they go, though they must in the end be supplemented by values of a more intuitive and transcendent cast.

About the Contributors

CHARLES BURKHART is Professor of English at Temple University, and he has been a member of the editorial board of *ELT* since its beginning. He is the author of books on I. Compton-Burnett, Charlotte Brönte, Ada Leverson, and Barbara Pym.

PIERRE COUSTILLAS is Professor of English at the University of Lille. Most of his three dozen published titles have been written in English and devoted to Gissing—volumes of correspondence, critical editions and anthologies, and translations. His other books concern Elizabeth Gaskell, Trollope, Hardy, Moore, Hudson, Conrad, Kipling, and Jack London.

DAVID B. EAKIN, an instructor at Auburn University, completed his dissertation on Oscar Wilde and George Moore under the directorship of Hal Gerber at Arizona State University. He is Associate Editor of *English Literature in Transition* and co-editor, with Hal Gerber, of *In Minor Keys: The Uncollected Short Stories of George Moore* and, with Robert Langenfeld, of *George Moore's Correspondence with the Mysterious Countess*. He has published articles on George Gissing, James Joyce, and Oliver St. John Gogarty, and he is author of the Moore entry in the *Modern British Dramatists* volume of the *Dictionary of Literary Biography*.

IAN FLETCHER was appointed Assistant Lecturer at Reading University in 1956; Lecturer in 1958; Reader in 1966; and Professor in 1978. He joined the faculty at Arizona State University in 1982. He has edited Lionel Johnson's and John Gray's collected poems; *Romantic Mythologies; Meredith Now;* and *Decadence and the 1890s;* and he has published articles mainly on W. B. Yeats and the 1890s.

WENDELL V. HARRIS, Professor of English at Pennsylvania State University, is the author of *Arthur Hugh Clough, British Short Fiction in the Nineteenth Century*, and *The Omnipresent Debate: Empiricism and Transcendentalism in Nineteenth-Century English Prose*. He has published essays on Victorian poetry and prose, English literature in the 1890s, and contemporary theories of literary interpretation.

ALAN JOHNSON teaches Victorian literature at Arizona State University, Tempe. He served as an associate editor of *English Literature in Transition* from 1976 through 1982. He has published essays on Arthur Symons's prose in *ELT* and the *Journal of Modern Literature.*

ROBERT LANGENFELD is the Editor of *English Literature in Transition*. He has published on Moore, Sassoon, Shakespeare, and Hemingway. He is editor of two forthcoming works: *George Moore: An Annotated Secondary Bibliography* and *Considering Aubrey Beardsley: Essays, with an Annotated Secondary Bibliography.*

FREDERICK P. W. MCDOWELL is Professor Emeritus of English at the University of Iowa. He has written books on Ellen Glasgow, Caroline Gordon, and E. M. Forster and is an authority on Bernard Shaw. He has also written essays on Robert Penn Warren, Conrad, Hardy, Lawrence, Woolf, and Angus Wilson.

HAROLD OREL is University Professor in the Department of English, University of Kansas. Major publications include editions of Thomas Hardy's personal writings and Rudyard Kipling as well as critical assessments of Victorian literary critics, of Rebecca West, and of Irish and Scottish culture.

BERNARD QUINT is the Program Associate and Assistant Director for the Arizona Humanities Council. He has taught at various colleges and universities, and his principal publications are translations of medieval Latin liturgical texts.

WILLIAM J. SCHEICK is J. R. Millikan Centennial Professor of English Literature at the University of Texas, Austin, where he also serves as editor of *Texas Studies in Literature and Language*. His books include *The Slender Human Word: Emerson's Artistry in Prose; The Half-Blood: A Cultural Symbol in Nineteenth-Century American Fiction;* and *The Splintering Frame: The Later Fiction of H. G. Wells.*

ROBERT C. SCHWEIK is Distinguished Teaching Professor of English at the State University of New York, College at Fredonia. His publications include *Reference Sources in English and American Literature, Hart Crane: A Descriptive Bibliography,* and, most recently, the Norton Critical Edition of Thomas Hardy's *Far from the Madding Crowd.*

STANLEY WEINTRAUB is Evan Pugh Professor of Arts and Humanities and Director of the Institute for the Arts and Humanistic Studies at The Pennsylvania State University. Among his books of biography and cultural history are *Private Shaw and Public Shaw, The Last Great Cause, Journey to Heartbreak, A Stillness Heard Round the World: The End of the Great War, Four Rossettis, Beardsley, Whistler, Victoria,* and *The Unexpected Shaw.*

Index